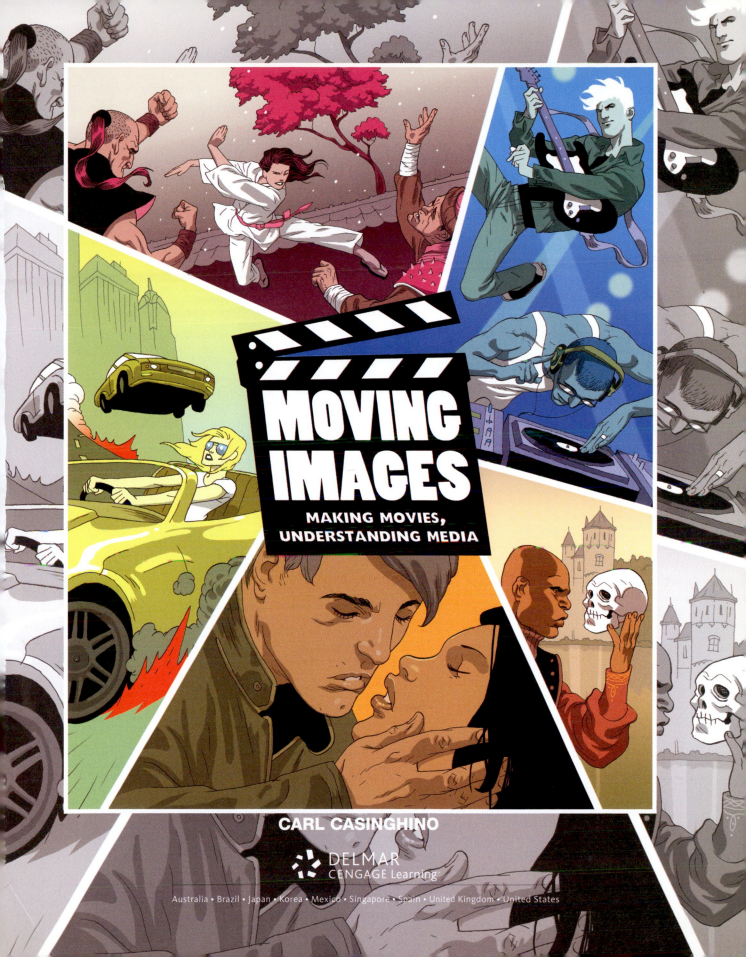

MOVING IMAGES

MAKING MOVIES, UNDERSTANDING MEDIA

CARL CASINGHINO

DELMAR
CENGAGE Learning

Australia • Brazil • Japan • Korea • Mexico • Singapore • Spain • United Kingdom • United States

DELMAR
CENGAGE Learning

Moving Images: Making Movies, Understanding Media
Carl Casinghino

Vice President, Career and Professional Editorial: Dave Garza

Director of Learning Solutions: Sandy Clark

Senior Acquisitions Editor: Jim Gish

Managing Editor: Larry Main

Associate Product Manager: Meaghan O'Brien

Editorial Assistant: Sarah Timm

Vice President, Career and Professional Marketing: Jennifer McAvey

Marketing Director: Deborah Yarnell

Marketing Manager: Erin Brennan

Marketing Coordinator: Jonathon Sheehan

Production Director: Wendy Troeger

Senior Content Project Manager: Glenn Castle

Art Director: Joy Kocsis

Cover design and illustration: Asaf Hanuka www.asafhanuka.com

Library of Congress Control Number: 2009933908

ISBN-13: 9781435485853
ISBN-10: 1435485858

Delmar
5 Maxwell Drive
Clifton Park, NY 12065-2919
USA

Cengage Learning is a leading provider of customized learning solutions with office locations around the globe, including Singapore, the United Kingdom, Australia, Mexico, Brazil, and Japan. Locate your local office at: **international.cengage.com/region**

Cengage Learning products are represented in Canada by Nelson Education, Ltd.

To learn more about Delmar, visit **www.cengage.com/delmar**
Purchase any of our products at your local college store or at our preferred online store **www.CengageBrain.com**

Printed in the United States of America
1 2 3 4 5 6 7 X X X 13 12 11 10

Table of Contents

Preface

Introduction

Media literacy, collaborative team building, creative problem solving, project management: these cross-curricular skills are among the most vital for students today, and they form the core of *Moving Images: Making Movies, Understanding Media.*

Moving Images is a comprehensive media studies and motion picture production textbook designed for effective classroom use in secondary schools and introductory undergraduate courses. Students of the twenty-first century need to develop skills in understanding, interpreting, and using moving image media, as has been established by publications of the National Standards for the English Language Arts, Common Sense Media, National Institutes of Health, and state guidelines across America. Young people today face a dizzying array of images and sounds, and it is crucial that they develop abilities to evaluate and utilize the messages and tools of moving image media.

To address this need, *Moving Images* is written for *all students,* just as textbooks for math, social studies, science, and other subjects are written for a broad range of learners in order to give them a solid foundation of knowledge and abilities for further academic study, professional life, and personal enrichment. Moreover, for students with a strong professional interest in motion picture communications, *Moving Images* will provide bountiful opportunities to develop creative and analytical skills in all key areas of motion picture communication and literacy.

Background

Why teach motion picture studies and production? In film and video classes, are educators training all of our students to be filmmakers? Of course not—no more than math teachers are preparing all students in their classes to become professional mathematicians. Schools are helping learners to develop cooperative skills, to enhance their problem-solving abilities, and to participate in cultural and social processes as capable, engaged interpreters. As schools offer our students opportunities to develop their ideas and communicate them through characters, images, and stories that play upon screens, they enable them to negotiate collaborative solutions with peers, to explore the creative potential of their own voices, and to articulate a deeper understanding of motion picture media.

As a teacher of motion picture studies and production at the high school level, I know that it is vital to offer a text that is easily used in the classroom and adaptable to a wide variety of contexts. *Moving Images* is formulated as a core text for courses in media studies that can be designed to function in communications, technology, English, arts, or cross-curricular departmental offerings at a high school or university. The work in the text is not tied to any specific technology, computer programs, or individual motion pictures. Support for the technological resources selected by a school can be found on the textbook website. In fact, the work of this course has been done with a few VHS cameras and a couple of VCRs (although I would not recommend this route).

This project is a culmination of my years of work as a teacher, filmmaker, and writer, and it is designed to offer a flexible tool for educators to develop media studies and motion picture production courses that meet the needs of learners in varied educational contexts. Having engaged in cinema studies as an undergraduate at Princeton University, then film production in New York University's graduate film and television program and on shoots in the United States and Europe, I was able to draw upon a diverse academic and professional background to create and write curriculum and coursework for motion picture classes at Suffield High School in Suffield, Connecticut. At the core of this text are everyday experiences of the high school classroom and lessons that have been developed amidst the difficulties and successes that I have encountered as a teacher.

Twenty-first century educators know that they must engage students in a variety of ways in order to be effective teachers. With this textbook, differentiation of instruction is facilitated by the use of multiple approaches for the mastery of skills and concepts in visual literacy and communication. *Moving Images: Making Movies, Understanding Media* is designed to maximize learning opportunities for secondary and undergraduate students by developing creative, analytical, and collaborative skills.

Contemporary educational experts have consistently singled out the benefits of cooperative learning and teaching for creativity. Although collaborative methods have been shown to be among the most fruitful modes of learning, the lack of texts designed to facilitate collaboration has hindered more widespread use of cooperative techniques in classrooms. In addition, engagement with creative activities is consistently cited as a boon to student achievement, yet students typically have less opportunity for creative problem solving at the consecutive steps from elementary to middle to high school. Through the exercises in this textbook, students are called upon to share tasks as they generate original solutions and individually demonstrate the skills necessary for understanding and using motion picture media.

In *Moving Images: Making Movies, Understanding Media,* students are consistently provided with contexts to understand the sources, traditions, and developments of moving image media. At every juncture, they are asked to reflect upon and seek creative and critical solutions to essential questions of motion picture communication. Artistic, historical, sociological, scientific, economic, and personal perspectives on the story of moving images are woven throughout the text. As a result, numerous opportunities for cross-curricular learning are imbedded into the modules of this textbook.

Organization

Moving Images: Making Movies, Understanding Media offers a series of thematically driven units that provide opportunities for collaborative learning, enhancement of creativity, and development of higher order thinking. The textbook is made up of eight chapters that are designed for approximately one month of coursework each. Thus, each four-chapter half of the book corresponds roughly to a semester of work. Chapters are arranged thematically, so students investigate topics to develop a basic understanding of motion picture technology, history, and artistry through selected examples that illustrate each subject. They complete analytical work and creative exercises to develop skills in evaluation, cooperative problem solving, writing, and visual storytelling.

In the first half of the book, students are introduced to the essential building blocks of motion picture communication: the language of moving images, the technical development of cinema, the integration of sound, and the fundamentals of cinematography.

In the second half of the book, students deepen their perspectives on the range of opportunities and sources in motion picture communication. They consider formats and genres of movies, including narrative or non-narrative and fiction or documentary. They are introduced to a wide range of filmmakers working in a variety of cultural and professional contexts. In the final units, students deepen their skills in evaluating and writing screenplays and then explore the full production process.

The text is organized so that skills are built incrementally and topics are explored from paired themes. Chapters 1 and 2 revolve around the growth of visual communication; Chapters 3 and 4 focus on the craft and technical underpinnings of moviemaking; Chapters 5 and 6 investigate the forms that movies take; and Chapters 7 and 8 concentrate on the development and production of stories on the screen. Following is a brief overview of the chapters.

Chapter 1: Motion Picture Language

In the first unit of the text, students are introduced to basic methods of communication through motion pictures. The class members learn essential concepts linked to framing and sequences, and they complete exercises designed to develop skills in creating basic shots and series of images.

Chapter 2: Inventions and Origins

Having explored the concept of motion picture language, the students are introduced to the birth of photography and the cinema. They learn about the physical process of filmmaking and the discoveries and creations of early filmmakers. They write character descriptions, shoot their own non-dialogue films, and analyze a variety of silent movies.

Chapter 3: Sound and Image

In this unit, students begin to explore the full integration of sound in the cinema. They learn about the essentials of production recording, sound design, and mixing. Sound initiates the use of spoken dialogue; therefore, students begin to explore more fully the basics of writing for the screen. They study character, motivation, conflict, and story structure in a series of short films and a feature film and then develop an idea for a promotional motion picture. Finally, class members collaborate in groups to produce a promotional short with dialogue and multi-tracked sound.

Chapter 4: Storytelling with Light

Students return to the visual aspects of the medium to explore the technical, historical, and artistic developments of cinema from the twentieth to the twenty-first century. In particular, they study the qualities of light and color and the parameters and effect of screen size. This is followed by a coordination of visual communication with the storytelling skills that have been developed throughout the textbook. In this unit, students produce their first major individual project.

Chapter 5: Personal Expression and Studio Production

In this unit, students explore connections between motion picture creators and viewers. Films from the contemporary era are used to illustrate a range of approaches to filmmaking, including independent and non-narrative traditions in motion pictures. Commercial uses of the moving image are also explored, including promotional subjects and corporate uses. As a warm-up to the next chapter, we study the use of non-fiction in motion pictures and produce a portrait of a person or a place.

Chapter 6: Recording and Presenting Reality

Students investigate key aspects of documentary filmmaking through representative historical and thematic examples, including the mixing of forms, techniques, and subject matter between fiction and non-fiction. They explore a variety of content domains, stylistic methods, and journalistic concerns in contemporary non-fiction motion pictures of diverse lengths and formats. In this unit, class members focus on directing an individual non-fiction short.

Chapter 7: Page to Screen

Students return to the fundamentals of writing for the screen. They explore the basics of screenwriting, including character development, dramatic conflict, and narrative structure. Class members investigate storytelling examples and write their own short screenplays for production with this chapter or Chapter 8.

Chapter 8: The Production Process

In this unit, students review the full range of positions on a typical professional motion picture. They complete investigations of particular areas of interest, and the class evaluates movies from various craft viewpoints. For this project, they work on major productions from scripts that have been developed since Chapter 7.

As a final note on the organization of the text, the two halves of the book follow an additional paired pattern to facilitate pedagogical planning. Chapters 1 and 5 ask, "What are movies?" Chapters 2 and 6 investigate the historical origins of movies and filmmaking traditions. Chapters 3 and 7 discuss the relationship of verbal and sonic communication and examine screenwriting. Finally, Chapters 4 and 8 offer a "putting it all together" summation of each half of the book that culminates in an independent production.

Pedagogical Resources and Benefits

- *Units are organized with classroom flexibility in mind.*
  - The lessons of *Moving Images* are organized for incremental skill development with students of varying abilities. Concepts and skills are introduced thematically, so instructors are never limited to a particular product or technology. Multiple opportunities for student demonstration of mastery enhance differentiation of instruction.
- *Collaborative work is built into each unit.*
  - In this textbook, students work in groups to build production skills through both guided and open-ended projects. The organization of exercises facilitates effective implementation of cooperative learning through clearly delineated tasks and management of group work.
- *Analytical and creative work imbedded in each chapter.*
  - In order to understand and master a field of endeavor, it is highly beneficial to be able to think critically and creatively about its subject matter. Students explore the themes of each chapter through critical analysis and creative problem solving. This approach enhances skill-building and understanding of visual media through a range of learning styles using higher-order thinking. Students also assess their progress through reflective personal evaluations.
- *Every chapter includes features for classroom interaction and personal perspectives.*
  - **Framing the Discussion** provides questions to initiate and guide classroom discussion and reflective individual responses to unit themes.
  - **Close-Up** offers interviews with leading figures in motion picture professions to share personal reflections and experiences linked with chapter topics.

- **Viewfinder** presents quotes about moving images to stimulate group discussion and individual reflection on the subjects of the text.

- *Inclusion of technical, evaluative, and creative skills offers curricular flexibility.*
  - Through its focus on media communication, this text can serve as a catalyst for development of curricula in English, technology, or other departments.

- *DVD offers interactive files for editing exercises.*
  - Students will have the opportunity to use files from the DVD included with every copy of the text in order to build editing skills. Scenes included have been designed to reflect the content of each chapter.

- *Short films for study are included on DVD.*
  - Teachers and students will be able to view a selection of short films that are used for investigation of the concepts in each chapter.

Notes for Students and Teachers

As its title indicates, *Moving Images: Making Movies, Understanding Media* is designed to facilitate the most widespread opportunities of investigation into motion picture media—from celluloid films to digital video and from feature films to commercials on television and the Internet. However, it was clear that in order to function properly and easily as a source for introductory motion picture media courses, the work with the textbook had to be designed for live-action production. Thus, animation techniques are not covered in this book, although animated movies are used as learning sources and investigative tools throughout the text, and there are many references to animators and various types of animation.

At the end of each chapter, students are offered three types of exercises: *Analysis, Writing,* and *Projects.* In addition, many more activities are offered for the classroom in the Teacher's Resources package that accompanies the text.

Analysis

Analysis work is provided to develop students' understanding and evaluative skills in motion picture media. The questions included in the student and teacher resources are written to facilitate conceptual understanding of unit material, so they can be applied to motion pictures that appropriately illustrate those themes. Movies are provided on the textbook DVD, and additional selections are available through Cengage on the Internet. Lists of additional motion picture resources for each chapter are included in the instructor CD-ROM and through the textbook website.

When viewing and reacting to motion pictures, we are affected in a multitude of ways. One must consider many factors when examining the meaning and impact of moving images. In his book *Thinking in Pictures,* director John Sayles says "Narrative film, what we ordinarily think of as 'the movies,' is a combination of literary, theatrical, and purely cinematic elements." His analytical breakdown of motion pictures offers a useful organizational strategy for any discussion of movies. When completing Analysis work, consider this structure of three areas to organize thoughts, reactions, and analyses.

- *Cinematic*—All of the factors particular to the cinema, including:
  - Cinematography: visual elements, composition, movement, light, color
  - Editing
  - Sound design (all dialogue recording, effects, music)
- *Literary*—Elements experienced in the study of literature, such as:
  - Story and plot
  - Dialogue and written elements
  - Theme
- *Theatrical*—Factors associated with the theater, particularly:
  - Acting and performance
  - Blocking—in theater, blocking is the positioning and moving of actors around the set, and this term can be applied to motion pictures in terms of "staging" or working from sets. However, it is important to see this as becoming cinematic when it is directly interpreted by the vantage point of the camera and the visual choices inherent in cinematography.

Keep in mind that these categories can be useful to organize analyses and discussion, but in many ways they can overlap and become blurred. For example, when discussing typical storytelling devices such as symbol, metaphor, or irony (which many would list under "literary"), they can stem from purely visual or musical sources. So, you should consider these titles to help with analytical work, while the overall goal is to develop an understanding of the distinct expressive and creative capacities and messages of motion pictures.

Writing

In each chapter, you will complete creative writing assignments to develop screenwriting material and skills. There is a writing exercise at the end of each chapter, and there is a selection of additional assignments in the Instructor Resources package. These can be used to generate narrative ideas or other storytelling material or to produce alternative scripts. The writing you generate for any of the assignments can be used for production exercises, and you will have the opportunity to produce scripts that you draft for group work or independent projects.

Projects

The third end-of-chapter component is the motion picture project. As with *Analysis* and *Writing*, along with the *Project* at the end of each chapter there is a selection of additional shooting assignments in the Instructor Resources package. These may be used in class to develop formative skills and explore avenues of creative inquiry investigated in the chapter.

Collaborative work is at the heart of most motion picture production, and cooperative learning forms the core of the work appearing in this textbook. The projects in this textbook have been designed for individual responsibility and collaborative support to reach personal goals and group objectives. Thus, it is important for groups to delineate responsibilities clearly for fairness in assessment.

In addition, all students will have the opportunity to write and direct the stories that they devise. If individual students do not have the chance to create a movie from an original concept at a particular time, they *will* have the opportunity to produce that story for a project during the following chapters. Over the course of a series of units, all students have the opportunity personally to write and direct a project of their choice, which generally stems from material generated in the preceding lessons. This will be the case throughout the work associated with this textbook.

Reports

Reports are provided for each major *Project* in this text. They are to be written for the following reasons:

- To formulate in-depth self-evaluation by each student regarding the exercises done in class.
- To record a shoot-by-shoot analysis of successes and failures of group work so that students can improve both individual performance and inter-personal skills.
- To provide full information to the teacher for proper evaluation of each student's work. They are to be used as an assessment tool in addition to classroom observation and notes.

Instructor Resources

To accompany the textbook, there is a wide range of supporting materials and information available through the Instructor Resources CD and the textbook website. These tools integrate a range of pedagogical approaches and offer many opportunities to develop curricula for diverse classroom needs.

- *Instructor Resources CD-ROM features:*
  - Sample syllabi and lesson planning materials.
  - Alternative and optional work for each unit, titled Class Activities, Creative Journal, and Critical Notebook.
  - Rubrics and holistic evaluative tools.
  - Test generation resources for formative and summative assessments.
  - Vocabulary lists per chapter.

- Resource lists per chapter for short and feature films and reading options.
- PowerPoint slides present highlights of each chapter.
- Supporting information for use of the DVD footage and short films.

- *Textbook website offers:*
  - Technical information and links for instructors and students regarding digital editing resources and moviemaking tools.
  - Regularly updated lists of chapter-aligned motion pictures.
  - Streaming video of supplemental short films and additional educational content.
  - Full filmmaker interviews, supplementary readings, and links to academic resources and related texts.
  - Author blog.

Author Biography

Carl Casinghino has drawn on many years of work in motion picture production, studies, and pedagogy to write *Moving Images: Making Movies, Understanding Media*. Carl earned a B.A. at Princeton University, where he wrote his senior thesis on director Marcel Carné, then entered the graduate film and television program at New York University. There, he wrote and directed several shorts and served in the camera department on a number of films, including a feature on the history of Princeton University and the award-winning short *The Architect*. After working full-time at New York University, he moved on to production jobs in Paris, France, followed by a return to the United States, where he began teaching in the late 1990s.

At Suffield High School in Connecticut, Carl has created curricula and coursework for film and video classes that he has been teaching for over a decade. As a teacher of media literacy and digital video production at the high school level, he developed this textbook in conjunction with work in the classroom and graduate studies that he completed for a Masters in education at Union Institute and University. In particular, significant segments of the studies he fulfilled in this program focused on collaborative learning and teaching for creativity, both of which are key foundations of *Moving Images: Making Movies, Understanding Media*.

Acknowledgments

This project would not have been remotely possible without the support, patience, and enormous contributions of its primary editor and chief sounding board, Alexandra Casinghino. Her keen critical analyses and bountiful spirit have been integral to its genesis. It was only through my wife Alexandra's generous collaboration that this textbook could be completed.

This book would also not exist without the support and input of filmmaker Adam Keker. Adam offered much of the initial inspiration and encouragement for this project and has provided indispensable assistance with many of the artistic and technical issues covered in the text. Adam has been *the* catalyst in soliciting cooperation from many independent filmmakers for this project. The daunting challenges of the scope of this endeavor could not have been met without Adam's expertise and friendship.

The kind contributions of many directors, producers, photographers, and artists were an enormous boon to *Moving Images*, and I wish to thank them sincerely for sharing their work: Nash Edgerton and Blue-Tongue Films; William Farley; Tony Gerber (www.marketroadfilms.com); Jon Jost; Agnès Varda and Ciné-Tamaris; Mike Chase; Eugene Corr and Tamsin Orion; Dan Geller; Estelle Grosso and The Cinema Guild; Amanda Micheli; Paul Saltzman; Christopher Benson; Laurent Carmé; Robert Casinghino and Fresh Music Library (www.freshmusic.com); S. Smith Patrick (www.shuttersmith .net); Kaarina and Derek Roberto; and Khadija Al-Salami. I greatly appreciate the generosity and sympathetic exchanges with research specialists, authors, and archival sources, notably Rita Altomara and the Fort Lee Library; Tim Bodzioney; Lisa DePaolo; Alison McMahan; Trond Trondsen (www .nostalghia.com) and Lars-Ol of Löthwall; Stephen Wainwright and the George Groves family; the Henry Mancini Estate; the Eames Office; Andy Malcolm and Footsteps Studios; and Buddy Weiss, Todd Ifft, and the team at Photofest. For their timely aid in the creation of the *Close-Up* feature of this book, I express heartfelt gratitude to Nanette Burstein, Greg Butler, Nash Edgerton (again!), Kevin Goff, Pamela Gray, Deborah Hoffmann, Hiro Narita, and David Riker.

In addition, the production of the DVD was made possible through the work of many people. Emily Doe of Wholphin DVD magazine (www.wholphindvd .com) provided crucial help. Brian Spellman and Ryan Sindler produced many segments of the DVD footage for student use. Of course, the short film portion of the DVD would not have been viable without the willingness of gifted filmmakers to believe in this educational mission, and I extend my gratitude to Emile Bokaer, Eva Ilona Brzeski, Nash Edgerton, Richard Levien, Kimberly Miner, Mark Osborne, Steve Pasvolsky, Rob Pearlstein, Matthew Silva, and Sasha Wolf. Finally, it took the dedication and substantial efforts of a talented individual to oversee the entire DVD project and to complete its significant technical, logistical, and editorial tasks: Ross Martin. Most important, Ross *understood* the mission of this textbook right from the beginning, and this fact was vital throughout the progress of our endeavor.

A number of the names in the preceding paragraphs bring me to the group that deserves the greatest thanks for this textbook, the reason that it exists at all: my students. Our mutual adventures in learning and moviemaking in the Fundamentals and Advanced Film and Video courses at Suffield High School in Connecticut began over ten years ago. When I reflect on this book, I imagine all of the students who have shared in these experiences from the frustrating days to the joyful ones. Having already mentioned the contributions to this book of Mike Chase, Ross Martin, Kim Miner, Kevin Goff, Matt Silva, Brian Spellman, and Ryan Sindler, I must add thanks to Colin Packard for his screenwriting, Conor Nicoll for the use of his coffee mug story in Chapter 8, Kendelyn Ouellette for her photography, and the filmmaking participants for their time and efforts. It has been a true pleasure to work with these former students who have become respected collaborators. Along with this continued creative exchange, I must reiterate that *all* the SHS students who have been in my classes have been a part of this book. From the first group in the fall of 1999 to those with me at this writing in the fall of 2009, I thank all of the learners who have taken part in our mutual discoveries.

Thanks to the many educators who have contributed to this book through their work: professors Frank Bellizia and Michael Duni for their oversight of my Masters degree work at Union Institute and University; Gaetana Marrone of Princeton University for her support and guidance during and after my undergraduate years; and my many fine teachers whose inspiring examples have served as pedagogical models. I wish also to thank my colleagues in the Suffield Schools for their high professional standards and dedication to their students and our community. In particular, I extend my gratitude to Dennis Picard, the English Media and television studio pioneer in Suffield, and Stephannie Holland, who has provided tremendous opportunities to students in media and theater arts; their support has been valued. Finally, I would like to express my deep appreciation to Nancy Lombard, whose abundant contributions to Suffield's learning community are sincerely uplifting and whose encouragement and friendship have been invaluable to me.

The professional team at Delmar Cengage Learning has been phenomenal. Jim Gish has made it all possible through his lucid comprehension of the purpose and substance of this undertaking, and I have sincerely appreciated his hard work and enthusiasm. Meaghan O'Brien labored tirelessly through all of the angles of the project, and I greatly respect her calm demeanor and thoroughness. Thanks so much to Erin Brennan for her energy and expertise in bringing this book to classrooms. It has been a true pleasure to work with such a talented group of collaborators, including Sarah Timm, Joy Koscis, Wendy Troeger, Glenn Castle, and Chris Catalina.

Last, I wish to thank my mother, father, and our entire close-knit family for their support and affection. And I must conclude with a most profound thank you to Alexandra and our children, Matteo, Lucie, and Vincent, for their inspiration and love; they have been my sources of motivation and energy during this entire project.

Dedication

This book is dedicated to Matteo, Lucie, and Vincent

Delmar Cengage Learning and I would also like to thank the following reviewers for their valuable suggestions and technical expertise:

Paul Bancroft
Teacher
RHAM High School
Hebron, Connecticut

R. Steve Parr
CTE Instructor
Bethel High School
Spanaway, Washington

Dr. Amy Friedman Phillips
Program Chair, Communications & Media Production
The Art Institute of Fort Lauderdale
Fort Lauderdale, Florida

Philip Rockey
Teacher
South Windsor High School
South Windsor, Connecticut

Roxanne Russell
Associate Professor/Studio Manager
George Washington University
Washington, DC

Heidi Whitus
Communications Department Coordinator
Communications Arts High School
San Antonio, Texas

Julie York
Teacher
South Portland High School
South Portland, Maine

Questions and Feedback

Delmar Cengage Learning and the author welcome your questions and feedback. If you have any suggestions that you think would benefit others, please let us know, and we will try to include them in the next edition.

To send us you questions and/or feedback, you can contact the publisher at:

Delmar Cengage Learning
Executive Woods
5 Maxwell Drive
Clifton Park, NY 12065
Attn: Media Arts & Design Team
800-998-7498

Motion Picture Language

CHAPTER IN FOCUS

In this chapter you will:

- create short motion pictures using visual planning techniques
- investigate standard shots and techniques that are the foundation of a visual language
- evaluate the effect of continuity and other editing techniques in motion picture sequences

Screens

You wake up in the morning, and you prepare for the day. As you go about doing various tasks to get ready, with what screens do you come in contact? Do you light up a computer and check your messages? Is there a TV on in the kitchen? Do you watch a show or play a game on a hand-held device? When you arrive at school, you will probably look at screens, whether pulled down from the ceiling or lit up in front of your keyboard. When the weekend arrives, you may go out with friends to see a movie on a big screen or stay at home and watch shows on a little one.

Screens are a constant part of our lives, from those of televisions or computers to the white screen at the front of the standard American classroom. Public spaces are littered with them, whether one is waiting for jury duty or barraged by fifty televisions at a sports restaurant. At the beginning of the twenty-first century, research has indicated that the average adult spends almost nine hours daily in front of a screen, whether it is a television, computer,

Figure 1-1 Screens in *The Dark Knight,* directed by Christopher Nolan, with, left to right, Michael Caine, Heath Ledger (on screen as The Joker), and Christian Bale. *(Courtesy Warner Brothers/Photofest).*

- *What are the meanings of the word "screen?"*
- *How do we use screens? What types do you look at and in what situations?*

- *In what ways can screens limit a view? Blind the viewer? Distort a view? Give as many examples of screens as you can—not just movie screens!*

mobile device, or other screen featuring moving images. The typical American is surrounded by a variety of images on these screens: What do we make of this flux of shapes, colors, words, and sounds? How do we navigate their meanings and fully utilize their communicative potential?

Moving image media are key modes of communication for storytelling, advertising, commerce, journalism, and research for societies across the world. Consequently, the comprehension, analysis, evaluation, and creation of motion pictures are vital skills for students of the twenty-first century. As movies light up different screens to inform, entertain, challenge, and inspire us, it is important for us to understand and use their images effectively.

For many people, making motion pictures involves picking up a camera, hitting the record button, and pointing the lens at a subject. This attitude is reflected in the passive viewer, slouched into a couch and letting the images stuff themselves into the mind.

Let's think about *active* choices in filmmaking and *active* viewing. These are our goals in this educational, collaborative, and creative experience. We want to develop abilities so that we can consciously use the moviemaking tools at our disposal and develop an awareness of the screen language that permeates our society.

Communication on the Screen

There is a good chance that you have already thought about these issues as a filmmaker. If you have a video camera, you might go out with your friends and shoot some **footage** of a variety of activities. Perhaps you are making a

Figure 1-2 As part of a motion picture, these three shots form a sequence. *(Courtesy of Kendelyn Ouellette).*

school project, or you are recording skateboarding or snowboarding action, or you are exchanging moving images with peers using the Internet. As part of these processes, you may have imported footage onto your computer and used an **editing** program to cut up the material.

Each time you hit the record button and then hit the pause button, you have created a **shot**, which is the basic building block of motion pictures. Recorded shots can be as short as the limits of a high speed camera (for example, 1/2000th of a second) and they can be as long as the length of the material on which you are photographing and recording (perhaps ten minutes for film or one hour or even more for digital video). When you begin the editing process, you will cut and move these shots to create **sequences** that will make up your completed motion picture, whether short or **feature** length.

From the origins of humanity, people have communicated visually. They crawled into caves and drew fascinating images from their world, particularly the animals that they hunted. Through the ages, civilizations have sought to develop a variety of methods to depict their lives, to plan their works, to create stories, and to express spiritual and philosophical ideas.

Evolution of Moving Images

In the nineteenth century, a new method of portraying the world was developed: photography. Through scientific research and discovery, Niépce and Daguerre (photographic inventors who are discussed in Chapter 2) developed the first processes for capturing light and transferring images onto fixed surfaces. At this time, there already existed devices that displayed movement through a rapid

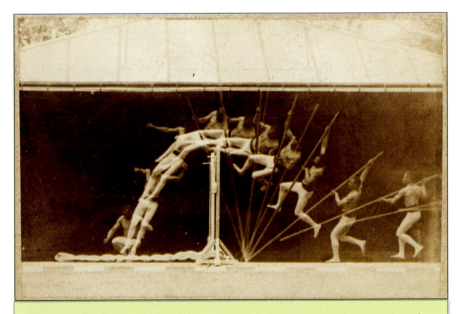

Figure 1-3 Study of a pole vaulter by Etienne-Jules Marey, inventor of the chronophotograph. *(Courtesy Getty Images)*.

Figure 1-4   A man looking at the moving images of the praxinoscope invented by Emile Reynaud in 1877.

succession of still images. As the versatility and quality of still photography progressed through the nineteenth century, it started to become clear that the phenomenon of photography and visual principles of animation toys could merge to lead to a new medium of expression.

By the end of the century, motion pictures had been invented. The process took many steps and involved a variety of creators, including Eadward Muybridge of Britain, W. K. L. Dickson working in the American Edison studios, and the Lumière Brothers in France (all discussed in Chapter 2). The first movies were made up of a single shot that lasted approximately a minute. Some are quite interesting to watch, others rather dull. However, it took the development of the idea of editing—or cutting together different shots to create a sequence of shots on film—to transform it to the medium that we know as the cinema. It is generally when shots work in juxtaposition that we can develop a complete perception of the full creative potential of motion pictures.

What we are talking about here is **motion picture language** (also sometimes called film language, screen language, or film grammar). What does this mean? Motion picture language is the way in which visuals on the screen convey information and express ideas and emotions without words. We use this term to describe the communication through sequences of images on the screen along with the sound that accompanies them.

When you pick up a camera and begin to shoot footage, you are already making decisions that affect how you are communicating to the viewer. You are framing shots, and by those choices in framing, you are selecting what viewers see and determining how they understand what is being shown. In order to discuss shots in motion pictures, filmmakers use a variety of terms for standard framings.

When you review the following terms for shots, keep in mind that use of framing vocabulary varies in different traditions, such as for feature films, television shows, or commercials. The terms used in this book have been selected for functionality and the widest application across motion picture history. When we discuss framing in motion pictures, our reference points are generally based on the most typical subject of moving images, the human figure.

The Building Blocks of Visual Communication

The most familiar framing term is the close-up, which is understood to be a shot of a person or object that is framed relatively close and shows a feature in detail, most commonly a human face. An **extreme close-up (ECU)** is a shot that displays a portion or detail of a subject or a small object. An extreme close-up of a human face shows only part of the face, such as an eye or the mouth. A **medium close-up (MCU)** is a close-up in which the frame is generally filled by the face, with the face framed at the forehead or through the hair and below the mouth or chin. A **full close-up (FCU)** roughly includes the entire head down to around the shoulders.

Two other key terms aid us in explaining the placement of the human figure in the frame: **head room** and **lead room.** Head room indicates the amount of space between

Figure 1-5 Extreme close-up. *(Courtesy of Carl Casinghino).*

Figure 1-6 Medium close-up in which the wide screen allows for significant amount of background. *(Courtesy of Carl Casinghino).*

Figure 1-7 Full close-up. *(Courtesy of Kendelyn Ouellette).*

a character's head and the top of the frame and lead room is the space between the "front" of the character's face and the side of the frame towards which he or she is turned.

The rest of the framing descriptions continue to expose more of the human figure. The shot that moves us to a view that does not exclusively feature the human face or a detail of an object is the **close shot (CS)** in which the frame line crosses the character's chest. A **medium shot (MS)** puts the frame at the

Figure 1-8 Full close-up with some head room. *(Courtesy of Kendelyn Ouellette).*

Figure 1-9 Framing that includes lead room in the direction that the actor is looking and moving. *(Courtesy of Kendelyn Ouellette).*

Figure 1-10 Close shot. *(Courtesy of Kendelyn Ouellette).*

waist of the character, and a medium close shot is between the medium and close shots, or across the stomach. Moving outward, a medium full shot cuts across the knees, while a **full shot (FS)** includes the entire human figure.

When two people are featured in a shot, this is called a **two shot**. For example, a shot that frames the characters at the chest line and includes both in the shot would be a "close two shot." If the camera is placed behind one character so that part of the frame shows the edge of the character's shoulder (and possibly neck and head), this is an **over-the-shoulder shot**. When we arrive at a shot that includes multiple figures in a view of an entire scene, such as a room or a field, this is a **wide shot**. If the camera is far away from the subjects, then it is called a **long shot**.

Figure 1-11 Medium shot. *(Courtesy of Kendelyn Ouellette).*

Figure 1-12 Characters running in full shot in the film *Side Streets*, directed by Tony Gerber, cinematography by Russell Lee Fine. *(Photo by Seth Rubin, Courtesy Market Road Films).*

Figure 1-13 Two shot. *(Courtesy of Kendelyn Ouellette).*

Figure 1-14 Over the shoulder shot. *(Courtesy of Kendelyn Ouellette).*

Figure 1-15 Wide shot for this scene – note that there are many possibilities for a wide shot, but the term is used in relation to the space of the scene and usually indicates a wide-angle lens (or wide setting on a zoom for a consumer digital camera). *(Courtesy of Carl Casinghino).*

Figure 1-16 Long shot – as with the wide shot, there are a variety of interpretations of the long shot, but this shot generally indicates a significant distance between the camera and the scene and may also be a shot that uses a long lens (or telephoto setting). *(Courtesy of Kendelyn Ouellette).*

Using Images to Communicate

When early filmmakers first chose framings for shots a century ago, they were not following a set of rules. Definitions of shots are general descriptions of what viewers see on a screen, and they are not a menu of choices for how to make a movie. These terms can simply help in describing what you see on the screen or in preparing to set up a shot you want to execute for a project.

Motion picture language is *not* the collection of words used on a set by the people who make movies. It is not simply "filmmaking vocabulary." It is a concept that expresses the process by which motion pictures communicate ideas to the viewer through the visual and aural articulation of actions, ideas, and emotions on the screen.

Linking Shots

For example, imagine seeing a shot of a character sitting at a kitchen table. After a few moments, there is a **dissolve** (which is when one shot fades away as another emerges into view) and the same character is standing near the far wall, at the kitchen counter making a cup of coffee. As this action continues, another dissolve begins and in the next shot that emerges as the previous one fades the character is standing to the right of the frame, looking out the window while the coffee cup is sitting on the table. In each of these three shots, the framing stayed the same. What do we guess from this sequence? Why were there dissolves between the shots? The dissolves were done for a few purposes, but one of the main reasons was so that the viewer would understand that time passed between each shot.

Viewers comprehend this because of motion picture language: you did not need to see a message on the screen telling the time or to hear the character tell you "boy, I've been waiting a long time!" in order to realize that some time has passed. In a similar way, the **fade in** can be used to introduce a scene or a new moment in a story, while the **fade out** can be used to bring a scene to a close like the curtain closing at the end of a scene in a play.

In a scene from the animated movie, *A Bug's Life* (1998), Flik, an adventurous ant, is about to leave his colony and is being seen off by little Dot and two skeptical ant "children." This sequence communicates with the viewer using a wide array of expressive tools of motion picture language built on the *physical reality* of filming live subjects.

Think about this: This is a movie made entirely of **computer-generated imagery**, so there was no real camera shooting a bunch of ants out on a field. Yet, it uses elements of **live action** shooting to show us the scene. For example, early on in the sequence, there is a **focus pull**. A focus pull occurs during shooting when a camera operator or assistant alters the point of focus on the lens of the camera, for example, from someone close to the camera to someone far away. In the sequence from *A Bug's Life,* this is done to draw our attention to a particular action on the screen and we react immediately because of our understanding of this device.

In fact, in this scene, there are a number of clear examples of motion picture language at work:

- The **point of view shot** as Flik looks down.
- The swooping feel of the "camera" as Flik takes off, duplicating a similar feel in live action shots.
- The "camera" continues when Flik hits the rock; the visual joke is accentuated by our understanding of shot movement and of its use timed with Flik's "splat!"

Figure 1-17 A focus pull: the cinematographer changes the focus in the shot from the flowers to actor Dan Wallace. *(Courtesy of Kendelyn Ouellette).*

Sometimes, when we think about "communication," we only think of words. However, as you can see from these examples, there are many ways in which we exchange information, ideas, and messages.

The Viewer's Perspective

In the decades after the invention of cinema, filmmakers developed techniques for using multiple shots in sequences. As they did this, they discovered that when putting one shot next to another, the viewer interprets them in relation to each other. It is only natural that we refer to our own perspective when we do this.

Imagine a Civil War battle scene. In the first shot, you see soldiers wearing Union blue moving across the frame from left to right. There is a cut to another shot: What will you see in this shot? You probably anticipate seeing the opposing army: What do you expect to see? If you see Confederate soldiers in gray moving across the screen from right to left, what do you conclude? What do you infer if you see them running from left to right?

If you see the opposing army in gray advancing from right to left, you expect that they are moving towards their enemies in blue, and that in an upcoming shot they will be fighting. If, however, you see them running from left to right, then you expect that they are retreating from the other army. Or, perhaps, they are chasing the other army. You are not sure yet. If one of the two groups looked behind themselves as they were running, you would expect that this group was fleeing.

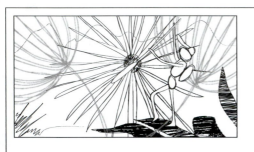

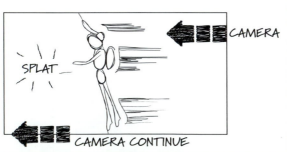

Figure 1-18 In this storyboard showing an example of a sequence in *A Bug's Life,* the first shot shows Flik picking his mode of transport, the second shot shows his point of view while flying, and the third shot shows the moment when he hits the rock and the "camera" continues to move.

Figure 1-19 Battlefield scene from *Glory,* directed by Edward Zwick and starring Denzel Washington. *(Courtesy TriStar Pictures / Photofest).*

How do you know all of this? It is because you have developed a visual understanding, a mode of communication that you understand. No one had to tell you this verbally. There probably was no **voice-over** telling you what was happening (or at least this was not necessary). You understood this because of your fluency in motion picture language, and this demonstrates that you comprehend such concepts as **screen direction** and the **axis**.

Establishing Continuity

It is from these juxtapositions of shots that we encounter one of the main concepts of this unit: **continuity editing**. Continuity editing is a method of editing that is designed to make cuts seem relatively invisible to the viewer. As one shot cuts to the next shot in a sequence, the motion picture moves forward in a continuous and clear way in relation to time and space, and the cutting is not noticeable or jarring to the viewer. In order to make a smooth cut between two shots, there needs to be a significant change in angle between camera and subject and often in framing, as well as proper treatment of issues of time, action, and space. Actions and movements of characters and objects progress smoothly from shot to shot using techniques such as **match cuts**.

With a match cut, there are visual elements that help to make the edit smooth or feel invisible to the viewer. For example, there can be a matching action between the two shots, in which a gesture or action begins in a first shot, then a cut is made and in the next shot, the action continues from the exact point at which it ended in the first, such as the opening of a door or the throwing of a punch. Match cuts can also be made from similar actions or forms of different characters or objects, such as characters in a dance sequence or the bone/spaceship match cut in *2001: A Space Odyssey* (1968).

Remember that a key aspect of match cuts on action is created during filming when there is a change in position for the camera. The framing

Figure 1-20 Match cut on action: the camera cuts from outside to inside as the door is opened. *(Courtesy of Carl Casinghino).*

needs to be changed significantly, particularly with the angle of the camera in relation to the subject of the shot.

The key to the concept of continuity editing is that there is a screen and a viewer. When you look at the screen, it is as if you are sitting in front of the scene that you see in front of you. How things move in that world can be seen as making logical sense or not. The two concepts we need to think about for this are *space* and *time*.

Continuity Editing: Time

When we watch a movie, the editing can show us time in a variety of ways. It can show us ten years rushing by in ten seconds or it can use slow motion and editing to make ten seconds pass by in a number of minutes—or even through an entire movie, if the filmmakers wanted to do this! As we watch movies, we are reacting to time passing on the screen, and how we interpret that time is a key to how we experience and interpret the movies we see and hear.

When filmmakers encountered the challenges of editing motion pictures, they observed a variety of effects as they cut shots together. They noticed that if there was a shot of a woman sitting in a chair followed by a direct cut to the woman standing on the other side of the room and opening a door, it would seem like there had been an abrupt passage of time. On the other hand, if the director simply let the woman get up from the chair and *leave the frame* in the first shot, then the cut to the person opening the door would not be as odd, because we would feel that our sense of time had not been disrupted.

The term continuity editing makes us think of the word *continuous*, and that is exactly what this concept is about: a style and system of editing designed to make time seem relatively continuous on the screen. But does time *have* to feel continuous when we are watching movies?

Jumping Time

To ask the question another way, can we make the first cut described above—from the person in the chair to suddenly opening a door—and say that it's "okay?" Of course! However, it's useful to make the decision consciously and for the effect that is intended. Such an edit is typically called a **jump cut**.

Framing the Discussion

- *Can you think of examples of films or shows that use continuity editing consistently?*

- *Can you think of an example of a motion picture you have seen recently that shows examples of filmmakers not using continuity editing? Describe the sequence or movie.*

- *What types of moving images do you usually see (on television, in a cinema, on the Internet, and so forth) and what editing styles do they typically use?*

An example of a very obvious jump cut begins from when a person is in a close up. There is a cut to the next shot, and it is the same person in the same **composition**, now talking at another point in time. This is a technique used sometimes in documentary film when the filmmakers have footage from an interview. One example is from the opening of *Spellbound*, a 2002 documentary directed by Jeffrey Blitz about a group of contestants in the National Spelling Bee. In the first sequence of the movie, one of the participants in the competition is trying to spell a word, and his attempt to do this is cut into a series of shots from what was originally one long shot recorded during the event. With this particular sequence, it adds energy and humor to the opening while it compresses time in an interesting way.

If you watch this sequence, or one like it, you will see that it plays with our concept of time. Filmmakers use the tools of editing to play with time in a variety of ways. Jump cuts are very rarely seen in classic Hollywood cinema, but they have become normal, even fashionable, in movies, television shows, and commercials of the late twentieth and early twenty-first centuries.

Continuity Editing: Space

As viewers watch the screen, they are also reacting to the space created on the screen in front of them. Remember the two armies facing each other? Not only is it important to pay attention to *time* when we make cuts between shots, but it is also important to consider *space* when we make edits, just as when we saw the armies running at each other.

In order to respect relationships of space in continuity editing, think about our concept of viewer and screen. The world on the screen in front of the viewer generally seems to be a continuous one, unless we are led to react to it in a different way. When we see the two armies fighting, we watch them from one side of the battlefield. If the camera suddenly switches to the other side of the battlefield, we will lose the perspective that we were given initially. The screen direction that was initially established has been altered, and now it will look as if the opposing army is actually running away.

Understanding the Axis

Imagine there was a line drawn between the two armies. In cinema, this is called the axis. To preserve continuity, the camera must always be set up on one side of the axis. Otherwise, there will be a change of screen direction that can be confusing and cause the sequence to seem jumbled or odd.

In Figure 1-21a, you see a boy throwing a ball. When you see his little brother catching the ball, what will be the angle for the shot? In Figure 1-21b, the camera has stayed on the same side of the axis when we cut to the younger boy catching the ball. Now consider a different angle: in Figure 1-21c, the

Figure 1-21a–c Consider the two edits created by cutting to either **Figure 1-21b** or **Figure 1-21c**: in which cut did the camera cross the axis?. *(Courtesy of Carl Casinghino).*

camera was moved to the other side, and the screen direction for the cut from Figure 1-21a to Figure 1-21c looks odd: It is as if the ball is moving from the wrong direction.

Visualize two people in a room, facing each other and talking. Now picture a sequence of shots back and forth between them as they engage in a conversation. If the camera is always placed on one side of the axis, the actors will look like they are addressing each other, since the screen directions will seem logical. In fact, the two actors could even shoot their close-ups separately and never be together in the room!

Figure 1-22 When we see these two shots filmed from one side of the axis, we assume the characters are talking to each other because of a match cut between their glances and other visual cues. *(Courtesy of Kendelyn Ouellette).*

When filmmakers set up the sequence of shots between the actors, they will generally decide on shooting the scene from one side of the axis, which is this imaginary line between the two subjects. In the boys' game of catch, the path of the ball creates the line. Even though this concept seems quite easy to apply when shooting, it can become very tricky when characters move or if there are more than two characters talking to each other. In a group conversation, it can be very important to get screen direction exactly right in order to know who is addressing whom at specific moments.

Another way to imagine this is on a film or television set with three walls. If the actors are sitting at opposite ends of a table in the middle of the set, the camera crew will set up the camera on the open side of the set to always have the walls of the set in the shot. If you moved the camera to the other side of the table—crossing the axis line between the actors—the completely open side of the room (or the audience, if there is one watching a show being taped) is revealed.

Directorial Decisions

As we asked before with the concept of time, one question is "Do we *have* to follow this rule?" Again, the answer is "Definitely not!" However, it is important to understand why one would employ this technique or not. If the style that is being established in a movie expresses a clear, measured tone in the look and editing of its sequences, it is generally appropriate to respect the axis in editing. If the axis is crossed by the camera at random moments, it could simply look amateurish and confusing, as is sometimes the case in poorly directed films.

On the other hand, many directors play around with space to compel the viewer to look at the scene or the space in a variety of ways or from a confusing viewpoint. Many action movies of the twenty-first century are deliberately disorienting and cross the line during fights and chase sequences, as in segments of *The Bourne Supremacy* (2004) or *The Fast and The Furious: Tokyo Drift* (2006). One exaggerated example of broken continuity is from the beginning of the film *Baghdad Café* (1987) directed by Percy Adlon, in which the director shows us the angry breakup of a couple by shattering virtually every "rule" of continuity editing in an off-kilter, intentionally jarring opening sequence. As with the example of time in continuity editing, contemporary filmmakers also play around with the axis and screen direction to accentuate perspective and tell stories in provocative and original ways. In fact, crossing the line has become a commonly used practice in late twentieth century and early twenty-first century motion pictures in order to establish a distinctive, kinetic, and more jarring style than with traditions of smoother cuts.

Composing a Style

Some of the most important aspects of moving images are often the hardest to describe. It is easy enough to explain the plot or events of many movies, and that is usually what people start with when they talk about a motion picture. Often, it's the only thing they talk about.

On the other hand, how we react to a motion picture is often summed up in its *feel.* As filmmakers use color, movement, sound design, or pace and rhythm in editing, the expressive means of the motion picture arts work together to create what we call style and tone in any communicate, creative work. As Sidney Lumet, the director of many films including *12 Angry Men* (1957), *Fail-Safe* (1964), and *Dog Day Afternoon* (1975), explains:

> . . . the way you tell that story should relate somehow to what the story is. Because that's what style is: the way you tell a particular story. After the first decision ("What's this story about?") comes the second most important decision: "Now that I know what it's about, how shall I tell it?" And this decision will affect every department involved in the movie that is about to be made.

Throughout your analytical and creative work with this text, you will be learning about the ways that motion pictures reflect the choices of style and tone by their creators, including you. When you arrive at the final chapter of this text, we will return full circle to Sidney Lumet's observation by investigating the tasks of individual departments in a feature film production.

Framing the Discussion

- *Earlier, you came up with examples of movies that follow continuity editing and one sequence that does not. Can you think of specific sequences that do not follow continuity of time in their editing? Why do they do this?*

- *Can you think of specific sequences that do not follow continuity of space in their editing? Why is this so?*

Using Composition

When you learned about framing of shots and the ways shots are edited together, you were introduced to key foundations of style and tone in a film. When a filmmaker sets up a particular framing for a shot, the way in which people, objects, background, and other visual elements are arranged in the frame is called composition. As you learned earlier, there are terms to describe basic approaches to composition, such as close-ups or wide shots. Filmmakers must consider many factors as they devise unique solutions to compose shots and establish a visual style in a motion picture.

When devising composition for a shot, reflect on the size of the screen and the effect of where things are placed in the space of the frame. The motion picture screen is flat, so the width and height of the frame are immediately obvious to the cameraperson and the viewer. Head room and lead room are important factors in creating a framing style. Excessive head room can look amateurish or it can help to create a humorous look, and lead room can help to direct the audience's attention or create tension by a tight framing. When you look at a picture, what draws your interest? What types of arrangements seem dynamic or interesting to the viewer? What compositions are chosen for a straightforward presentation of information, such as a televised press conference or video of a person speaking at a town meeting?

Many of the essential concepts of composition are shared with other visual art forms that use flat frames, such as painting and sequential art (comics or graphic novels). Although there are sometimes major differences in frame dimensions between different media, the ways in which space and

Figure 1-23 What is shown in a composition can be as important as what is not shown. When viewers see two shots in succession, they interpret meaning from how the shots are presented. *(Courtesy of Carl Casinghino).*

perspective are depicted and utilized have been studied for centuries and can provide many lessons. For example, one common strategy shared with artists of other visual media is to divide the frame into three equal parts horizontally and vertically.

Figure 1-24 Live high school morning announcements. *(Courtesy of Carl Casinghino).*

Figure 1-25 Frame from a digital short separated into thirds. Note the strong placement of the foreground actor at the top right intersection point. *(Courtesy Brian Spellman and Ryan Sindler).*

Rule of Thirds

This lesson, called the **rule of thirds**, is employed to show artists that more forceful impact is achieved by placing important visual elements, such as a character's face, at one of the points of intersection of the dividing lines in the frame. The aesthetic impression and design possibilities of a composition may be enhanced by reflecting this pattern. Like many "rules" in the arts, this concept should be looked at as a creative tool to be used when appropriate. Certainly, some of the most successful compositional choices in the history of the arts have been those in which the center of interest is exactly in the middle of the frame. After all, Leonardo da Vinci's *Mona Lisa* still seems to attract quite a few visitors, and many filmmakers find that the greatest impact in a particular shot is achieved by placing an actor in close-up at the center of the frame.

Like the canvas of a painting or the page of a graphic novel, the motion picture screen is flat. Creators working in all these media share a common challenge: to bring the image to life by giving it depth. A filmmaker must consider the ways in which three-dimensional space can be used to give shape to the world on the screen. Placement, movement, lighting, and camera position all affect what the viewer perceives in the frame, and the establishment of depth can help the visual storyteller to portray the actions and events occurring in the story.

Figure 1-26 Sometimes a centered, balanced composition can be appropriate in a shot, as in this motion picture still featuring Taryn Scozzari. *(Courtesy of Carl Casinghino).*

Figure 1-27 Choices of composition face artists working in a variety of media, as seen through the point of view, placement of figures, and depth seen in *Law Office,* an oil painting on linen by Christopher Benson. *(Courtesy Christopher Benson).*

Depth of View

Relationships between two or more characters can be powerfully enhanced by placement in the **foreground** or **background** of a shot. The foreground of a shot refers to whatever subjects are closer to the camera, and the background is composed of the visual elements and setting that are at the rear of the image. If there is enough depth to what is seen in the shot, the people and things that are placed in between these two planes are in the middle ground or at middle distance. For example, in the opening dramatic scene of the film *The Graduate* (directed by Mike Nichols, 1967), Benjamin Braddock, played by Dustin Hoffman, is towards the background of the scene, his head framed by an aquarium, and his father sits in the foreground in the left part of the screen (see Figure 1-28). The depth of the shot communicates a great deal to the viewer: Benjamin is in focus, drawing our attention to him, while his father, representing Benjamin's adult life, is fuzzy, out of focus and out of sync with his son visually. He constantly obscures Benjamin who is framed by the tank, examined and peered at like the fish and stuck in a situation that feels artificial to him.

In *O Brother, Where Art Thou?* (2000), a comedy by the Coen Brothers, three convicts have just escaped from a chain gang and then a fiery trap in a barn. They are in the woods trying to figure out their next move when two of them, Ulysses Everett McGill (George Clooney) and Pete (John Turturro), get into an argument because Everett has stolen a watch from Pete's cousin (who subsequently betrayed them). The shots cut back and forth following their dialogue, and in an over-the-shoulder shot of Pete that puts Everett in close shot, we begin to perceive characters clad in white walking in the woods behind Everett (see Figure 1-29). In this way, the filmmakers use

Figure 1-28 Frame from *The Graduate*, directed by Mike Nichols, with William Daniels as Mr. Braddock and Dustin Hoffman as Benjamin Braddock. *(Courtesy Embassy Pictures/Photofest).*

Figure 1-29 Frame from *O Brother Where Art Thou,* directed by Joel Coen, with George Clooney as Everett (facing the camera) and John Turturro as Pete. *(Courtesy Buena Vista Pictures/Photofest).*

depth of composition to introduce one of the mysterious interludes of the story. These robed worshippers emerge from the background and effortlessly dissipate the conflict between Everett and Pete, reflected by the spiritual they are singing.

Compositional techniques are shared with other visual arts that use frames, but in motion pictures, the images are *moving in time* from the perspective of the lens on a camera. Where you place the camera, what you show or hide, and how you move the camera and what is in the frame are all cornerstones of style and tone. For example, a point of view shot can be used to establish a closer identification of the viewer to a particular character or to reveal information from a distinct perspective. The height of the camera also affects the impact of a shot. A **high-angle** shot, in which the camera is placed above the subject with the lens facing down, has been commonly used to make a character appear vulnerable or to allow the audience to look over a scene from a contemplative vantage point. A **low-angle shot,** in which the camera is significantly lower than the subject, offers a perspective that accentuates the stature of the people or objects in the frame, sometimes distorting them or giving them force and power. Of course, relationships between characters or a particular viewpoint of a character within a scene can be accentuated by cutting between high- and low-angle shots.

Figure 1-30 High-angle shot.

Figure 1-31 Low-angle shot.

Moving the Frame

If the camera holds its frame steadily, such as when it is locked in place on a tripod, this is called a **static shot**. Sometimes this is the most appropriate way to frame a shot. However, movement is also at the heart of the medium of motion pictures. The roll of film is advancing as the projector turns. The

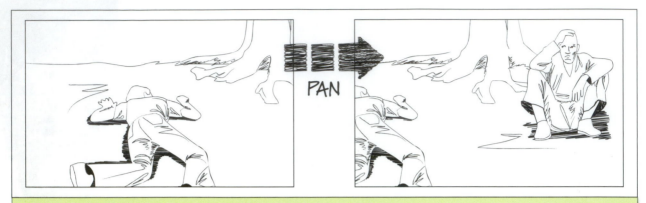

Figure 1-32 Storyboard indicating a pan right of the camera.

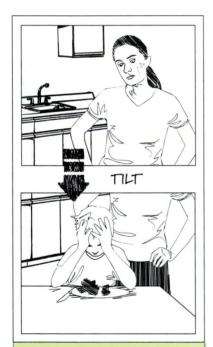

Figure 1-33 Storyboard indicating a tilt down of the camera.

disc spins in the player to make light move on the screen. And just as figures move in front of the camera, filmmakers are naturally compelled to move the camera around to shift its viewpoints and exploit the kinetic experience of moving perspectives.

From their invention, cameras were steadied by placing them on tripods. Most primitive shots duplicated the fixed frames of still photography. Although most early films were shot from a lock-down position, eventually filmmakers began to **pan** the camera side to side or **tilt** it up and down. This was commonly seen in travelogue films in which filmmakers strove to provide a full view of a landscape, much as tourists do today.

Filmmakers also realized that they could place the camera on a moving device. They discovered that they could put the tripod onto a wheeled platform or set up carefully leveled railed tracks to film a tracking shot. Any moving shot from a wheeled device became known as a **dolly shot**, and this technique became one of the most expressive storytelling methods available to directors. It allows directors to pass across the action for a graceful view of the scene, to move towards a subject to add dramatic emphasis, or to pull away from a view to widen perspective. For a larger movement that provides a longer view than a dolly or a significantly higher angle, filmmakers can mount a camera on a device that raises or lowers the camera significantly for a **crane shot**.

Today, small movements known as **push-in** and **pull-out** are often used for quick dramatic emphasis. A push-in can provide accent to move a sequence along and a push-in or pull-out can bring it to a close, like a punctuation mark. For example, they are used many times in the *Lord of the Rings* films directed by Peter Jackson.

In twenty-first century films, camera movement is quite common through **hand-held** use of the camera or an invention of the 1970s known

Figure 1-34a–b These two frames are from one shot in which the camera pushes in on a dolly towards the actress for dramatic emphasis. *(Courtesy of Kendelyn Ouellette).*

Figure 1-35a–b In this case, the camera pulls back at the end of a shot. *(Courtesy of Carl Casinghino).*

as the **Steadicam**. This device, which is mounted on the operator of the camera, is used to allow smooth movement of the camera like a dolly shot without being limited to the wheels or tracks of a dolly. Directors can opt for a camera style that feels unrehearsed or chaotic by using a hand-held camera or they can choose the fluid approach of the Steadicam.

Investigating Tone and Style

As you have seen, *style* is the way that the images or story are presented. Throughout the chapters of this text, you will explore the issues raised by the following questions. As you watch and make movies with your work in this book, you will consistently return to these concepts. Think about the following elements:

- Composition of the frame
  - How are people, objects, and places presented, and how do they move around?
  - Where is the camera positioned and how does it move?
- Use of light, dark, and color in photography.
  - Are there ways in which you can describe the "look" of the film?
  - What is typically sharp or blurry?
  - How would you describe light and dark or color in the film?
- Use of editing of shots.
  - What rhythms are established by the edits?
  - What are some typical juxtapositions of shots as they line up in a sequence? How do they reveal or hide information?
- Stylistic choices in the approach to acting; sound design and use of music; production design (sets, costumes, props, and so forth); and visual effects.
  - Is there a particular tradition and context in which the actors are working? Do the performances in the movie fit together well and follow an approach that reflects a cultural, social, or historical context?
  - How does sound affect the impact of the images? How does sound work to add to, contradict, or comment on the events of the motion picture?
  - How are production design and visual effects used to create a believable or artistically cohesive world on the screen? In what ways do production design and visual effects add to the story being told or the impact of the images on the screen?

Tone can sometimes derive from the type or genre of a particular movie and is expressed through the emotional qualities, ambiance, and mood of a motion picture. You can apply this to any format, whether a feature film, a television program, a commercial, or an instructional video. There are many ways in which we can describe the *tone* of motion pictures:

- Is it *quiet* and *reflective*, or is it *brash* and *aggressive*?
- Is it *dramatic* but with a *slightly comic* tone (like some James Bond films), or is it *brooding* and *menacing*?
- Does it tell its story or relate information in a straightforward way (such as in a *clear* tone), or does it establish a *sarcastic* attitude about characters or other aspects of the story or message?
- Does it follow a certain format that you are familiar with, such as romantic comedy, action adventure, horror, or other recognizable type?

You can start with some adjectives as you begin to describe films, but try to move on to more complete and satisfying descriptions of the motion pictures that you see.

Motion Picture Language in Action

Now it is time to think about developing your own style and creating your own tone. In the moviemaking exercises with this chapter, you will work on visualizing and executing short projects. To do this, you will use the most valuable tools that filmmakers use to prepare for filming: **shot lists** and **storyboards**.

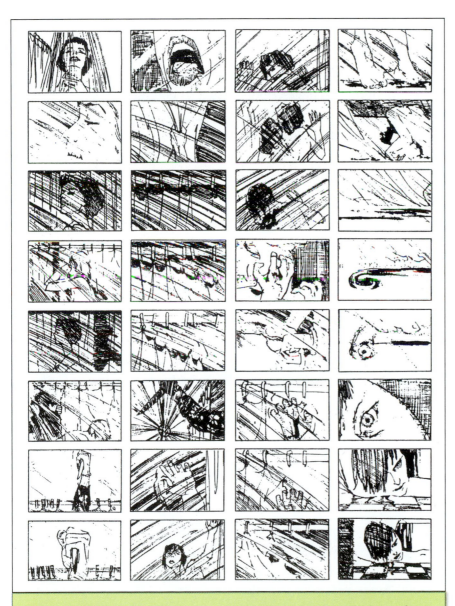

Figure 1-36 Storyboard sequence by artist and designer Saul Bass for Alfred Hitchcock's film *Psycho. (Courtesy Paramount/Photofest).*

Throughout this text, you will explore foundations and methods of storytelling and of media communication. In this chapter, you will use provided scripts and generate simple story ideas in collaborative teams. Your primary task is to translate these simple scenes into motion pictures. There are two common initial steps taken by filmmakers to prepare to shoot footage.

Often, the first step directors take to devise a plan for recording moving images is to prepare a shot list. This is a list of the shots that they plan to record from the information in the script or story, compiled in the order they will run in the finished motion picture. With completed scripts, scenes are numbered starting with 1, so a shot list will use letters for the shots. Thus, scene 1 will include shots 1a, 1b, 1c, and so on, and scene 2 will proceed with 2a, 2b, and so on. Shots are described briefly using framing descriptions (MCU, Close Two Shot, and so forth) and other pertinent information such as camera movement or other shot descriptions (such as point of view).

Storyboards are one of the most familiar tools used by filmmakers. In fact, one of their earliest uses was by the Walt Disney Studios, which employed them in early animated productions to plan their stories. Story developers and illustrators would break up into teams to prepare sequences of the motion picture, and then they would present completed scenes to the production team (headed by Walt Disney sitting in an armchair front and center in the screening room). The story developers would explain the **narrative** that was shown through the individual panels which were posted on large boards. Later in feature film productions, the use of storyboards was applied in the

Figure 1-37 Walt Disney confers with songwriter Johnny Mercer in front of a storyboard sequence for the film *Song of the South*. *(Courtesy Getty Images)*.

preparation stages for live action films as well, and they are used today by many filmmakers.

In a storyboard, the director or an illustrator creates a series of sketches that show the planned shots for a motion picture. They are done in sequence just as they are envisioned in the completed movie. The drawings can be very simple, using stick figures and simple lines for backgrounds or important objects, or they can be complex illustrations that show compositional perspective and a significant amount of detail.

These preparations can be an invaluable help during production. In particular, by having a plan, certain ideas can be reflected on in advance and confidence can be built before stepping into the shoot. The challenges to be faced on set will not be completely unexpected, since these preparations have forced the filmmakers to imagine shots ahead of time. As a result, shot lists and storyboards can free up filmmakers to devise spontaneous creative solutions when they are necessary. Director Robert Wise, whose films include *The Sound of Music* (1965), *The Haunting* (1963), *The Andromeda Strain* (1971), explains his first use of storyboards for the 1949 boxing movie *The Set-Up*:

Figure 1-38 Director Robert Wise looking through a viewfinder to set up a shot. *(Courtesy United Artists/Photofest).*

> *Very often you plan something in the office and when it gets on its feet with the actors on the set and gets started, sometimes it just doesn't want to play that way. The actors will find new things, new dimensions that you can't anticipate. It's only through the doing, the playing of the scene that that happens. Then you have to be able to work what the actors develop into what you planned or say, "Listen, that isn't going to work. Let's try and make our move this way, or change the set up and go another way." So you have to be flexible, but story boarding, and having a start, gives you a good handle on how you approach the film or what the feeling is going to be and what the continuity and the look is going to be, whether you change that within it or not.*

Exploring Motion Picture Language

Motion pictures reflect a diverse array of factors, including artistic goals and concerns, traditions and cultures, history and contemporary events. In turn, we are influenced by our own societies, backgrounds, and values. As you watch movies in conjunction with the work of this text, it is important to remember to keep an open mind and to make an effort to learn from the movies you see. Typically, when we encounter new places and people in life, we come to these new experiences with expectations and biases. It is important to recognize our perspectives and see from a variety of vantage points, including the contexts of the creative works we encounter.

When you engage in analysis of motion pictures, whether with works presented to you or those made by you and your peers, it is important to be constructive and precise with criticism and to avoid personal or strongly emotional language. This also is true of the collaborative work with which you will be engaged as you make your way in this text. Collaboration works when people are able to communicate effectively and move forward together. Divisive comments and personal attacks lead to a breakdown of continued cooperative work and inevitably result in bitterness and frustration among those involved in the work. A study of the studio system in Hollywood provides plenty of lessons in this subject!

It's a Wrap!

In this chapter, you examined the ways in which moving images communicate ideas and narrate events using motion picture language. In order to describe what you see on the screen, you studied a variety of terms and concepts to classify, analyze, and interpret various types of motion pictures. As you will learn throughout this text, the use of moving images and sounds present infinitely exciting challenges to us as we attempt to express ideas, stories, emotions, and imagery to viewers. Now you will begin work with the concepts we have been discussing through *analysis*, *writing*, and *exercises*.

VIEWFINDER

"[What surprised me during] my first film was the unbelievable number of constraints—financial, temporal, human, and artistic—that could rise up between the director's vision and the final result. I thought that a director's job was, above all, to have good ideas. I realized instead that it mainly consisted of managing all kinds of outside elements to create the right environment to bring those ideas to fruition."

–Takeshi Kitano–

Japanese director and actor whose films include *Kikujiro* (1999) and *Hana-bi [Fireworks]* – (1997)

Analysis: Communicating through Images

A. Basic Information: Character, Place, Tone – *For the first section of this Analysis exercise, you will watch the opening sequences from a selection of movies. Answer the following questions in relation to each sequence:*

1. What characters are revealed in the opening, and how are they introduced? Are there any clues indicating who will be main characters in the movie?

2. Using the vocabulary from this unit, describe one sequence of at least three consecutive shots from the selection. What does the sequence tell you?

3. What information is revealed in the opening? How is this done—through shots? Sound? How does shot selection show or hide information?

4. After examining your answers for **1, 2, and 3,** what do you think will be the tone and style of the movie?

B. Creating a World: Inhabitants, Landscapes & Interiors, Atmosphere – *For Part B, you will watch* Inja *by Steve Pasvolsky (see included DVD) and other selected short films. Take notes on the movies to prepare your answers to the following questions. After all of the shorts have been screened, you will analyze one of the films or complete a comparison and contrast of two of the films. You choose the one or two films and use the questions below to guide your writing. For each of the short films you view, answer the following questions:*

1. How are the characters introduced? Through the course of the movie, how do their actions define who they are?

2. How is the setting portrayed? What is the sense of space in the movie—what do you see or not see in the world that these characters inhabit?

3. What types of shots do you see in the film? How do the filmmakers use photography to set a tone and style?

4. What is the pace and style of the editing? Describe two cuts in the movie: between what shots do they occur and at what points in the story? In what ways do any edits add meaning to the shots or help the flow of scenes?

5. What visual and sonic elements create a strong impact? What are your reactions to the short movie? Consider both your thoughts and emotions.

Writing: Writing Pictures

You have probably heard the phrase "a picture is worth a thousand words." Well, you won't need to write a thousand words for this assignment, but you will focus on describing **images** *as you tell a brief story. Once you have completed this assignment, you may keep it for future reference. You may end up using it for a script you write at some time in the future.*

A.   Think about an interesting action event you have witnessed in person during the past month. It may involve one person or multiple people. For this writing exercise, you will describe that event *as if you were describing a series of moving images, one after another.*

1.   Introduce the scene.

   a.   What is the setting?

   b.   What led up to the event? Is there any description that can help to set the scene properly and dramatically?

2.   Describe the actions of the scene. As you present us with a person or people, have their actions define their character. You may also give physical description.

3.   At the end of the scene, remember to present only a physical description of the actions that you witnessed and the last descriptions of what was seen.

B.   After you have completed the assignment, it is a good idea to share it with a group of collaborators. All the members should share their writing. Use the following questions to lead group discussion or a personal evaluation:

1.   What could be some approaches in filming this scene? Do you visualize any particular point of view or style for this sequence?

2.   How could the filmmakers use the camera or sound to create a strong impression during the film?

Project: Motion Picture Language

For this exercise, you will begin working in collaborative groups to shoot complete scenes that will be edited by a group member. Two or more students will serve as actors in a scene with a prepared script. Others will serve as director, cameraperson, boom operator, and editor.

A. You have been provided with two scripts from which you will select one. In the scripts, minimal action and setting details have been indicated. Your group needs to create actions and determine a specific setting for the scene you choose. You **may** make changes to the script, but the primary context of the scene should remain the same. See below for indications on how to proceed, and devise answers to the following questions:

   1. Who are these two characters?
   2. What led up to the event?
   3. How will the short begin? What action or image will initiate the scene?
   4. What will bring about an end to the scene? With what image will it close?

B. For the film, complete the following preparatory work:

   1. The director meets with the actors, rehearses the scene, and determines location, actions, and context in consultation with them.
   2. The cameraperson, editor, and any other crew members review the script and write out a shot list for the scene. For the shot selection of the scene, follow these guidelines:
      a. There must be a variety of shots, including at least four framings defined in the chapter.
      b. Do not use any zooms during shots—any movements must be done using a dolly or movement of the camera operator.
      c. Use a tripod for at least one of the shots, if one is available.
   3. The production team meets and reviews the prepared materials to finalize the plan for the shoot. If there is lack of consensus, the director proposes a solution to the plan and presents the proposal to the instructor for evaluation.
   4. The crew and actors shoot the scene.
   5. The editor cuts the scene in consultation with the director.

C. **Guidelines** – For all of the projects you do in association with this textbook, you need to follow the guidelines established by your instructor and your school. School and community rules concerning language, controversial topics, defamatory or injurious depictions of groups, and representations intended to malign or cause harm to any individual must be strictly respected. Situations that involve injurious violence, bodily harm, or danger to any person or animal involved in the making of any motion pictures are not permitted.

Script A

INT. ROOM - DAY

ROBIN enters room. CHRIS is in the room.

                        ROBIN
            I don't think there's any way
            he could have done it.

                        CHRIS
            I'm sure it's him - I'm
            positive!

                        ROBIN
            How could YOU know?

                        CHRIS
            Look, just believe me.

                        ROBIN
            Why should I? Tell me why!

                        CHRIS
            Look - just trust me.

                        ROBIN
            But why should I NOW, after
            all the rest?

                        CHRIS
            Let's forget about all that.

Script B

```
INT. ROOM - DAY

ROBIN enters room. DANA is in the room.

                    ROBIN
          Where is everybody?

                    DANA
          I don't know. I guess it's
          cancelled.

                    ROBIN
          But you called me.

                    DANA
          Yeah.

                    ROBIN
          Like, WHAT? Come on, you knew
          there wouldn't be anybody.

                    DANA
          I didn't.

                    ROBIN
          Come on, admit it.

                    DANA
               (Pause)
          Well, OK. I didn't want anybody
          else to be around.

                    ROBIN
          What?

                    DANA
          I've had enough of him. I want to
          do something.

                    ROBIN
          I don't want any part of it. I'm
          leaving.

Robin leaves.
```

Report

For this report, complete all information with a full description of pertinent examples and analysis. Provide supporting details where necessary, and use a variety of descriptive terms from the chapter. See the instructor with any questions. If indicated by the instructor, you may include information from all class activities in this report.

A. Exercise Work – Write a minimum of one paragraph describing your work on Exercise 1. Comment on the *process* of creating this video. Note the following:

1. Your position and the completion of your tasks in the preparations.

2. Comment on your contributions in completing the requirements for the assignment. Did you complete the scene? Why or why not?

3. Difficulties that were encountered as a group and possible solutions that were devised—or not!

B. Video Analysis –Write a minimum of two paragraphs to evaluate the sequence you shot. Comment on the effectiveness of the motion picture in reference to the following elements:

1. Framing of the shots: Are compositions effective for the scene?

2. Length and juxtapositions of shots: How are the edits?

3. Performances: Are they consistent with the group objectives for the scene?

4. Overall effectiveness of movie and story: Are you satisfied with the scene?

Glossary

Axis – In filmmaking, "the axis" is an imaginary line perceived between two or more characters in a scene used for purposes of continuity editing.

Background – In relation to the depth of space depicted in the frame, the background is made up of the visible elements (people, spatial elements, walls, and so forth) that are the farthest from the camera.

Close shot (CS) – Shot of a subject's face and upper body in which the lower frame line crosses the person's chest.

Composition – The arrangement of visual elements in a motion picture frame. This includes all people, objects, settings, and other visuals as they are seen in terms of width, height, and depth, and as they move in the space of the screen.

Computer-generated imagery – Also known as CGI, this term refers to moving images created by the manipulation of digital information generated using computer graphics programs.

Continuity editing – The cutting and arrangement of shots designed to make sequences feel continuous in time and space.

Crane shot – A shot in which the camera is mounted on a device that raises or lowers the camera significantly, such as a crane or a jib arm.

Dissolve – A transition between two shots or sequences whereby the first gradually fades out as the second fades in with some overlap.

Dolly shot – A shot in which the camera is on a moving device, such as a dolly with wheels, either independently mobile or on tracks. If the camera is moving on a dolly mounted on tracks, it is often called a tracking shot.

Editing – The process of selecting and cutting shots (separating them and altering their length), then moving them and determining their proper arrangement in sequences.

Extreme close-up (ECU) – A shot that features a portion or very close view of a subject, such as a detail of a face or a small object.

Fade in – An image gradually appearing from a black or monochromatic screen or other image.

Fade out – Process in which an image gradually fades away to a black or monochromatic screen or other image.

Feature – A motion picture intended as a prime attraction for theatrical distribution (as opposed to short films or media for other formats, such as television or the Internet), generally from eighty minutes to three hours in length.

Focus pull – A change in the distance at which the image is sharp during a shot, which can be done manually on the lens, through the camera, or by a remote device.

Footage – This term can refer to: (1) the numerical measurement of film in feet or time; (2) the length of moving images recorded by a camera, in an unedited state.

Foreground – In relation to the depth of space depicted in the frame, the foreground is made up of those elements (people, objects, and so forth) that are closest to the camera.

Full close-up (FCU) – Framing that includes the subject's head and shoulders.

Full shot (FS) – A composition that includes the entire human figure.

Hand-held – A shot in which the camera is held directly by the cameraperson, sometimes with the aid of a brace.

Head room – The amount of space in the frame that is above the primary character(s) head(s). Excessive headroom can be a sign of amateurish photography.

High-angle shot – A shot in which the camera is higher than the subject and tilted down.

Jump cut – An edit between two shots from a single sequence that makes time or space shift abruptly or in a jolting manner: not continuous.

Lead room – When a character is facing to one side of the frame or the other, this is the area in the frame between the character's face and the edge of the frame towards which he or she is facing.

Live action – Moving images featuring living subjects in the physical world, as opposed to animation.

Long shot – Shot filmed at a significant distance from the subject.

Low-angle shot – A shot in which the camera is lower than the subject and tilted up.

Match cut – An edit in which an action or visual form in the first shot is matched with one in the second shot to create a smooth transition between the shots.

Medium close-up (MCU) – A shot in which the face occupies a substantial portion of the image. The top of the screen frames the face from the forehead to near the top of the head while the bottom frames the person below the mouth or chin.

Medium shot (MS) – Shot framed at the waist of the subject and including the entire upper body of the person.

Motion picture language – Motion picture language (or film language or screen grammar) is the "language of images" that stems from the meanings that we derive from the moving images created by anyone making movies. These meanings are generated by the visual elements of shots, their juxtaposition into sequences, and the use of transitions, animated frames, and visual effects.

Narrative – This is the broad category of films that primarily consist of sequences of events that are linked by cause and effect following continuity of time and space.

Over-the-shoulder shot – A shot taken from the vantage point of behind one of the characters, and including the person's shoulder and/or back of the head.

Pan – The turning of the camera to the left or right, such as when mounted on a tripod.

Point-of-view shot – A shot that is from the point of view of a character in the film. This can be quite obvious, such as a hand coming into the screen, or it can be more subtle, such as from the context of other shots in the sequence.

Pull-out – A shot in which the camera moves away from the subject, widening the view.

Push-in – A shot in which the camera moves towards the subject, narrowing the view.

Rule of thirds – In an image, the height and width can be equally divided into thirds. According to this principle, the four points in the space where the two vertical lines and two horizontal lines meet are the areas of most dynamic interest to the viewer, and the top and bottom thirds of the frame are where horizon lines should stretch.

Screen direction – The movement of subjects in relation to the camera, particularly to the left or right sides of the screen.

Sequence – A series of shots that form a distinct storytelling unit or unified passage in the film, much like a scene in a play.

Shot – A recorded series of images that show a view, either fixed or moving, which duplicates a passage of real time. It can be cut into smaller pieces through editing. Also, the passage of time can be lengthened or shortened by recording more or fewer frames than is technically appropriate per second of normal time, commonly known as slow or fast motion.

Static shot – Shot in which the framing does not move; generally, the camera is mounted on a tripod for stability.

Steadicam – A camera-stabilizing system introduced by Garrett Brown in 1976, worn by the operator for steady camera movement. The Steadicam rig is generally used to photograph smooth-looking shots while the camera operator is moving on foot.

Storyboard – A series of still images, usually drawings, representing individual shots arranged in sequences for motion picture production.

Tilt – Adjusting the angle of the camera in an upwards or downwards fashion, as when mounted on a tripod.

Two shot – A shot that includes two characters; often a close or medium shot.

Voice-over – A voice heard with moving images but not spoken out loud by any character who is physically part of the sequence shown on the screen.

Wide shot – A shot that takes in most or all of the space of the scene in view, whether a room or an open space, often filmed with a wide-angle lens.

Close-Up

Behind the Scenes with Director
Nanette Burstein

Director Nanette Burstein on the set of *American Teen* with cinematographer Wolfgang Held. Her other directing credits include *The Kid Stays in the Picture* and *Going the Distance,* and she has produced such projects as the television series *Film School. (Courtesy of Nanette Burstein)*

Q In what ways did you first become involved in making movies?

A I went to NYU film school and started making short fiction films and during that time I started my junior year interning in the edit room for a documentary series. I got hired as an assistant editor, and then they ran out of funding and I offered to edit the last movie in the series for very little money, which they let me do. So I was pretty young, I was 21 when I had my start at a professional documentary, and it was an interesting experience because the directors weren't involved in the editing room, they were just hired to go out and shoot the film and then it was left to the editor to figure out the story line, so there was a lot of freedom which made me really excited about documentary.

Q What were your next steps?

A Through having made my own short fiction films I had to do a lot of jobs myself. It's very hands on. And then following that up with editing non-fiction films, when I went to make my first feature-length documentary, I had both of those experiences in fiction and non-fiction and I decided to meld the two and shoot a non-fiction film, to film real people but have in mind a story that has a narrative and can be shown in a three-act structure and not be a meandering story. Something that would appeal to me thematically would be compelling to me as well, and I could develop a style that is appropriate for that subject. At the time of this project, that warranted being very gritty because I didn't have any money, so it had to be gritty. So all of these experiences led up to shooting my first film.

Q How have you used motion picture form to develop storytelling?

A For me, the style is always dictated by the subject matter. If I have a subject matter that I'm interested in telling, I try to find the most appropriate style to communicate that cinematically. And if you move between varied projects, the style can change quite a bit too. And so, my first film, *On the Ropes*, was about boxers in Bed-Stuy, a very poor neighborhood, and it was very important that the film not be heavily stylized or glossy, that it be real and gritty and that the soundtrack came from those streets.

Any kind of "making of" story has endless conflict because to arrive at a final product there's just so much fighting and heartache that happens along the way. So *Film School* is about showing the conflict that's happening in trying to collaborate which invariably appears. And then we also chose to come up with animation to show the fruit of their idea, the idea at the beginning that described what their movie is. We wanted to use animation to show a storyboard of the film in their head.

Q What are some comparisons and contrasts between fiction and non-fiction moviemaking?

A Ultimately, you're trying to arrive at the same goal, to tell a really honest, compelling story and use the same sort of dramatic structure for either medium. The route to get there is rather different though. For a fiction film it's so important for your script to be as good as can be, because you're going to shoot your script. You're going to be limited with your choices in the edit room. Whereas in a non-fiction film, you have a very high shooting ratio but you also have little control, comparatively.

In a fiction film that I made, I directed performances to make them feel as honest as possible, and as real as possible, like in a documentary where you try to get your subjects to feel as honest and real on camera, because they have a camera in their face and you are sort of altering reality. In a way, you are trying to figure out "how can they be themselves? How can they be most natural?" The difference is they are that person rather than embodying a character through lines they're supposed to say.

In documentary filmmaking, you are asking people to open up their lives to you, and you have to gain their trust, and with actors in fiction films—even though they're a trained professional playing a part—you are guiding them into how they should appear on screen and they equally need to trust you in a different way. They need to trust that they're in good hands and that when you ask them to do something in a certain way they won't end up looking like fools but they will actually be complimented by that process.

Visit the textbook website to read the entire interview with Nanette Burstein.

Inventions and Origins

CHAPTER IN FOCUS

In this chapter you will:

- produce a short motion picture in a collaborative group using principles of visual storytelling
- investigate the origins and basic optical principles of motion pictures
- evaluate the effectiveness of visual communication in a variety of moving images

Light Moves

For many of us today, it is probably hard to imagine life without photography and motion pictures. We have become accustomed to seeing ourselves and those who surround us in snapshots and filmed sequences. Flashes of our lives are captured in the light that passes through lenses and is recorded on a variety of media.

Picture human beings two hundred years ago, when the only possible inscribed image would have been recorded through drawing or painting (and even this would have been relatively rare). As you think about their perspective on time and memory, imagine the effect of seeing a photograph of yourself for the first time. Or of a loved one who has passed away. When we hear stories of the first motion pictures shown to audiences, it is important to keep in mind the enormous impact of these new ways of recording the visual world.

All of these concepts revolve around the most basic element of our visual world: light. The many developments that progressed and coalesced to result in motion pictures stem from the understanding and use of light. **Photography** is all about the capturing and transferring of light to a preserved state. In fact, many essential elements of photography are reflected in the source of our own relationship to the visual world: the eye.

As we examine fundamental concepts of visual storytelling in motion pictures, it is useful to understand basic elements of the origins and invention of cinema. Key steps in the development of photographic media offer insight into the cultural, historic, and artistic importance and uses of motion pictures.

Figure 2-1 *Feeding the Baby* directed by Louis Lumière in 1895 and featuring Auguste, Marguerite, and baby André Lumière. *(Courtesy of Photofest)*

Figure 2-2 Over a century after *Feeding the Baby*, images are constantly used to capture everyday life. *(Courtesy of Carl Casinghino)*

Figure 2-3 Compare human eyesight to photography.

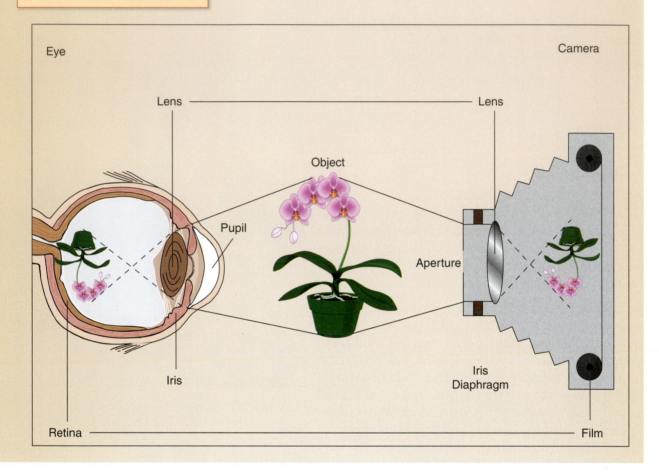

Framing the Discussion

- *When do you take photographs? When do you look at them?*

- *Do you regularly use a motion picture camera? Does anyone in your family or do any of your friends use one? When do you watch motion pictures you have made?*

- *How would your life be different if there were no photographs or motion pictures? How would it alter your perceptions of life? How would it change your activities?*

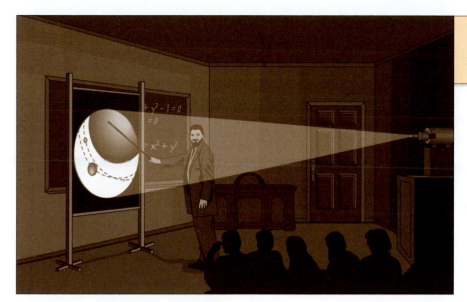

Projecting Light

In the last unit, we discussed the earliest recorded impressions that humans made of their world, painted on cave walls. Humanity has constantly sought diverse ways to tell stories and record and enact impressions of their world, and among these methods has been the use and manipulation of light. From ancient examples of using one's hands or body to create shadows that outline figures in a story to the expressive cutouts of shadow theater in Asia, people have used light projected on a surface to communicate with an audience.

A major step towards what we think of as the cinema was initiated with an apparatus that was used for centuries in Europe and Asia: the **magic lantern**. Over five centuries ago, artisans had used very primitive lanterns that created candlelit projections of shadows to entertain spectators. By the seventeenth century, devices with a light source, lenses, and mirrors were used to project images and writing on walls and screens. These magic lanterns, which are essentially precursors to the modern slide projector, allowed people to see shows that thrilled and amused with images of ghosts, demons, or painted scenes. By the 1830s, traveling storytellers used glass plates with painted scenes that sometimes incorporated movement, and audiences could even see slides dissolve into each other, an effect that later became a key cinematic technique.

The next major component of motion pictures, a succession of images that blends into a sense of movement, is seen in the many devices developed during the first half of the nineteenth century, such as the **phenakistoscope** or the **zoetrope**. When we see a rapid succession of images, our eyes and brain process the stream of images as a perception of movement. Although previously attributed to the concept of "persistence of vision," contemporary

Figure 2-5 The phenakistoscope, invented in 1832 by Belgian physicist Joseph Plateau.

scholars have defined the more appropriate **short-range apparent motion**. This phenomenon is the illusion of real-time action produced by a rapid succession of still images capable of producing smoothly perceived movement. The capacity of the human eyes and brain to process a quickly-moving series of images as a flowing succession of movement is essential for optical spinning toys and motion pictures. This illusion is so powerful that we feel as if we are watching the smooth progress of time and space of the real world when we watch motion pictures.

As the nineteenth century advanced, the devices using a spinning mechanism to display a succession of images that blend into movement became more effective and intricate. From Plateau's phenakistoscope to the stroboscope, zoetrope, **praxinoscope** (see Figure 1-4), and **zoopraxiscope**, the latter of which

Figure 2-6 Emile Reynaud projecting an animated film to an audience using the Théâtre Optique.

combined elements of the zoetrope and magic lantern, viewers were first presented with a continuously moving row of images and later with a series of quickly passing shuttered views of single frames. By 1892, Emile Reynaud had adapted his earlier invention, the praxinoscope, to create the Théâtre Optique (pronounced "tay-at-truh op-teek," meaning optical theater), a relatively complex device that projected animated films onto a screen for audiences.

Although they use a different process from what we know as films, Reynaud's moving images were the first animated motion pictures. But to arrive at the full development of the cinema as an expressive medium, we need to examine the last component of its existence: photography.

Printing Light

Photography is a process by which light is captured and reproduced. Normally, the light passes through a lens into a camera and falls on a light-sensitive surface. This can take place through chemical, magnetic, or digital interaction and registration between the light and the surface.

Key practical steps in the development of this medium were taken long ago by Ibn al-Haytham of Persia, when he fully explained and produced the **camera obscura** and **pinhole camera** in the eleventh century. Some essential elements of photography are seen in these devices, such as the controlled admittance of light into a closed area so that an image falls upon a surface for recording. However, the need to control light and to increase its quality required the use

Figure 2-7 The pinhole camera, a box that allows no light other than through a small hole, making it capable of photography even without a lens.

of lenses. In order to develop the potential of reproduction, many discoveries came into play, including silver nitrate and silver chloride.

In 1816, French inventor Nicéphore Niépce achieved success in registering a temporary photographic image on paper after having been interested by the idea for years. How did he do this? By this time, the primitive pinhole camera had been improved to integrate a lens at its front to focus the light, and Niépce wanted to find a way to record the image that was projected at the back of the box (until then, such a device had been used to help with drawing and painting). He built a camera and then placed paper coated with silver salts at the back of the box, and it recorded an image that turned to black in daylight. The question then became: how to make the image permanent?

After experimenting with a variety of chemical compounds and processes, in 1826 Niépce produced the first permanent photograph, which he called **heliography** or "sun writing." It took eight hours to expose the photosensitive chemicals that he coated onto a plate of pewter. Niépce later began working with Louis Daguerre to improve the process and reduce exposure time, and after Niépce's death in 1833, Daguerre developed the **daguerreotype** in 1837. Through most of the nineteenth century, photographs were produced by using a box camera with a lens that focused the image on a light-sensitive plate (generally a glass plate coated with an **emulsion** of silver salts).

By the second half of the century, certain basic elements of photography had been established. Typically the camera **lens** is made up of pieces of glass that work to focus the light so that it will be projected in a controlled, tight band as it passes through its transparent width. To control the length of time that the light is allowed to pass through the lens, a **shutter** opens and closes to admit the light for a specific length of time.

At the time of of Louis Daguerre, Fox Talbot, an English inventor, developed different methods for producing photographs which pointed the way for photography to move in the more fruitful direction of reproducible **negatives**. Although negative processes had become the norm by the mid-nineteenth century, photographs from this period were made onto hard plates. In order to create the rotating spool of images necessary for motion pictures, a transparent, flexible film **base** was necessary to support a coat of light-sensitive emulsion. The **film roll** was commercialized by George Eastman in 1888, although Reverend Hannibal Goodwin had patented and used a supple photographic base in 1887 and won a lawsuit years

Figure 2-8 The first photograph: View from Nicéphore Niépce's window at Gras. (Courtesy of Getty Images)

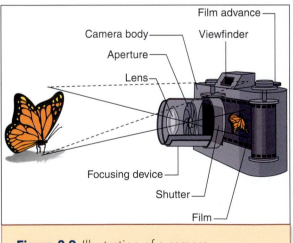

Figure 2-9 Illustration of a camera.

later against Kodak. This invention brought live action motion pictures much closer to becoming a reality.

From Still to Moving Image

A medium as dramatic and viscerally engaging as motion pictures appears to have been driven by stories that are just as engaging and compelling as many of those we see on our screens. One of the most memorable stories of the founding of motions pictures belongs to Eadward Muybridge. In the early 1870s, Leland Stanford, the governor of California, initiated a challenge—and legend tells of a bet for a large sum—to prove that a horse's hooves all leave the ground as it gallops, as he believed. Muybridge took up this challenge and—with key help from John Isaacs—set up a test on a racetrack with a series of cameras attached to trip wires. The series of photographs not only proved that a horse does bring all four hooves off the ground while galloping, but the photographs realized the idea of a series of quickly snapped photos to capture movement.

By 1880, Muybridge furthered his work in capturing and showing motion with his invention the zoopraxiscope, which combined elements of the zoetrope and magic lantern. That year, he held a series of well-documented showings of motion pictures in San Francisco. At these events, viewers could see motion pictures of different animals and people running, trotting, jumping, and kicking. The *Alta California* concluded its article on the event as follows: "Mr. Muybridge has laid the foundation of a new method of entertaining the people, and we predict that his instantaneous photographic

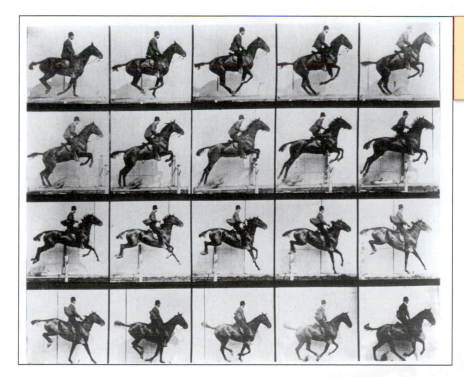

Figure 2-10 An Eadward Muybridge study of a horse in movement from 1887. *(Courtesy Photofest)*

magic-lantern zoetrope [the zoopraxinoscope] will make the rounds of the civilized world."

Many inventors and entrepreneurs were working on ideas associated with photography and movement at this time, and numerous advances fed the development of cinema. An invention that furthered the possibilities initiated by the work of Muybridge was a photographic gun developed by scientist Etienne-Jules Marey. With one camera, he was able to record a quick series of images by having the shutter open and close quickly in rapid succession. Using this portable camera, Marey was able to pan to follow the moving subject, and he recorded the first motion pictures of birds in 1882. These discoveries fed the developing plans of Thomas Edison, who met with both Muybridge and Marey in 1888 and 1889.

The Edison Studios

Edison wanted to develop a device that would complement his recent invention for recording sound. In fact, he simply thought of such an apparatus as a method to exploit more fully his existing phonograph. He entrusted a man working at Edison Laboratories, W. K. L. Dickson, with the task of creating such a device. Documentary evidence tells us that Dickson is responsible for

Figure 2-11 Man looking into the viewer of the Edison Kinetoscope. *(Interior seen in cross-section)*

the work of developing and realizing the **Kinetograph** and **Kinetoscope** from Edison's initial conceptualizations that were close to his previously developed cylinder phonograph.

Once Dickson and Edison had recently available **celluloid** film at their disposal, one of the final necessities for motion pictures was in place. For a while, Dickson continued to try to work on Edison's original conception of a cylinder device, but this would not work. By 1891, he had produced two devices that would create and show motion pictures: the Kinetograph and Kinetoscope. The Kinetograph was a camera that would record the footage, and the Kinetoscope was a viewing device through which a single person could watch a motion picture on a small screen. By the final stages of the creation of these devices, Dickson originated many of the standards in motion picture technology, such as placing four **sprocket holes** per frame.

The first public use of the Kinetoscope was in 1893. By 1894, the machines had achieved great popularity, and viewing parlors were opening across the country. However, the concept of a projected picture was still not realized, and Edison absolutely opposed the idea of projection.

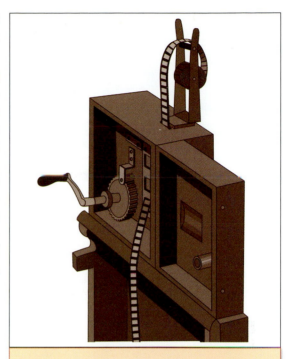

Figure 2-12 The Lumière Cinematograph.

The Beginning of Cinema

The final major step in the birth of motion pictures was brought by two French entrepreneurs, Louis and Auguste Lumière. Having seen an Edison Kinetoscope in Paris, the brothers were inspired to create a motion picture machine of their own. With a family-owned laboratory and factory at his disposal, Louis invented a piece of equipment that created motion pictures that would be seen projected onto screens in front of audiences: the **cinematograph**. Key innovations with this camera were the hand-cranked motor and a pull-down claw that advanced the film roll through perforations in the film that Louis administered by hand (see **Figure 2-12** and **Figure 2-13**).

With the cinematograph, the Lumière brothers patented a lightweight, attractive device that functioned as camera, projector, and printer. Louis shot a number of films, including *Leaving the Factory, Card Party,* and *Sprinkling the Sprinkler.* On December 28, 1895, the Lumières held a public screening of their motion pictures for a paying audience, and soon many viewers were amazed and thrilled to see these movies that lasted about a minute each.

It is important to note that through their invention, the Lumière brothers not only brought about the first use of a practical device that would create films of a significant length, but they also created motion pictures that generated far more interest than the early Edison shorts. The quality of exterior photography adds significantly to the value and interest of many of their scenes, such as in *Baby's Meal* and *Snowball Fight.* Additionally,

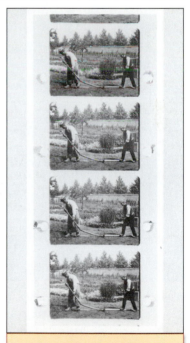

Figure 2-13 Frames from the Lumière film *Sprinkling the Sprinkler.* Note the sprocket holes. *(Courtesy Photofest)*

Figure 2-14 In *Arrival of a Train at La Ciotat,* the train has traveled from the distance and is now pulling into the station and towards the viewer. *(Courtesy Photofest)*

the choice of framing and use of perspective with such films as the well-known *Arrival of a Train at La Ciotat* contribute significantly to the audience's engagement with the material, as shown through the fearful reactions of some of the spectators.

Projecting Motion Pictures

The limitations of the motion pictures as unveiled by the Lumière brothers in December 1895 were answered by both technical and artistic means. The projection system used in the cinematograph would not support the tension of long rolls of film, and this was solved through the Latham Loop, an advancement named after its inventors, the Latham family, in which a small loop was incorporated into the path of the film through projection. This reduced the tension on the film rolling through the projector, so longer reels could be used without assured breakage.

The next improvement was with the pull-down mechanism of the claw in the projector. R.W. Paul pioneered a solution known as the Maltese Cross, which uses a pin to pull down the film frame-by-frame in intermittent motion as the cross rotates. It was fine tuned by 1905 and became a permanent pull-down mechanism for **35-millimeter film**.

Remember that a film roll is a long strip of light-sensitive material that must be developed to produce an image. The standard size of film established by the Edison studios and the Lumières was 35mm, and later other sizes of film were created, such as the smaller and cheaper 16mm and 8mm and the larger 70mm for increased quality when projected. Later in the twentieth century, **videotape** recording was introduced, in which magnetic tape was used instead of the film negative. The medium that you are probably most familiar with is **digital video (DV)**, in which sensors record images as digital information.

Louis Lumière brought his camera to record events in front of a factory, at his brother's house, and on streets. If the Lumières can be seen as the originators of non-fiction films with their minute-long, motion-picture documents of daily events, the filmmaker who provided a number of the first strong creative breakthroughs in fiction film is Georges Méliès.

Figure 2-15 35mm film being inspected and edited by British director Thorold Dickinson. *(Courtesy Getty Images)*

The Illusionist

Cinema is built on illusion: We believe we are seeing movement in front of us on the screen. In fact, as first indicated by scholars Joseph and Barbara Anderson, our brains are actively seeking to create this illusion as we are working to

Figure 2-16 Cameras and their recording platforms: film, video, and digital formats.

see and make sense of the light in front of us. Thus, it is entirely appropriate that the man who fully embraced the potential of this new medium built on illusion was, in fact, a professionally trained illusionist, a magician.

Georges Méliès began to explore the more expressive aspects of this medium soon after he acquired a camera. At first, he filmed travel scenes and everyday events in the mode of the Lumière studios, but Méliès capitalized on a chance occurrence while shooting in Paris. This discovery reflects a "stop-trick" first seen on kinetoscopes in a brief 1895 film by Alfred Clark, *Execution of Mary, Queen of Scots,* in which an actor was replaced by a dummy when the camera was stopped and "beheaded" once the shot was resumed. As you see, interest in gruesome effects has been around since the beginning.

Méliès made his discovery when the camera jammed while photographing a shot on a busy street. After fixing the jam, he continued to shoot the reel of film. In the space between the two moments of running the camera, a "jump" occurred: An omnibus that had entered the shot turned into a hearse as it exited the shot. By the end of that year, 1896, he had made *The Vanishing Lady* in which a woman "disappeared" from the scene and *The Nightmare* in which a sleeper's visions transform abruptly. During these years, Méliès was not only stopping and starting the camera but making actual edits—cutting between frames of film to remove a section and pasting the remaining two pieces together.

In 1897, Méliès built a glassed-in film studio and began to shoot films using the conventions of magic shows and theater. In this working space, he produced and directed hundreds of films, acted in many of them, led a studio staff, and oversaw the creation of a body of work from conception to printing. Building on his initial realization of a jump cut and the possibilities of working within and between motion picture frames, Méliès developed and utilized **superimposition**, **matte** shots, dissolves, and simple camera movement.

An Emerging Form of Communication

During this time, many filmmakers were creating shorts that reflected the style and tone of Méliès's work, and there were a number of innovations. In Britain, R. W. Paul and G. A. Smith made many short films. Smith began

Figure 2-17 The rocket reaches the moon in Méliès's *Trip to the Moon.* (*Courtesy Star Film/Photofest*)

to launch himself as a true film pioneer in *The Kiss in the Tunnel* (1899), in which he created a sequence of three shots that began to establish a sense of continuity in film by starting with an exterior train shot entering a tunnel and cutting to the interior of the train (for the kiss by a man and woman on the train), followed by the exiting train. In *Grandma's Reading Glass* (1900), Smith used close-ups and developed basic point-of-view shots as a boy looks at objects in close-up using his grandmother's magnifying glass.

Close-up framings and simple cuts between shots may seem like obvious techniques to us now, but when watching the standard films of 1895–1905, it is important to recognize that the innovations that Méliès, Smith, and others brought to filmmaking were simple yet also revolutionary. They represent the basic building blocks of filmmaking as we know it today.

Director Edwin S. Porter

In the United States, Edwin S. Porter's work shows advances in editing and cinematic storytelling with *Life of an American Fireman* and *The Great Train Robbery*. In **Figure 2-18**, you can follow the shots of *Life of an American Fireman* of 1903. In the first shot, seen in the two top left frames, you see a fireman daydreaming, which Porter shows through a visual effect that illustrates his warm thoughts about his wife and child. Next, a fire alarm is pulled, and you can track the images that tell the story (each shot in the illustration is shown as a pair of frames that proceed top to bottom in two columns) of a fire rescue of the wife and child from a burning building. Porter shows the

Figure 2-18 The individual shots from Edwin S. Porter's *Life of an American Fireman* shown in two frames each, read top to bottom in two columns. *(Courtesy Photofest)*

same rescue twice, both from inside and outside of the building. In the years to come, we see filmmakers advance greatly as they begin to use **cross-cutting**, through which the viewer would see back-and-forth shots between interior and exterior during the rescue, as is seen in re-cut prints from later versions of *Life of an American Fireman*.

Later that year, Porter directed *The Great Train Robbery*, a landmark film. Suddenly, audiences were shown an exciting tale with an exploding safe, a fight atop a moving train, and an innocent passenger gunned down. The last shot of one of the outlaws shooting directly at the spectator cemented the outcome of grabbing the viewer's attention. This western tale shot in New Jersey featured an effective series of shots that built up its story well, and although it does not feature any intricate cutting, its use of action and staging in depth were thrilling to viewers at that time.

Pioneer Alice Guy Blaché

The use of a close-up as an actual part of narrative can be seen in French director Alice Guy Blaché's daring film, *Madame Has Her Cravings* from 1906. In this film, a pregnant woman on a park bench sees a little girl with a candy stick, shows her desire for it, and steals it. The woman is seen in close-up enjoying her prize, and then she and her husband (and their baby in a carriage that the man is pushing) are confronted by the little girl's father. In the series of scenes that each feature a close-up, the pregnant woman proceeds to guzzle a man's drink, smoke a pipe, and deliver her baby in a cabbage patch! A number of Alice Guy Blaché's films from this period

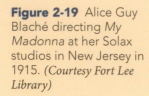
Figure 2-19 Alice Guy Blaché directing *My Madonna* at her Solax studios in New Jersey in 1915. (*Courtesy Fort Lee Library*)

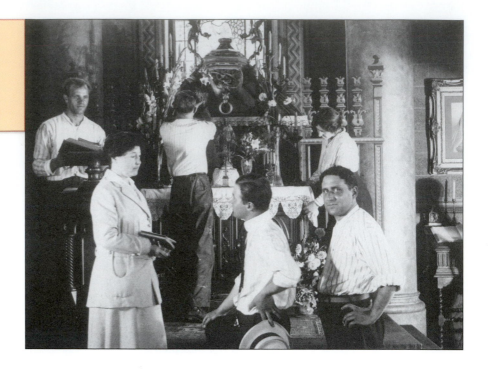

feature individual character development, inventive use of city locales, and dramatically expressive compositions.

As you can see, in this first decade of film, certain building blocks of cinematic form and technique began to emerge. At first, movies typically mimicked still photography and theater: a view that uses the stage as its frame, and a single, unedited shot or series of theatrical tableaux. However, through the advances shown in the work of innovative filmmakers, key basic methods emerged to convey visual ideas more effectively, to tell simple stories, and to enchant and entertain.

Framing the Discussion

- *Edison and Dickson's kinetoscope was designed for a single viewer. The Lumière brothers' cinematograph was made to project films to an audience. How did this development alter the context, uses, and impact of motion pictures?*

- *What traditions involve an audience facing a performance or show? What artistic forms involve*

a frame? How does this influence the types of work produced for these formats?*

- *In what ways are motion pictures similar to the theater? How are the two art forms different? How is the cinema similar to and different from painting?*

The Establishment of Motion Picture Storytelling

During the next decade, movies grew longer and more complex and inventive, particularly in terms of establishing the basics of narrative. Many directors across the world developed ways to tell stories that took advantage of the movie camera's ability to show us a scene from a particular vantage point and then to cut the views into a sequence of images that reveal information in a variety of ways to heighten drama, emotional impact, and perception. Sweden's Victor Sjöstrom; Russia's Yevgeni Bauer; France's Louis Feuillade, Maurice Tourneur, and Alice Guy Blaché; and the United States' D. W. Griffith, Raoul Walsh, Cecil B. DeMille, Lois Weber, and Allan Dwan all made films that, overall, established more effective staging in depth; masking and revealing of characters and objects; dramatic, expressive lighting; and cutting that became more smooth and complex.

Directors began to see the compositional possibilities offered by the unique vantage point of the camera and its lens. When filming, the camera basically duplicates the vantage point of a single viewer. Filmmakers began to explore the possibilities of what can be exposed to the audience or hidden from view. There is the width of the scene that is photographed by the camera, determined by the type of lens and the physical placement of the settings or objects that frame the shot. The height of our view is determined in the same way.

Next, there is the apparent depth of the shot that was discussed in Chapter 1, measured by the appearance of people, objects, and settings that are relatively closer and farther from the camera. By the mid-1910s, filmmakers such as those mentioned previously were directing scenes in which the stories took

Figure 2-20 Willot-Fox studio stage in New Jersey with glass ceiling for maximum light and ample space for building of sets. Actress Theda Bara, seated, is being addressed by the director with camera at right. (*Courtesy Fort Lee Library*)

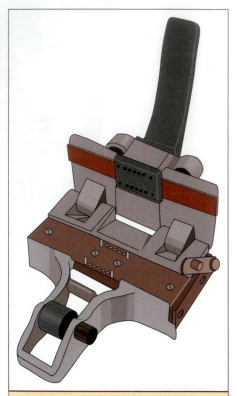

Figure 2-21 One model of a film splicer.

on much more significance and displayed energetic artistry through their use of the width, height, and depth of the screen.

Cinematic storytelling developed both *within* shots and *between* shots. In the last unit, we discussed the concept of continuity, including the use of the axis and screen direction. It was during this time that these concepts first started to emerge in the practices of filmmakers. As directors created films that used well arranged and blocked takes in longer films, they also began to display more use of a variety of framings arranged into sequences of shots. They began to understand that by placing shots in relation to each other, they tended to function more or less effectively depending on their timing and relationship to each other.

The Development of Editing

To edit film, it is first necessary to cut the piece of celluloid. This is done using a razor, which is part of a standard editing tool: the **splicer**. Editors cut the film precisely between frame lines, remove unwanted lengths of film, and reattach the selected shots together. As different pieces of film are cut, editors manage the footage by hanging the pieces in **trim bins** so they can use the strands of footage when they need them. **Non-linear editing**—the type of editing seen in computer programs—is a direct replication of this process. You may have noticed the appearance of razors or metal bins in the icons of digital editing programs because of their significance in film editing.

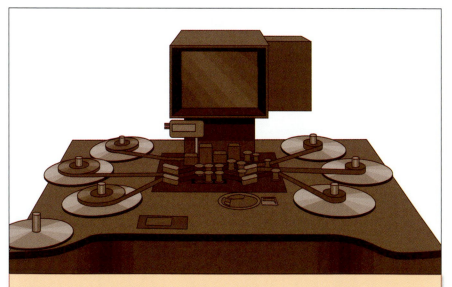

Figure 2-22 Flat-bed editing machine in which the reels of picture and sound travel across the viewer and sensors from left to right, allowing for forward and backward movement of synchronized picture and sound.

Figure 2-23 Twenty-first century digital editing home studio setup of editor Ross Martin with computer linked to two monitors to track picture and sound edits and view full screen picture. *(Courtesy Ross Martin)*

When you edit digitally, you look at a screen just as film editors have stared at devices such as the **Moviola** or **flat-bed editing machine**. You are also able to move around the pieces of film in any arrangement because you can cut them apart and piece them back together freely, just as editors did when they had to splice and paste each segment of film together by hand.

Continuity through Cutting

During the mid-1910s, directors and editors were making astonishing progress in advancing the complexity, precision, and expressiveness of cinematic art. By the end of this period, a range of editing traits can be observed in numerous films produced by a variety of directors. Editors began to use match cuts to move action forward from one shot to the next. Directors would establish screen direction by filming from one side of the axis, such as the previous example of a battlefield sequence. Continuity also was established in matches between the **eyelines** of characters looking at each other in a scene.

When you think of a standard dialogue scene today, what comes to mind? The pattern of shot and **reverse shot**, moving the camera from one side of a scene to its opposite viewpoint, so that two characters looking and talking to each other can be seen from each perspective, was also established during this period.

How about when you see a brief close-up of a weapon that a character is secretly taking out of a pocket in order to attack another character? This example of an **insert shot** is first seen during this period and became a standard technique during the 1920s. A common insert from this time was a close-up of a letter or page being read by a character. Directors often use insert shots to provide a dramatic detail that adds important information, and it can be shot separately from the primary takes with all the actors.

Figure 2-24 Sequence that starts with a close shot, followed by a match cut reverse shot of the second character, back to the first character in a full close-up, and then an insert shot that heightens the drama of the scene.

Cutting Away

Storytelling techniques also were enhanced by cross-cutting (mentioned earlier when discussing Edwin S. Porter's films), in which the motion picture moves back and forth between two or more developing scenes. This was a recurring technique of D. W. Griffith and is commonly used in motion pictures today, particularly for dramatic buildups. In *Ocean's Thirteen* (2007), a heist movie directed by Steven Soderbergh and starring George Clooney as Danny Ocean, the climax features cross-cutting between different members of Ocean's team completing their parts of a plan to destroy casino mogul Willy Bank (played by Al Pacino).

A similar editing effect is seen as the heist group enacts their revenge on Bank. In the midst of the main action as the entire casino shakes as if in an earthquake, there is a **cutaway shot** to Terry Benedict (Andy Garcia) as he reacts to what is happening while he is completely apart from the action. The cutaway is a single shot that is separate from the primary action of the scene. Editors will cut to a shot that is not part of the main sequence to add information or commentary to the entire story being told, to build suspense, or to create parallels with other characters or events. From the time of silent films, filmmakers have developed the practice of shooting cutaways for the editor. For example, a cinematographer might shoot cutaway shots during a street sequence to record reactions from individuals in a crowd or small details separate from the main characters and outside of the principal thrust of the action.

The Effect of Editing

In the 1920s, the establishment of a wide range of storytelling styles, powerful imagery, and meaningful themes is evident in films from many directors. Across the globe, filmmakers began to use editing in expressive ways and noted how individual shots could be used in juxtaposition to create dramatic, provocative meanings. In the Soviet Union, filmmakers studied and wrote about the effect of linking shots in sequences, and director and theoretician Lev Kuleshov originated the conception that came to be known as the

Figure 2-25 An illustration of the Kuleshov effect: compare the effect of seeing each of the shots on the right juxtaposed with the same shot of the actor. We interpret the character in relation to the other shot.

Kuleshov Effect. In his workshops, it was observed that when a shot of a relatively blank-faced actor was juxtaposed with different shots: an empty bowl, a dead body, an attractive woman (the accounts and examples have differed), the interpretations of the character's behavior and the reactions to the actor's performance change.

Thus, the meaning of what we see in motion pictures is determined not only by what we see in individual shots but by the messages and ideas that are created between the juxtapositions of the shots. For example, Kuleshov showed how we can see a scene in which people are talking and we do not even need to see the people together in the shot. We link them together even though we have not actually seen them together at all, as long as the information gathered between the shots is significant enough. Normally, a sequence will begin with an **establishing shot** that shows the setting of the scene with its characters, but as Kuleshov demonstrated in his editing experiments, an establishing shot is not necessary, as long as the information is clear, because of the *interaction* of the shots.

Most notably in France and the Soviet Union, filmmakers were writing about movies and making them in ways that enhanced their creative potential through provocative cutting that strived for dynamic rhythms, striking juxtapositions of shots, and forceful imagery that ranged from the poetic to a rapid collision of visual cues. In particular, these filmmakers focused on the aspects of motion pictures that were unique to the cinema and worked on the development of means of expression—a language, in essence—that was particular to filmmaking. A vital passion for the expressive powers of the cinema is seen in the works and writing of such filmmakers as Eisenstein, Pudovkin, Dovzhenko, and Vertov in the Soviet Union, and Delluc, Vigo, and Gance in France.

Through editing, filmmakers were expanding the range of possibilities for movies to tell stories and express visual ideas and imagery in ways distinctly suited to motion pictures. The sense of discovery, invention, and teamwork is reflected in comments by many filmmakers of this period. Talking about her work with editor and director Dorothy Arzner, screenwriter and actress Bebe Daniels commented that assisting in the editing process "taught me more about writing for motion pictures than anything in the world could have taught me." Dorothy Arzner, who worked as an editor in the 1920s before moving on to become a director, explained:

> *I cut something like thirty-two pictures in one year at Realart . . .*
> *I also supervised the negative cutting and trained the girls who cut*
> *negative and spliced film by hand. I set up the film filing system and*
> *supervised the art work on the titles. I worked most of the day and*
> *night and loved it.*

Figure 2-26 Director Dorothy Arzner leaning on a tripod as she holds a combination viewfinder and megaphone while cinematographer Alfred Gilks stands behind the camera for *Get Your Man* from 1927. *(Courtesy Hulton Archive/Getty Images)*

The emerging artistry of cinema was seen not only in editing but also through the progress of cinematography, musical composition, and acting suited to motion pictures.

The Growth of an Art Form

Cinematographers and directors put the camera onto dollies in order to create new perspectives for the viewer, add dramatic emphasis to scenes, and augment the creative potential of visual artistry and storytelling in the cinema. By the mid-1920s, camera movement became another tool commonly used by directors to move through a space, reveal details, and enhance action in a dynamic way, such as in films by those mentioned earlier and Murnau and Lang in Germany, Bernard and L'Herbier in France, Ito and Shimizu in Japan, Borzage and Vidor in the United States, and Kozintsev and Trauberg in the Soviet Union.

Filmmakers also paid more attention to the quality of photography through the manipulation of light and art direction. Once again, artistry and advances in technology are intertwined to tell the story of the cinema. In the 1910s, references began to be made in relation to painting and the attention artists give to light in the depiction of a scene. Technically, cinematographers began to work in studios where complete illumination of a scene was required, thus allowing them to experiment with varied styles of lighting. Conversely, some films used real locations to capture busy or gritty urban settings, such as Paris or New York, or exotic locales, from ice-bound regions to jungles to deserts.

When surveying motion pictures from this period, it is clear that film had developed into a fully expressive art form, and virtually all of the basic tools of filmmaking seen today were in place. Stunt work became quite remarkable in a variety of films, from the adventure movies of Douglas Fairbanks to the comedies of Buster Keaton and Harold Lloyd. Visual effects were present from the beginning of film history, starting in the studios of Georges Méliès and seen in the sophisticated matte work of early glass plate painters who contributed to Hollywood motion pictures from the 1910s and became an element of the studio system from the 1920s.

The variety of work necessary to produce movies that told interesting stories was becoming more intricate and called for increasingly complex solutions. Filmmakers needed to set up a convincing world in front of the camera and to arrange shots into sequences that pulled the spectator along effectively. Discussing the art of comedy in motion pictures, Buster Keaton observed,

> Comic effects are fleeting. They must be initiated at a very precise moment, allow the audience the time to recover themselves, then following that circumstance, to be pushed to the brink or to recover their progression. In their rhythm, it is necessary for them to have a mathematical precision, and this rhythm is a science whose responsibility is entirely dependent on the film director. A film comedy is assembled with the same precision as the inner workings of a watch.

Figure 2-27 Buster Keaton and friend in the MGM film *The Cameraman*, which Keaton co-directed in 1928. *(Courtesy MGM/Photofest)*

Sound and Motion Pictures

Another area in which motion pictures progressed during the years of the silent cinema was in the use of sound. Although it seems very odd to talk about sound with "silent films," it is important to note that the term "silent" is quite misleading. Movies are a visual medium, but they are also a sonic medium. Sound is at the core of the experience of motion pictures, and it deserves ample consideration in any discussion of film and video.

Films have been linked to sound right from their beginning. When Dickson developed the early versions of the kinetograph, he was able to produce primitive versions of motion pictures with matched sound using the Edison phonograph. In the first decade of the 1900s, hundreds of early sound films were made using the **chronophone** system of Gaumont and other methods.

Live Music and Voices

From their first years, movies were screened with musical accompaniment, so in fact virtually none of them were truly "silent." Whether complemented by a piano, an organ, or a full orchestra, movies have nearly always featured sound as part of their artistry. In fact, a pianist was present at the first screening of the Lumière cinematograph, and many silent films featured scores composed specifically for their screening. In the late twentieth and early twenty-first centuries, there has been a revival of recording and composing for silent films, and a number of small and large musical ensembles have produced music for early classics of the cinema.

Silent films also incorporated the voice before the widespread projection of sound films: some early films were paired with narration, and in Japan this was viewed as one of the most important parts of the moviegoing experience. In fact, the *benshi*, or film narrator, was an important profession in the Japanese film industry.

Just as there were optical effects in the early cinema, there were also sound effects. In some venues, individual performers created a wide variety of noises for projections. There were also sound effect machines, such as the Allefex or Kinematophone, that were developed by 1908. By this time, it was clear to filmmakers and distributors that sound could function as an integral and expressive creative component of motion pictures.

Exploring New Horizons

Motion pictures came about through technical achievements and business ventures, and those two reasons for the existence of movies have affected every aspect of their development. The creation of films quickly established itself as a rather costly, labor-intensive practice, and in America the business groups who held the rights to manufacture moviemaking tools and control distribution asserted strong control over their use and practice. This dynamic has remained at the core of the story of motion pictures. Throughout the history of moviemaking, it is necessary to inquire: who controls this process? Who is making movies? How are they allowed to make them? Why are they making them?

When discussing the first decades of motion pictures, many of the filmmakers and technicians who were involved in its growth describe feeling like explorers, searching uncharted territory and making amazing discoveries. They were developing new ways in which to tell stories, enact dreams, visit remote corners of the earth, record life as it passed, and exchange ideas and information. Upon this screen where images were suddenly flashing and transforming before viewers, there existed a new and compelling reflection of our own sense of perception, the image-driven aspect of our own minds, home to observed events, visions, dreams, and memory.

It's a Wrap!

In Chapter 2, you investigated the evolution of motion picture technology and the communicative discoveries of early filmmakers. In the work of this unit, you will explore the basics of cinematic narrative using visual sequences to articulate your thoughts, stories, and emotions. Like the early filmmakers, you will also have sound as an expressive resource as you transmit ideas visually.

VIEWFINDER

"As an editor, you must relate strongly to the characters. You have to. The question of who do you cut to, when, why, and how, is not a technical question. It's really a matter of taste and making the scene play… Because there are thousands and thousands of options and decisions to be made every second."

–Dede Allen–

Editor of numerous classic films including *Bonnie and Clyde* (1967), *Dog Day Afternoon* (1975), *The Breakfast Club* (1985), and *Wonder Boys* (2000)

Analysis: Non-Dialogue Film

For this chapter, you will watch a series of non-dialogue films including More *by Mark Osborne (see included DVD), both from the early cinema and contemporary examples. For each short film, indicate the following:*

A. The Establishment of Story

1. How does the movie begin? How is the context of the story introduced?

2. How are key characters introduced? Is there much detail given to the characters?

3. How are the characters' actions shown and how do these actions propel the story?

4. How is the setting established? How do location changes occur?

5. What are key turning points in the story? How are they shown?

6. How do the filmmakers conclude the movie?

B. Cinematography

1. Is the camera used to establish particular points of view?

2. Do camera angles show or hide characters and particular information?

3. Does the camera move? How and when?

4. Can you give examples of changes in perspective of the camera?

5. In what ways does photography help to tell the story and give the movie a particular style or tone?

C. Editing

1. What is the pace of the editing? Approximately how many cuts occur?

2. What brings about cuts between shots? Give two examples of the motivations for edits in the movie (if there are any edits).

3. How does the story advance as cuts are made? Describe at least one sequence of shots in which cuts between shots help to tell the story.

D. General evaluation: Describe the use of moving images to express story, themes, and emotions through the short.

   1. Overall, how is this story told visually?

   2. How do the actors' performances fit with the content of the story and style of the movie?

   3. Are there individual moments or passages that are particularly successful to you?

   4. What are the central themes or messages of the movie? What emotions, ideas, or reactions did it generate for you?

Writing: Character Development

In non-dialogue sequences or films, characters become alive and understandable to us through their actions and gestures. For our writing exercise for this chapter, you will compose character sketches that will be based on the direct physical presence of actors essential for silent films. Next, you will write short, simple scenes that explore physical interactions of each character with their world.

A. **Sketching them out** – You will create three characters for this exercise. We will use three steps to this process. You are encouraged to use these characters for later writing exercises and film shoots, so it is a good idea to create characters that will be feasible to bring to the screen. In particular, the characters should be those that you will be able to cast (age, gender, ethnicity, and so forth).

It is difficult for many of us to create detailed descriptions of people or to describe things that we see every day. If the following steps are very difficult for you, spend some time looking at people today (for example, at lunch or when you are waiting for something or someone) and note very specific actions and physical details that you observe. You can use them to feed your character descriptions or to find inspiration.

1. **Face** – Describe the face of the character. How would you describe the eyes? Are there any typical movements or attributes of the character's face? How is the head usually held?

2. **Body** – Describe the character's body, in particular how it moves. Is there a particular walk? Typical gestures? Shoulders, elbows, hands, knees, and feet are all sources of expressive movement and distillation of character.

3. **Waking Up** – Imagine your character getting up in the morning. Write a brief paragraph (approximately four to six sentences) about the character's first actions of the day. The paragraph must start with the character's name and use the verb "wants" in the first or second sentence.

B. **Solo scenes** – Now you are going to write a "solo scene" for each one of your characters. The character must be alone or in a situation in which there is no interaction with any other character. Use this writing to explore details of the character and establish physical interactions with the world that surrounds the character.

1. **Place** – Where do you see your character all alone? If one place is quickly obvious to you, write a short description of that location. If not, brainstorm a list of possibilities, writing down any places in which you can imagine this character. Then, select one of the spots and write a brief description of that place.

2. **Action** – Now describe at least one action that the character can perform. These can be everyday tasks, chores, or activities. Note the details of any action.

3. **Scene** – Write a solo scene for the character. Make all descriptions physical—avoid any writing about thoughts of the character. Only write what we can see!

Project: Visual Storytelling

Now you will develop your skills in visual storytelling, although you may use some dialogue. The trick for this project is to find out a way to tell your story with images even though the characters can speak. The scene has three characters (you can use those from the Writing exercise or create new ones) and takes place in one or two locations.

A. **Individual preparation** – *Before the class period when you meet with your group to share ideas and decide on a story line, consult these guidelines to write a two to four sentence summary to propose an idea for the scene. Here are the instructions:*

1. **Characters** – Three who are all part of a class, team, business, or family.

2. **Narrative** – choose **one** of the following ideas to begin your story:

   a. A secret

   b. A project that needs to be completed

   c. A desired item

3. **Location** – There need to be at least two separate locations.

4. **Dialogue** – You may have up to six lines of dialogue in the scene, although you can also make it completely non-dialogue. Follow these requirements:

   a. You cannot express any *emotional* aspect of the scene through dialogue (Such as "I think you're so cute!").

   b. Characters cannot ask or answer any questions.

   c. The gist of the sequence must be understood without sound. If we turn off the sound, viewers will comprehend the scene.

   d. When you write the script, you do not have to write out actual lines of dialogue. You may indicate that one character says something to another character without saying the exact words.

5. **Length** – The scene should last between three to eight minutes. Run through the scene in your head. Imagine the events unfolding in your mind.

B. **Writing/Brainstorming** – *The instructor will organize the class into production groups for unit two. The producer will lead the meeting of the production team. During the first meeting:*

1. In your assigned production group, members present the ideas they have formulated.

2. Members discuss the ideas considering the following factors:

   a. Ability to cast the roles from available people

   b. Accessibility to locations

    c. Feasibility to capture the situations and events of the story

    d. Interest of the concept, characters, and cinematic elements

3. Members evaluate the concepts and see if they can arrive at a consensus. If there is lack of consensus, the director proposes a solution to the plan and presents the proposal to the instructor for consultation. From this outside evaluation of the project, the producer submits a choice to the group. If there is still lack of consensus in the group, the team must return to the instructor for a final decision.

C. Production

  1. Crew and talent positions

    a. Director – For each activity and exercise in class, the instructor will oversee the rotation of directorial positions. If possible, the person who offered the main idea for the script will finalize the script and function as the director. Working with the cinematographer, the director must prepare a shot list or storyboard for the scene. The director has the final say on decisions for how to shoot the scene (within the class guidelines, of course!).

    b. Cinematographer – This person will shoot the scene. It is important to work closely with the director and agree on the manner in which the scene is to be shot.

    c. Sound – If applicable and necessary, there can be a boom microphone for the scene. Remember, even if there is no dialogue, it may be important to record quality sound of the scene. The actors or the editor may serve in this position.

    d. Actors and editor – From among the remaining group members and possible outside sources, the three remaining roles must be cast. The editor of the project can be chosen from this group. As with the directorial position, the instructor will arrange rotation of editing roles for each exercise.

  2. Cinematography

    a. Tripod – A tripod must be used for at least two of the shots, if one is available.

    b. Movement – There must be at least one shot with simulated dolly movement: this includes using a wheelchair, an AV rolling cart, camera held on a steadying device (even including a tripod), or similar tool or method. If the director and production team feel that this is not appropriate for their project, consult with the instructor.

    c. **Shots** – The following shots should be included in the short. If the director and cinematographer have another proposal, submit it to the instructor:

        i. Close-ups (at least four), including reverse shots

        ii. Two shot

        iii. Wide shot

D. Final product

    1. Editor and director consult to create a final cut of the project that will be presented to the class. The running length of the completed movie is between three to eight minutes. If this is not the case, consult with the instructor.

    2. The edit of the motion picture must include credits.

Report

Remember to be specific in evaluating the work that you accomplished and in describing the motion pictures you have helped to create. Avoid generalizations and reliance on adjectives when discussing the projects. Use this writing to progress in your skills and to share a self-evaluation of your work.

A. **Collaborative Work** – Write a minimum of two paragraphs describing your work on this project (and class activities, if appropriate). Comment on the process of creating this video. Please note the following:

   1. Your position and all that you did. If you were a director or editor on a class activity, highlight this as well.

   2. **Requirements** – Comment on your ability to complete the projects appropriately.

      a. Were you properly prepared?

      b. Did you complete the shots?

      c. Was the edit complete with all of the appropriate elements?

   3. In what ways did the group work together effectively? What elements of the projects were possible through successful collaborative work? Give at least two examples.

   4. How could you improve production or post-production for the next project? Give at least one concrete example of an action you can take.

B. **Video Analysis** – Write a minimum of one paragraph to evaluate the sequences you shot and the work that your group accomplished. Comment on the following elements:

   1. Framing and camera movement

   2. Pacing of shots

   3. Juxtaposition of shots/cuts

   4. Performances

   5. Overall effectiveness of motion picture

Glossary

35-millimeter film – The standard size gauge of film stock (abbreviated as 35mm), which contains four perforations on either side of the rectangular frame.

Base – Flexible, sturdy substance typically made of cellulose acetate or polyester, used in the film roll.

Camera obscura – From Latin meaning "dark room." In this enclosed space, light is admitted through a small hole and falls on an opposite wall where the image facing the hole is projected upside down.

Celluloid – The transparent, flexible material—at first cellulose nitrate and later cellulose acetate—used as a base for photographic film.

Chronophone – Early film synchronization system of sound and picture achieved by attaching the cinematograph and phonograph through coupled electrical motors.

Cinematograph – Motion picture apparatus developed by Louis and Auguste Lumière which served as a camera, projector, and developer.

Cross-cutting – Editing that cuts between shots that would otherwise make up completely independent sequences, used to establish relationships between different events, usually occurring simultaneously events.

Cutaway shot – In a narrative sequence, this is a shot that "cuts away" from the main action (in a distinct change of space or time) in order to indicate passage of time or provide reference to the time, build suspense, show reactions, or provide outside information, after which there is a cut back to the primary sequence underway.

Daguerreotype – The first widely used type of photograph in which the image is recorded on a mirrored surface coated with silver halide particles. A daguerreotype is actually a negative image that is viewed as a positive because of the reflected metal plate, but it cannot be duplicated to print multiple images.

Digital video (DV) – Photography in which the images are recorded as digital information—a series of binary information (zeroes and ones)—that does not change from generation to generation. The overall topic of digital moving image capture is commonly referred to by the term digital cinematography.

Emulsion – A coating of light-sensitive silver salts, held in gelatin, that forms a layer on the base of a film roll. See also **Film roll**.

Establishing shot – A shot that clearly identifies the location of a scene, usually shown as the first shot of a sequence after a change in location.

Eyeline – The invisible line perceived between the eye of a person and what is being seen by that person. An eyeline match is an edit in which spatial logic dictates that the position of the eyes of a character in one shot matches the subject being perceived in another shot, including looks between characters.

Film roll – Photographic film is a transparent, supple, thin strip of material, such as celluloid or polyester, which is coated with a light-sensitive emulsion. The emulsion reacts to light, and when the film is developed it creates a negative image that can then be reproduced as a paper photograph, motion picture, or other type of viewable copy. With a piece of undeveloped film, the dull side is the emulsion, the shiny side is the base.

Flat-bed editing machine – Editing table featuring flat plates for horizontal running of picture, multiple sound reels, a viewer, and improved ease and quality of use over the Moviola.

Heliography – Photographic process invented by Niépce in the 1820s in which he coated a bitumen and lavender oil solution on a stone, metal, or glass plate, placed the varnished plate in a camera obscura, exposed it to light for many hours, and dipped the exposed plate in a lavender oil bath to leave an image.

Insert shot – A shot of a detail of a scene (such as an object or a small detail of a character or a gesture) which is later inserted into the sequence during editing.

Kinetograph – Motion picture camera developed by W. K. L. Dickson in 1891 from Thomas Edison's conceptualizations to produce films for the Kinetoscope viewing apparatus.

Kinetoscope – Motion picture viewing apparatus developed by the Edison laboratories in which a single spectator watched a movie through a small viewer. The movie ran in a single continuous band that passed between a long series of spools and was illuminated through an eyepiece.

Kuleshov effect – The meaning and significance created by two shots in juxtaposition that is not apparent in the shots when they are viewed separately.

Lens – A piece or series of pieces of transparent material, usually glass, that receive and refract light to form an image at a set distance behind the lens. The lens is affixed to or mounted on the camera and generally allows for control of focus and exposure.

Magic lantern – Image projection device that normally functioned through the use of a light source such as a candle, a lens, and transparent slides. Used from the seventeenth century, development of the magic lantern continued through the nineteenth century, during which lanternists would create dissolves between images and simulate movement on the screen by passing superimposed slides across each other.

Matte – A covering of part of the frame to block light for emphasis or introduction of another image.

Moviola – Editing machine usually equipped to handle a single reel of film and sound track. It featured a small viewer, synchronization of picture and audio, portability, and it was noted for its versatility.

Negative – In photography, a camera commonly produces a negative of the recorded image from which prints can be made. In filmmaking, the process of printing from the original negative is complex and can include many steps of making positives and negatives to produce the prints that will be seen in theaters.

Non-linear editing – In contemporary filmmaking, motion picture editing systems in which the footage has been shot in or transferred to a digital format and is edited using a program designed for random access to footage and unlimited cutting, pasting, and arranging of shots, combining characteristics of traditional film editing and computerized word processing.

Phenakistoscope – Optical toy invented by Belgian physicist Joseph Plateau, consisting of a flat disc with images along its edge. Above each image is a small hole. The viewer stands in front of a mirror, spins the device, and looks through the holes to see the images performing a simple movement, such as juggling.

Photography – The capturing and transferring of light to a preserved state.

Pinhole camera – A box with a hole in one side which acts as a lens to focus the entering light and display its inverted image on the box's back surface, like with a camera obscura.

Praxinoscope – Motion picture device invented by Frenchman Emile Reynaud in 1877, in which moving images are seen through rotating mirrors.

Reversal – A type of photographic film that does not produce a negative: the film running through the camera is a positive, and it is thus typically the only copy of the film that will exist. It has been used generally for amateur filmmaking (such as Super-8 films) and 16-millimeter student films.

Reverse shot – A shot that is taken at the opposite angle from the shot immediately previous to it. The reverse-angle shot is commonly used in dialogue sequences, to depict movement of characters from one distinct space to another, and to accentuate perspectives of characters in action sequences.

Short-range apparent motion – The phenomenon through which a viewer perceives real motion when observing a series of rapidly projected still images that are changing in small increments. Although each individual motion picture frame is a separate image and nothing is actually moving on the screen, the visual system of the eyes and brain allows viewers to perceive an image that is continuous and moving.

Shutter – A mechanism that opens and closes to allow light to pass through the lens into the camera and onto the recording surface (such as celluloid film). In motion pictures, the shutter typically opens and closes twenty-four times per second.

Splicer – A device used for cutting and attaching individual pieces of film. There are different models of splicer, including the cement adhesive splicer (such as the hot splicer) and tape splicer. With the Rivas model tape splicer, perforated transparent tape is placed across the edit to adhere the two pieces of film.

Sprocket holes – These are the small, regular holes on the sides of a strip of film that the camera uses to move the film forward. For 35-millimeter film, there are normally four holes per frame; for 16-millimeter film, there is one hole per frame.

Superimposition – The application of two or more images in the same space of the frame simultaneously, as in double exposure.

Trim bin – An open-topped container designed to store individual pieces of film during the editing process. Supports at either end of the bin hold a crossbar that has many thin hooks on which film strips can be hung using sprocket holes.

Videotape – A motion picture medium in which image and sound are recorded on a magnetic tape by a video camera.

Zoetrope – Although similar devices appeared centuries earlier in China, the European development of what became known as the Zoetrope occurred in 1834 by William Horner. This cylinder spins on a base and the viewer looks through holes in its sides to see the moving image of the illustrated band below the slits on the cylinder's interior.

Zoopraxiscope – A device that combined elements of the zoetrope and the magic lantern. The early zoopraxiscope presented a continuously moving row of images, and the later zoopraxiscope presented a series of quickly passing shuttered views of single frames.

Close-Up

Behind the Scenes with Visual Effects Supervisor

Greg Butler

Visual effects supervisor Greg Butler, whose credits include the Lord of the Rings *series,* Harry Potter and the Order of the Phoenix, Charlie and the Chocolate Factory, Prince Caspian, *and many other movies.* (Courtesy of Greg Butler)

Q In what ways did you first become involved in making movies?

A In 1989, I went to a small liberal arts college initially to study history and avoid math. In my first semester I applied to get into both film and video production courses, both of which were very popular. I didn't get into either, but I did get a work study job in the engineering department. I quickly found that my combination of curiosity, technical aptitude, and a set of keys to all of the video production facilities was getting me all sorts of new connections and acquaintances in the film and video departments. I started helping older students and some of the professors with their productions. In my third year, I was asked to be the director of photography for a friend's final video project. After graduating, she got a job at Industrial Light and Magic. She helped me to get an internship and later my first job. I started at ILM in the commercials division and quickly transferred to an entry level job in the new computer graphics department.

Q What were some of the most important early lessons you learned?

A One of the most important things I learned about the filmmaking process is that it is incredibly interdisciplinary and requires a tremendous amount of planning and organization. As a result, films of any significant length can rarely be completed without a large number of people working closely together. A film can succeed or fail at so many different points. Everyone involved needs to keep focused on their job and work well with everyone else.

Q How did you move on from those initial steps?

A I started in the film industry just at the moment that the transition to digital was occurring. While I was a camera engineering intern at ILM in 1992, they had just completed *Hook* and *Death Becomes Her*. Both films effects used some digital compositing, but were mostly created with traditional techniques such as hand inked rotoscoping and optical printing. At the same time, the small computer graphics department was doing tests of digital dinosaurs for *Jurassic Park*. When I returned a year later to start my first job, the company had almost completed its transition. The optical printers were being dismantled and a number of departments had disappeared or been computerized (fx camera, rotoscoping, opticals). Computer graphics in visual effects had graduated from one-off "gimmicks" like the water creature in *The Abyss* to become an integral part of the filmmaking process.

In 1996, I worked at Tippett Studio on *Starship Troopers*. Phil Tippett and many of my colleagues at the studio had worked in stop motion animation for years and were finding innovative ways of incorporating digital tools into their process. It's where I really learned about visual effects and animation. I was constantly surrounded by reminders that computer graphics are just a new way of working in a much older craft. The same rules still apply.

Q How does your role in the visual effects department fit into the entire process of film production?

A These days, very few films don't include some level of visual effects. Sometimes, it's simply to save money on locations or big sets, to increase the safety of actors or stunt people, or just to save time during the shoot. And of course, there's still a lot of demand for us to create what doesn't exist, like dinosaurs or space battles. The visual effects department is now part of the process from the very beginning; creating a budget, then planning the shoot, and finally working on all the vfx shots in post-production.

Filmmaking has always been an expensive and time consuming "group project." Visual effects and computer graphics have only increased the time and amount of people needed to make a film. With more people involved, there are many more decisions needed, both creative and technical. My collaborations are mainly with the film's overall vfx supervisor and the senior artists on my vfx team, such as an Animation Director or CG Supervisor. The film's director is always involved of course, in setting the overall goals, in terms of the story, style and the look of the film.

Visit the textbook website to read the entire interview with Greg Butler.

Sound and Image

CHAPTER IN FOCUS

In this chapter you will:

- produce a commercial or promotional short
- classify and utilize the types of audio that make up a sound mix
- evaluate uses of sound in a variety of movies

A Medium of Moving Pictures and Sounds

When people talk about their experiences at the movies, they often speak about moments or scenes in which sound is key: a line of **dialogue** or funny exchange, a song or musical sequence, the creak of a door or drops of rain, the swoosh of a spaceship or comical ping of a machine. On the other hand, when film educators, critics, and historians discuss cinema, many of them focus greatly on the concept of film as nearly exclusively a *visual* medium. Some talk about "pure cinema" as an art form that is only about the visual expression of narrative and ideas. However, it is clear that motion picture media have consistently been experienced as communicative vehicles that involve both image and sound.

In the first two units of this text, your learning centered on the fundamental underpinning of film: a series of images that move in front of us, as with our experience of time itself. When you use motion pictures to record events, tell stories, and exchange ideas, it is vital to consider the parameters and possibilities of visual expression and communication. In particular, you need to think about how to use images to communicate to the viewer and how to make choices that reflect what you want to express. Just as you saw in the first unit of this text, a great deal of the power of motion pictures lies in their potential as a means of visual communication. Therefore, it is useful to begin studies of moving images by developing skills in interpreting and creating movies from a visual basis.

We are used to speaking in order to communicate, in part because it is innate to humans—verbal exchange has been described as a fundamental instinct for our species. Spoken exchange comes quite naturally to the majority of people and is fundamental to typical interactions. This ease of expression manifests itself in motion pictures: spoken words are often used simply to *tell* viewers something rather than to *show* them. However, a great deal of our thinking processes occur through visual sequences—essentially, images in our minds. By relying too heavily on spoken words instead of images and actions in moviemaking, the direct visual expression of stories, emotions, and ideas can be weakened.

Figure 3-1 Sound helps to bring images to life. *(Courtesy Kendelyn Ouellette)*

In fact, when sound became a viable part of filmmaking in the 1920s, it was seen by some as a step backward in terms of film artistry. The development of film language through its *visual expressiveness* that crossed language barriers and cultures would now be bound to spoken words and the restrictive process of sound recording. In addition, the independent entrepreneurial and artistic spirit of early filmmakers was suddenly reined in by the crushing costs of sound recording and distribution and projection of sound films, which allowed the studios to control and industrialize the process of filmmaking in the United States to an unprecedented degree.

Figure 3-2 Set of an early sound film: note the camera stuck in a soundproof box on the walkway and the orchestra next to the stage. Sound mixer George Groves had to travel up and down six floors to shuttle between the sound booth and the set. *(Courtesy of http://www .georgegroves.org.uk)*

Figure 3-3 Capturing sound in a natural setting. *(Courtesy Kendelyn Ouellette)*

In some ways, these viewpoints in the 1920s are reflected in moviemaking styles of the years to follow, but within a short time, there were examples of filmmakers who found a balance between the creative potential of sound in films and the power of images to tell stories in gripping, lyrical, and informative ways. When you studied the filmmakers from the first decades of cinema, you observed how certain ingenious creators devised original and expressive methods and techniques for using the camera to record life and tell stories. Similarly, we can learn from the imaginative and clever uses of sound in filmmaking when recorded audio was integrated with movies.

Recorded Sound

As you learned in the last unit, Edison first made plans to develop a motion picture apparatus in order to increase sales of his **phonograph**. In fact, W. K. L. Dickson worked on synchronization of the Kinetograph and the phonograph in the late 1880s and eventually created a device dubbed the Kinetophone. The Kinetophone used Edison's cylinder phonograph housed inside of the Kinetoscope with the viewer listening with earphones. The music played to accompany the picture, but it was not a **synchronous sound** system, and the company gave up on satisfactorily linking the two.

Alongside the development of early motion picture cameras in the 1890s and 1900s, sound systems and devices were introduced by numerous inventors, including Demeny and Baron in France, Friese-Greene in England, and Messter in Germany, who married moving image and sound in various ways to project before audiences. As mentioned in Chapter 2, the Gaumont Company of France produced hundreds of chronophone motion pictures starting right at the beginning of the century. Subsequently, advances with **amplifiers**—such as with the audion tube developed in America by Lee DeForest—made it possible to reproduce sound in a large space.

Figure 3-4 Illustration of the chronophone.

Experiments in matching motion pictures to recorded sound continued through the first thirty years of film. There were two primary methods that technicians used to enable recorded sound to play along with movies: either sound-on-disc or sound-on-film (**optical sound**). Both were experimented with from the time of the invention of the cinema, but the first widely used system of synchronous sound with motion pictures was a fundamentally flawed system of sound-on-disc, the **Vitaphone**.

Sound-on-Disc

The Vitaphone, owned and marketed by Warner Bros., was a sound-on-disc arrangement in which a turntable playing 33-1/3 rpm discs (not 78 as was then standard) was linked by cable to the projector. The projectionist matched the start marks on vinyl records with those on the film for sync. However, the imperfections of such a system are immediately obvious: If there was even a slight skip in the record or a break or skip in the projected film, the synchronization between the picture and sound would be ruined.

Nonetheless, movies using the Vitaphone were shown starting in 1926, featuring recorded orchestral scores played in sync with the film. However, the film industry avoided this new development because studio heads were worried about the enormous cost of the shift to sound films, particularly through the installation of sound systems in cinemas across the country.

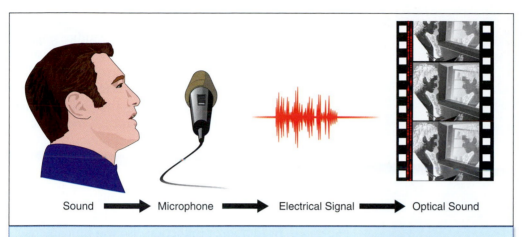

Figure 3-5 Basic steps in motion picture audio: sound is picked up by the microphone, which transforms noise into electric impulses. For optical sound, the audio track is printed directly onto the film and read by the projector. In contemporary digital processes, sound and image are stored as digital information, can be read by laser or from a hard drive, and are translated and projected using computer technology.

Sound ➤ Microphone ➤ Electrical Signal ➤ Optical Sound

Nonetheless, as is often the case in the history of moviemaking, financial profits led to change. In 1927, the enormous success of *The Jazz Singer* showed the studios that sound was here to stay.

In that movie, actor Al Jolson spoke during two scenes of the film, and audiences reacted overwhelmingly to seeing a character talk in an everyday way up on the screen. Actors had talked in movies before, but with this movie it occurred in a way that was natural and real to audiences. Moviegoers flocked to see the movie across the country, and *The Jazz Singer* reaped enormous profits for Warner Bros.

Optical Sound

In fact, studio heads had been avoiding the adoption of synchronous sound for nearly a decade. By the time the Vitaphone was making headlines with the success of *The Jazz Singer*, viable systems of sound-on-film, or optical sound, had existed for almost ten years. Optical sound is a system of reproducing sound visually. With optical sound, audio waves are recorded by a **microphone** and transformed into electric impulses that produce a visual pattern which is directly printed on film. The sound track, which runs along the side of the celluloid between the motion picture frame and the sprocket holes, is projected onto a photoelectric cell which reads the sound as the motion picture passes through the projector.

In Germany, the Tri-Ergon process of optical sound was patented in 1919. In the United States, Dr. Lee De Forest developed his own optical sound system during the 1920s and showed thousands of sound films from 1924 to 1927. De Forest offered his system to the studios, but they were not

Figure 3-6 Camera in the bulky, sound-proof box in 1929. *(Courtesy Photofest)*

interested in making the investment. Once sound films showed their enormous profitability, the studios engaged in an astonishingly rapid switch to sound films. In just two years, virtually all films being produced were sound films. After a brief period in which sound-on-disc films continued to be made, by 1930 superior systems of optical sound had won out and were adopted by studios and distributors across the world.

The Effects of Changing Technology

The effects of the conversion of equipment and theaters to sound movies on the economics of the film industry were enormous. In addition, production also was fundamentally altered in a variety of ways. In Hollywood studios, the demands of sound recording immediately dictated how movies were shot. Instead of being freely used to develop creative visual solutions to tell stories, the camera itself was now literally attached to the needs of sound recording. In addition to being stuck to cables, the camera now had to be isolated. The loud sound of a rolling camera would be picked up by microphones, so cameras had to be stuck in soundproof booths with windows for shooting.

However, some directors pointed out that a sound track was simply a new tool at the disposal of filmmakers and that the way to approach sound was to use it as a creative means of expression. In particular, Soviet filmmakers Eisenstein and Pudovkin and Frenchman René Clair pointed out the creative potential for the use of sound and went on to demonstrate provocative and artistic audio innovations in their films of the early 1930s.

The story of the transition to sound and its effects on the techniques, artistry, economics, and other aspects of filmmaking is typical in film history. As you saw in the last unit, motion pictures are grounded in technology. Just as technology tends to be developed as it is being used, motion pictures

Framing the Discussion

- *What have been the most important new developments in media technology over the past decade? Compile a list of at least five key changes or innovations.*

- *How have any of these developments altered how movies are viewed? In what ways are various types of motion pictures viewed today?*

- *How have these changes in media technology altered moviemaking in terms of access to filmmaking?*

- *What are the most important economic effects of these changes? Are there new challenges that have presented themselves to filmmakers, distributors, cinemas, or other sources of media? List the three most important challenges that you perceive.*

have been in a virtually constant state of change throughout their history. Discuss the following questions to examine the effects of modifications and new developments in motion picture technology through a variety of viewpoints:

As discussed earlier, the conversion to sound initiated a complete overhaul of the film production process and eventually added a new sector of work in filmmaking. The most important facet of sound recording was the one that made it such a sensation with audiences: seeing people speak on the screen. This was the aspect of sound recording that most greatly affected the film industry and the experience of viewing films.

Getting in Sync

The key to recorded sound in films is that the picture and sound match up. When we observe the mouth of a person move as he or she speaks on the screen, what we see and hear must correspond exactly or it sounds "off." Of course, this is true unless we want it to work contrary to normal sound and image. Synchronous sound, or sync sound, is sound that is heard exactly as its visual source moves or is seen or perceived to create that sound. Typical examples in movies are lips moving as that person speaks, footsteps heard as a person walks or runs, or a door closing as we see it happen. The image is said to be *in sync* with the sound.

What is needed for this to occur in movies? It is necessary to have both cameras and sound recorders that run at an absolutely constant rate. For movie cameras in the United States, this rate has been established at 24 frames per second for 35mm film. For synchronous sound to work, the camera must continually run at exactly this pace. The sound must be recorded and played back on a device that ensures an absolutely constant speed consistent with precision time. With digital media, time codes are used such as **SMPTE time code**.

Many people use motion picture cameras to record everyday events with family and friends. They turn on the camera, point to what they will shoot, and press to record. It seems like picture and sound are one and the same. However, it is important to understand and imagine picture and sound as two separate parts that come together to make up a motion picture.

Matching It Up

For movies that are made with celluloid, the camera only shoots film. The sound recording is preserved on a separate device. A sound recordist oversees the proper recording of sound for the movie (often using and mixing together a number of microphones, for example) while the cinematographer and camera staff are in charge of the photography.

In fact, this is why the **slate**, or clapperboard, exists. For most of the history of filmmaking, the slate has been necessary to match up sound and picture. At the beginning of takes that require sync sound, the clapsticks on the slate are snapped together by the clapper (often the second assistant camera on

Figure 3-7 Camera assistant about to mark a scene with a slate. *(Courtesy Kendelyn Ouellette)*

a film shoot) who then leaves the shot. The camera and sound source both record the precise moment in which the sticks produce a sharp snapping sound. The exact instant at which the noise is heard on the recorded sound is matched up to the precise frame in which the sticks are seen to come together. With the advent of digital techniques, there are electronic slates that feature a time readout that is linked to the sound recording device and can assist in syncing picture and sound.

Just as had occurred with the emergence of optical sound with motion pictures, we will first concentrate on the techniques and traditions of capturing sound on the set. During movie production, the craft necessary to select and record properly the sounds heard on **location** or the set is a demanding and intricate endeavor.

Sound Recordists and their Collaborators

What is sound? Sound is a wave motion caused by pressure changes that registers as an identifiable sensation through the ear, which we call hearing. Sound waves travel as vibrations through gas, liquid, or solid, and their particular qualities are created by the frequency, intensity, and phase of their cycles. Because these vibrations are constantly reacting to pressure differences, sound waves spread and bounce in all directions from their source, which makes them quite difficult to control and capture easily.

In moviemaking, most people tend to take sound for granted. When most of us use movie cameras, the sound is picked up when we push the record button and concentrate on capturing the pictures that we want. However, in order to develop our media skills fully, it is vital to understand the craft of using appropriate audio instruments and techniques and the artistry of achieving high quality and proper mix of sounds on location and in the studio.

Figure 3-8 In this scene from *Singin' in the Rain*, the director is showing his stars the importance of the microphone that will be recording dialogue for their first sound film. *(Courtesy MGM/Photofest)*

When filmmakers first began recording sound during motion picture production, the process was cumbersome and hampered creativity enormously. A great illustration of this is in the film *Singin' in the Rain* (1952), which inventively and comically demonstrates the complexities of the change to sound film. The scene featured in Figure 3-8 points out a number of the challenges to any sound recordist in capturing good sound, such as stray noises from costumes and objects, actors facing away from microphones, and the **dynamic range** of voices and other sounds in a scene. Sound technicians are consistently confronted with many factors as they place microphones to capture acceptable sound, and this can be the case, even with the most highly advanced hidden **radio microphones**.

Lowering the Boom

Since the early years of optical sound, the essential elements of audio recording have remained quite similar. Microphones are used to record the audio that is deemed necessary for the scene, and the sounds captured by these microphones are mixed. Sometimes a single microphone is used, particularly a microphone on a **boom** which is normally fitted with a **windscreen** for exterior shooting. An operator usually holds a boom—a retractable pole to which a microphone is attached—but it can be placed on a stand. The boom operator positions the microphone above or below the scene and then moves it in relation to the dialogue of the actors or other sounds happening during the scene.

Figure 3-9 Boom operator and sound mixer recording sound on location. *(Courtesy Kendelyn Ouellette)*

Figure 3-10 Boom microphone with windscreen being used to record sound on independent digital feature. *(Courtesy Mike Chase)*

There are two major considerations for the boom operator: to record the sound well and to stay out of the frame. It may seem very easy to movie viewers to keep the boom and microphone out of a shot, but there are a number of factors to consider, including a changing frame line, shadows created by various light sources, and the necessity to record high quality sound, which means getting as close to the actors as possible. The sound crew must weigh all of these factors in preparing to record sound, and during shooting, the boom operator often must be very active moving the microphone to maximize the quality of the recording.

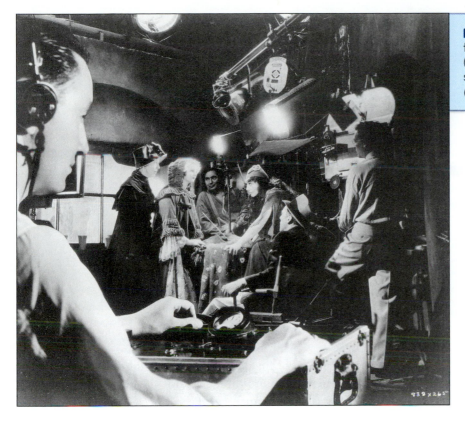

Figure 3-11 Production still from *The Tale of Two Cities* (1935) with the production sound mixer at left. *(Courtesy MGM/Photofest)*

Mixing on the Set

A number of microphones can be placed at different spots around the set or location, particularly in relation to the actors, in order to capture the dialogue and sounds occurring in the scene. The **production sound mixer** implements and oversees the proper placement and function of the audio devices on the set, often directing a team of technicians. Sound professionals must develop expertise with the selection and use of various microphones for the unpredictable requirements of location situations. For example, a **cardioid microphone** picks up sounds in a heart-shaped pattern in front of and to the side of its top while a **shotgun microphone** is used to record sound at a distance from a precise source.

When shooting takes place, the production sound mixer operates the device that records the sound during filming. Previous to the widespread integration of **digital recording**, audio was commonly recorded onto 1/4-inch magnetic tapes using a **Nagra**, a portable sound recording device ideal for synchronized sound recording at constant speed. As digital sound recording became available in the late twentieth century, production sound mixers began to use **Digital Audio Tapes (DAT)**, and have since shifted to other digital storage formats, such as **hard disk recording**.

Whatever the storage format is for the audio, the production sound mixer must set proper levels for each microphone so that sounds are captured within

Figure 3-12 The sound team strives to record all the audio necessary for a good sound mix and to avoid unwanted noises.

the dynamic range of the recording devices. As recording occurs, these levels are mixed to form the production sound track for the film. This is the most essential source of sync sound in many movies.

At the beginning of a take, the first assistant director will give the first call to begin a shot by declaring "roll sound." The production sound mixer begins to record sound and when there is confirmation that the audio device is recording at perfect rate, "speed" is called out by the mixer. The camera is now called out and started, and when it is running properly, the camera operator will say, "rolling" and "mark it." This means that the slate will be shown and clapped, which is preserved by both the camera and audio recorder.

The Elements of the Mix

It is possible for the sound of a motion picture to consist solely of the production sound track. In fact, the sound source for an entire film can be the audio recorded by a single microphone, such as a boom microphone. However, a mix of microphones is usually used during production to record sound, and the sound track of a film is nearly always made up of a number of audio elements that are mixed together to create the sound for the film.

Just as shots are edited together to create the sequence and mix of images that make up a motion picture, sound is edited as well. There are two basic elements to consider. First, editors must *cut* the sound into distinct pieces with a beginning and end, just as is done with the picture of a movie. Second, sound editors and designers *mix* the different tracks of sound to form the final composite track of the motion picture. Sound elements fall into a number of different types of audio material.

Figure 3-13 Recording wild sound with no camera running. *(Courtesy Kendelyn Ouellette)*

In Production

In fact, during production, sound mixers record more than just the sync sound as described. When on a set or location, the recordist generally provides other sounds to be used when sound editing for the film occurs. First, the mixer needs to record different samples of **ambient sound** in order to have this track for use during editing, particularly if dialogue needs to be replaced in post-production recording. Ambient sound is sound that is recorded during production to preserve the noise that is present on location or a set. This includes *room tone*, which is simply the noise that is present in an interior without any actors or technicians talking or making any noise.

The sound team may also record **wild sound**, which is non-synchronous sound recorded during production. It is recorded on location separate from the picture for possible use in the sound mix. Some wild sound consists of **sound effects**, which are noises other than dialogue created by people, animals, and objects during the movie. These sounds, such as footsteps or doors opening and closing, are added to the film during post-production. Wild sound also includes off-camera lines and non-sync dialogue recorded because of production difficulties.

Post-Production Sound

During post-production, sound effects can be added to match the actions on the screen. **Foley effects** are noises created to synchronize with the images recorded during production. In a sound studio with a projection or viewing system, foley artists use a wide variety of materials and objects to produce sound effects directly in sync with the motion picture as it is viewed.

All of these effects are brought together during the post-production process and mixed with the dialogue that is both in sync with the picture and **off-screen** (such as **voice-over**). In addition to sound effects, another typical step in post-production sound recording is **Automated Dialogue Replacement (ADR)**, also known as looping or dubbing, which is a system of recording dialogue in synchronization with the photographed motion picture. Through ADR, actors record their lines in sync with the picture as they watch the motion picture on a screen.

ADR is performed for a number of reasons. It is sometimes necessary to replace some dialogue that is faulty because of problems in the original production recording, such as traffic or other location noises. In addition, the lines may be unintelligible and need to be replaced. Finally, ADR is performed across the world to replace the original dialogue of the motion picture with a language for native markets. This is the most common meaning people understand when talking about dubbing a movie. Although this is often perceived comically in the United States through the well-known example of poorly dubbed Asian martial arts films, dubbing work can be of a very high quality when there is a well-developed tradition of synchronized dialogue replacement in a film industry, such as is the case in many European countries.

There are many tracks of sound that can be brought together to form the composite mix of motion pictures. We have considered the different types of audio recording that comprise the dialogue and sound effects of a motion picture. Finally, we must think about the type of sound that often enters the mix at the last stages of its development: music.

Music and Moving Images

Music was the chosen sound accompaniment to the first motion picture, and it has retained a central role in movies throughout the history of the cinema. Music is one of the most expressive and powerful means used by filmmakers to shape the tone and style of a film. In fact, its power is so strong that its *absence* is often just as important as its use at particular stages in a film.

As directors or filmmaking teams enter the pre-production of a film, they can consider two main approaches to the insertion of music in film: music that has previously been recorded, or music that is composed specifically for the movie. Motion pictures have included countless successful examples of both methods.

Music is regularly generated by composers who create scores specifically for individual projects. The score is recorded for the soundtrack by a musician, small ensemble, or orchestra, generally in front of a screen showing the edited movie. This can be one of the last steps in the creation of a motion picture, so that the composer can time the musical cues to the editing that has been completed.

Musical scoring of films has a long tradition dating back to the early years of silent cinema, and composing for motion pictures has been a source of

Figure 3-14 Composer Henry Mancini conducting a studio orchestra to record a score in sync with picture. The movie screen can be seen behind the musicians. *(Courtesy of The Henry Mancini Estate)*

creative and professional opportunity for many of the finest and most original musical figures of the past century. Some of the most profound and inspiring developments in cinematic storytelling traditions, styles, and themes have benefited from creative synergy between image and original music. Studies of musical scores and the ways that music can affect a film are extremely useful for a full understanding of motion pictures.

Music powerfully shapes many aspects of motion pictures. It is obvious to most viewers that music contributes to setting a tone for many movies and also helps to instill a style. In some cases, music establishes the feel of the movie virtually on its own! Choices of approach when creating an original score include the instrumentation, genre of music, and use of repetition or range of melodic and thematic material.

Lessons from the work of the most successful and renowned film composers consistently demonstrate original and distinctive choices in relation to the movie, whether they work as a complement or in contrast to the visual material of the film. These can be heard in the works of such composers as Alex North, Jerry Goldsmith, and Elmer Bernstein in the United States, John Barry and Roy Budd of England, Georges Delerue and Michel Legrand of France, Ennio Morricone and Nino Rota of Italy, Toru Takemitsu of Japan, and many others. There have also been numerous repeated collaborations between composers and directors, such as with Bernard Herrmann and

Figure 3-15 The collaborative process in the recording studio: at the podium, actress and singer Julie Andrews, composer Henry Mancini, director Blake Edwards. *(Courtesy of The Henry Mancini Estate)*

Alfred Hitchcock, Henry Mancini and Blake Edwards, John Williams and Steven Spielberg, Mark Mothersbaugh and Wes Anderson, Danny Elfman and Tim Burton, or Joe Hisaishi and Hayao Miyazaki.

It is also important to note the effect of music on continuity and pace. Music greatly influences the quality of continuity of a film and can help tremendously in smoothing out rough edges or putting accent marks on visual cues in the film's continuity. Additionally, music can have a tremendous effect on the tempo of a film. In particular, the addition of music to the scene can give the impression of enhancing the speed of a scene without a single frame cut from the picture, thus adding to its energy and possible emotional impact.

Songs in the Scene

When reflecting on the use of music in film, there is a key question to consider: is the music heard or created by the people on the screen, or is it not? If the music is actually present during the scene, such as played on a radio or actually performed by the characters, it is useful and often necessary to determine or create the actual tracks in advance. In fact, the first famous sound film, *The Jazz Singer*, was a musical, and one of the most significant uses of music in films is in the integration of musical performance and dance in such films as *On the Town, The Band Wagon, Funny Face, The Sound of Music, Pride & Prejudice, Dreamgirls*, and *Sweeney Todd*, among many others.

The choice of previously recorded music is the other primary musical possibility available to filmmakers. In contemporary cinema, the most obvious example is the use of popular songs. Filmmakers frequently began to embed contemporary songs into the soundtrack of films commonly by the

Figure 3-16 Scene from the contemporary musical *Dreamgirls*, with Jennifer Hudson, Beyonce Knowles, and Anika Noni Rose, directed by Bill Condon. *(Courtesy DreamWorks SKG/ Photofest)*

1980s. Notable filmmakers who creatively employed popular songs include Mike Nichols in his groundbreaking film *The Graduate*, George Lucas with *American Grafitti* (1973), and Martin Scorcese, who demonstrated integral use of songs to enhance such films as *Mean Streets* (1973) and *Goodfellas* (1990), although he has also worked with composers as he did with Bernard Herrmann for *Taxi Driver* (1976).

Previously recorded instrumental music has also been a soundtrack source for many motion pictures. In fact, many production studios have managed and drawn from libraries of music recorded by individuals, ensembles, and orchestras for use in various projects, including television series. In feature films, many types of music are used, from jazz to electronic to classical music as in Stanley Kubrick's *2001: A Space Odyssey*.

When filmmakers started using popular songs in their films, they were often driven by choices influenced by an artistic desire to reflect and illustrate the culture of the times and its full social and popular contexts. However, there is a relative ease to selecting songs for a film, so such a choice could quickly become limiting and lazy. Thus, it is important to weigh the use and reasons for using songs and instrumental themes from available sources. In addition, producers must consider the legal aspect of using prerecorded music. It is necessary to get permission from the publisher of the music and the copyright holder to the recording, which typically involves payment.

In the twenty-first century, some of the most active and fertile sources of interaction between moving images and music are found on the Internet. While the recording industry has struggled with consumers' access to music downloading, artists have used web portals to reach their audiences through music and spoken addresses often linked to moving images. Also, music linked to streaming video has been a source of both new media experiences and fresh twists on old forms like the movie musical, as seen in *Dr. Horrible's*

Sing-Along Blog (2008), created for Internet distribution and later adapted with sing-along commentary for its DVD release by director Joss Whedon and his collaborative team.

Designing Sound

With music added to the picture, we can see the many elements that combine to form the composite sound track to a standard motion picture. As mentioned earlier, the application of inventive ideas for the creation of the composite sound track was evident in the first years of sound, as was discussed regarding Clair, Eisenstein, and Pudovkin, and was later apparent in the work of the Disney studios and such filmmakers as Orson Welles, Jacques Tati, and Stanley Kubrick, among many others. As sound recording, mixing, and reproduction increased in complexity and range of methods and tools, the role of an architect to establish a blueprint for the structure of sound in the film and to oversee its creation was seen as necessary in many films. In contemporary cinema, sound design has become a key creative underpinning to the work of the sound recording and mixing teams.

In contemporary moviemaking, sound design is viewed as a cornerstone of the marriage of image and sound. This evolution in the role of recordists and mixers and the subsequent creation of the role of the sound designer stems in particular from the groundbreaking work of Walter Murch in the late 1960s and 1970s, most notably through his films with Francis Ford Coppola, including *The Conversation, The Godfather*, and *Apocalypse Now*. Sound designers oversee and guide the many choices of all the contributors who create the tracks of sound effects that are mixed together for the composite

Figure 3-17 Sound pioneer George Groves at an early mixing board. *(Courtesy of http://www.georgegroves.org.uk)*

track. They must help to provide the film with a sonic signature, an aural world that enriches and brings to life the reality present on the screen.

In sound design, there is an interesting tug between reality and imagination. You can hear this when you experience the work of the designers or supervising sound editors who fueled bursts of creative work in this field, as with Ben Burtt on the *Star Wars* films, Skip Lievsay on films by the Coen brothers, and Alan Splet on early films of David Lynch. They have devised imaginative solutions to the creation of distinctive noises that remind us of what we are used to hearing yet that can also depict fantastical settings using noises of the everyday. As Ben Burtt said about *Star Wars* (1977), "We wanted real motor sounds, rusty clanky things, to create the sense of a used world." Whether a film is set on a far-off world or in a typical home, it is sound that can complete the task of crafting a world up on the screen. As the efforts of the creative team working on a film come together, mysterious and imagined places and events can feel as real to us as everyday life, or the most mundane daily experiences can take on powerful resonance as we witness them on the screen.

As we have now reached the role of a professional whose tasks on a film stem from the complexity of contemporary movies with digital recording, multi-tracked surround sound, and teams of assistants, let's return to the true reason for audience excitement upon the arrival of sound: a person talking in a movie.

The Spoken Word

At the time of the integration of recorded sound into motion pictures, the addition of sync sound added a relatively new element for filmmakers to consider: spoken dialogue. Until then, the only actual words communicated to the audience were those written on the screen for the **intertitles** of silent films. Now, they could be heard.

By the 1920s, certain aspects of the role of the writer had been standardized in film industries, although roles for writing stories, scene breakdowns, and intertitles were often separated, vaguely defined, and regularly uncredited. However, some writers developed substantial careers writing for the silent cinema, such as Anita Loos, Frances Marion, June Mathis, and C. Gardner Sullivan. Significant conventions of screen storytelling were developed by

Framing the Discussion

- *Can you name three movies you have seen in which sound contributed greatly to the impact of the movie? Why was this the case?*

- *What are the sorts of sound systems that are used when you watch the different types of motion*

pictures that you see? How does this affect your experience?

- *Do you have any favorite places where you see movies or shows? Is sound a factor with this?*

Figure 3-18 Actor John Turturro playing a playwright struggling in Hollywood in *Barton Fink* by the Coen Brothers. *(Courtesy 20th Century Fox/Photofest)*

this time as movies increased in length and required character development and story structure that warranted longer running times.

With the arrival of spoken dialogue in films, characters could be defined not only by how they acted and looked but by the words that came out of their mouths. Since actors needed lines to be spoken during the production of films, screenwriting took on a new role in moviemaking. During the silent cinema, writing had developed some consideration as a craft, and there were screenwriting books, competitive awards, and advertising for writers. As sound films became the norm, strategies for composing cinematic dialogue and screenwriting standards took on a more crucial significance for the studios.

Yet again, *Singin' in the Rain* amply demonstrates consequences of the integration of sound in motion pictures. While making a new "talkie," the actors improvise insipid lines as they have in the past. During the first screening of their newly completed sound movie, the audience erupts in boisterous, unintended laughter when Gene Kelly's character melodramatically delivers horrible dialogue. Clearly, the time had arrived to bring in writers who could pen effective dialogue, whether dramatic or intentionally comic.

In fact, the central plot of the movie revolves around another aspect of the arrival of sync sound: the quality of actors' voices. In the film, actress Lina Lamont possesses a grating voice whose overwhelming Brooklyn accent is not particularly suited to roles such as one set during the French revolution. Problematic speaking and singing voices were an issue for a number of silent film stars, as well as the fact that acting talent now had to include the full range of abilities necessary for spoken performance.

Figure 3-19 Pierre Brasseur, Arletty, and Jean-Louis Barrault in *Les Enfants du Paradis,* directed by Marcel Carné and written by Jacques Prévert. *(Courtesy Pathé/Tricolor/Photofest)*

Writing for the Screen

In the 1945 film, *Children of Paradise* by Marcel Carné, written by Jacques Prévert, two of the main characters work on the stage, one a mime, the other a dramatic actor. Through this juxtaposition, the filmmakers compare and contrast the artistries of gesture and speech in the setting of early nineteenth century Paris while also commenting on the traditions of silent and sound film. Interestingly, their exploration of these differing modes of expression highlights underlying similarities in the search for engaging storytelling and efficacy of expression in both traditions.

This example could be applied to screenwriting as well. The core elements of writing for motion pictures stayed relatively constant from silent to sound film, although they seemed masked by the addition of dialogue. This remains true to this day. Many young writers spend little time developing a strong dramatic structure for their screenplays. What they spend most of their time establishing is dialogue. Perhaps they even mold their scripts around lines of dialogue that they like.

Usually, strong screen narrative results significantly from the actions that we observe on the screen, not from what the characters are telling us. This is why the most highly respected screenwriters and educators in the field highlight the importance of understanding the fundamentals of dramatic writing. Writing for the screen has evolved from traditions of storytelling that reach back to the beginnings of oral and dramatic narrative. These traditions involve such concepts as the Classical Unities of time, place, and action, and

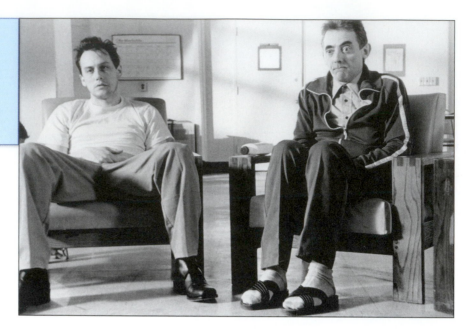

Figure 3-20 The main characters of *Joe*, a non-dialogue short film by Sasha Wolf in which the actions of the characters drive the events of the story. *(Courtesy Sasha Wolf)*

the nineteenth-century French "well made play." From these various methods and dramatic rules, there are a series of core principles that are vital for any screenwriter to investigate.

We will begin with the following three essential story elements: character, setting, and structure. Consideration of these essential elements can be found in virtually all stories that involve characters, whether the narratives are farcical comedies, realistic dramas, or action-filled adventures.

Character

Who is the main **character** of the story? Is there a group of primary characters? How do you describe the characters—physically, mentally, historically? It is typically useful to develop a full portrait of the character, including personal background, occupation, and interests. If an author develops detailed portrait of a character, it can help the story and the creation of the film even if a number of the details are not used in the script. These portraits are actually **characterizations**. On the other hand, characters take form through the actions and behavior that occur during the telling or depiction of a story.

What are some key elements in establishing characters?

- *Objective* – What are the **objectives** of the key characters of the story? What do they *want*?

- *Action* – From the basis of objective, what do the characters do to fulfill objectives in the story?

- *Conflict* – What is it that is stopping the characters from obtaining their objectives? **Conflict** is the basis of drama; it is the source of pressure at the heart of the story.

Setting

One of the three Classical Unities is that of a single place, but an essential function of the camera is its mobility, its ability to occupy and then to transcend limitations of place. Among the first decisions of the initial filmmakers was the choice of **setting**, whether an everyday location or an elaborate set.

- *Feasibility* – What are the limitations of the production? Where can the crew shoot or what can be created to set the movie in a particular space or locale?
- *Location* – In motion pictures, the depiction of a particular location or type of setting can be a core foundation of the movie. It is important for screenwriters to explore fully the qualities inherent in a particular setting or space and to ask key questions about the usefulness and appropriateness of settings described in scenes. Do the locations serve the drama of the story? Do the settings offer ample opportunity to develop the visual resonance of the story?

Structure

Many of the most acclaimed and successful screenwriters have stressed the point that the single fundamental goal of a screenplay is to provide a solid structure for the narrative. This means that the depiction of the pursuit of objectives and the conflicts and twists and turns on the course to resolution (or lack thereof) is grounded in a structure that serves the events and their outcome.

- *Plot* – In motion pictures, **plot** is the series of events that stem from the actions of the characters of the film and that serve to advance character objectives on their way to further conflict and potential resolution. In "character-driven" stories, the initial and subsequent actions of the individuals in the story drive the plot; on the other hand, "situational" or plot-driven narratives are regularly driven by outside forces and events that are then reacted to by the protagonist or central characters of the movie.
- *Tension* – The push and pull between the establishment of a situation and the complications that ensue revolve around tensions between what characters want and the opposing objectives or situations that get in their way. As a complication ensues, tension is created in the story and it tends to build and release at different times during the story. The structure of dramatic storytelling revolves around the manipulation of tension between characters and their situations.

As you can see, our first topics do not even mention dialogue. In your exercises, you will start with conceptions of character, setting, and structure to establish key elements in the development of dramatic narrative for motion pictures. Once a strong framework for the story is built, the writing of compelling and appropriate dialogue can be essential to the effectiveness and success of a script and final film. Now, you will complete your formal introduction to screenwriting by familiarizing yourself with the basic components of screenplay format.

The Essentials of Screenplay Format

Motion picture scripts are designed to put all essential story information onto the page so that the participants in the filmmaking process can use them easily in the preparation and shooting of a motion picture. The three basic components of screenplays are **scene headings**, **action**, and dialogue. From these three sources of information, the reader can tell when a location or major time change is indicated, the physical views and actions witnessed on the screen, and words and important noises heard from characters or other audio sources. Screenplays are written single spaced with a blank line in between scene headings, action, and each separate piece of dialogue. Some of the parameters of script format change depending on the type of production and the stage at which the script exists in the development and production process.

Scene Heading

At the beginning of each scene in a movie is the scene heading (also commonly called a slug line). This line of information in full capital letters begins with a reference for *interior* or *exterior* (abbreviated INT. or EXT.), followed by an indication of the location (dining room; school cafeteria; backyard garden; and so forth). Finally, after a dash (–) there is a word or two to tell the time of day or night (early morning; day; sunset; late night; and so on). In the screenplay format prepared for production, the shooting script, the scene headings begin with the scene number (1, 2, 3, etc.) at the far left and right. For a short film that will quickly go into production, this can be a useful inclusion to make.

Action

The part of the script that tells us about the actions we observe and important visual aspects of the world on the screen is the action (also called scene directions or body copy). Action is a description of actions and important stage directions, mood establishment for the scene, and key aspects of the physical setting. It is written in the present tense in paragraph form stretching from margin to margin on the page. When a character is introduced, his or her name is in full caps. Traditionally, distinct noises, props, vehicles, and special effects are also in full caps when introduced, although newer formats sometimes drop this rule so there is less capitalization.

Dialogue

The third key aspect of a screenplay is the dialogue. First, the name of the character who speaks the lines is placed in full caps on a single line of the script, at about 2 inches inside the full margin. If there are brief acting directions or other important information to the actor—called a parenthetical – that one word or short indication is placed in parenthesis on the line below the character's name, at about 1½ inches from the left margin. If dialogue is being spoken off-screen or through voice-over, this is also indicated using parentheses next to the character name (O.S. or V.O.). On the next line beneath the character name or any parenthetical, the actual dialogue spoken by that

```
INT.  JAY'S LIVING ROOM  -  DAY

SUPERTITLE:  12:16 P.M.

JAY, a senior in high school, passes the time trying to
balance a spoon on his nose, lacking inspiration to do
anything more.

The door bell RINGS.  In no hurry, Jay puts the spoon down,
picks himself up from the couch and heads towards the front
door. Waiting on the other side of the door is NORM, one of
Jay's classmates and good friends, holding a basketball and
ready to play.

                    NORM
          Hey, man.  You ready to throw the rock
          around!

He tosses the basketball to Jay who looks at it with
indifference and drops it to the ground.

                    JAY
          Eh...no.

Jay turns back into the house and Norm follows him in with
an extra hop.

                    NORM
          C'mon, you gotta braid your hair or
          something?

                    JAY
               (Unfazed)
          Shut up.

Jay falls back onto the couch and Norm follows.  Norm
tosses the tail end of a Power Bar onto the coffee table
and eyes a nearly empty bowl of cereal while Jay flips on
the TV.

                    NORM
          You gonna eat that?  I haven't eaten
          since like 12.

                    JAY
          What'd you do?  Run here?  It's only like
          12:15 . . . Yeah, you can have it,
          whatever floats your boat.
```

Figure 3-21 A page from the script for *Jay & Norm*, a short film by Colin Packard. *(Courtesy Colin Packard)*

person is placed in an interior margin 1 inch inside the left full margin and 1½ inches inside the right full margin.

It is important to note that there are many screenwriting tools available today, including a number of computer programs that automatically set up script format. Later in the textbook, you will explore further writing techniques and screenplay format details.

From Blueprint to Collaboration

You have investigated some of the basic principles and logistics of writing for narrative films. Remember that it is generally preferable to develop the characters, setting, and structure of your story before working on the dialogue of a script. Most writers and educators recommend this approach. Naturally, it is possible to begin work on the dialogue of a screenplay before the characters and story are fully worked out, but it is often most practical to complete significant work on the structure of the story before moving ahead with the characters' lines.

When preparing to design a new structure, an architect creates a blueprint for the building. A script can be seen as a blueprint for the finished motion picture. As you may imagine, filmmakers have devised many approaches to the creation of the "blueprints" to their future motion pictures. These blueprints can take on a variety of forms, although the most customary and accepted approach in the United States is seen through the use of the screenplay's standard format. Throughout the units of this text, a variety of approaches to writing and filmmaking will be explored, and you will complete a more in-depth study of writing for motion pictures in Chapter 7.

Persuading the Viewer

One type of motion picture that plays a major role in contemporary life is the advertisement. For your primary exercise project in this unit, you will collaborate to produce a promotional segment. To fulfill this assignment, you will apply the components of filmmaking you have been studying in these opening chapters: visual communication, editing techniques, and use of sound.

The generation of concept and writing of script are typically the initial steps in a motion picture project. For a commercial, the initiator of the project is the client, and filmmakers must devise conceptualizations, then scripts and storyboards, to sell the product or brand in question. They then present their concepts to the clients who decide which, if any, of the proposals are compelling to them.

As you have probably noticed from watching television and other media where advertising is seen, there are many types of commercials, from ones that show characters interacting in a scene to some that display a series of shots of the product (like many car commercials) to others that present a concept expressed through a sequence of associated images accompanied by the voice of an actor delivering the message of the advertiser. Although there are different issues to consider in the use of these varying approaches, they all include elements of what we have been studying about film language, sound design, and screenwriting. When writers prepare short advertising segments, they will generally consider the same factors you just reviewed: character (including just a voice), the appropriateness and feasibility of a setting, and structure of the story or message.

Cooperative Decision-Making

As writer Kevin Goff explains, "The first thing to consider is the time restriction. I've got either 15, 30, or, very rarely, 60 seconds to tell a story and sell a product. The challenge is to weave the two together with as few words as possible." Once the script is sold, the copywriter, art director, and producer with the advertising firm will seek a director for the project. From there, the production team, including the copywriter, director, and art director, will cast actors, scout locations, and complete the many preparatory tasks such as props and wardrobe. At each key juncture in the process, the client must approve the choices of the production team.

Working within such a short format, filmmakers often will point out the heightened importance of every detail. In his work as a copywriter, Kevin Goff highlights a few of the many issues he faces, "We're always trying to show [the product] as naturally as possible. How do you make the client happy by showing a close-up of a cheeseburger, and not make it an obtrusive cut? Or if the client wants a more broad delivery on a line, or a happier, more energetic beat to the spot overall, what can you do in the edit to make that happen, knowing you can't go back out and shoot more film?"

As collaborators move projects forward, the group members take care of the tasks they are individually responsible for, keeping track of progress and consulting on the completion of the work. Key parts of the filmmaking process are **casting** and working with actors, both for scenes and voice work. As you work with your collaborators on exercises associated with this textbook, use the written preparations and the goals you set for each project to guide the selection of actors and to clarify the indications they are given as they interpret their roles.

It's a Wrap!

In Chapter 3, you have explored the integral place of sound in motion picture communication. For the analytical and creative exercises of this unit, you will explore the interaction of image and sound and exhibit skills in visual communication, creative problem solving, and cooperative task management that you have developed over the course of these first three chapters. In this case, your goal offers the challenge described in the previous section: to communicate a message in a brief span of time. The visual elements of the shots, editing choices, design of the sound mix, and performances of the actors combine to bring a group's shared vision to life. That is what you will be evaluating in the movies you watch and the ones you help to make.

Analysis: Sound Analysis

From Individual Sounds to the Layers of a Mix – *For each sequence or short film, including the shorts* Joe *by Sasha Wolf and* Time Persists *by Matthew Silva (see included DVD), indicate the following:*

1. **Dialogue:**
   a. Is there any dialogue in the sound of the film?
   b. Is the dialogue heard alone, or are there other sounds present during the delivery of dialogue? If there are a variety of approaches, note them.
   c. Comment on the prominence and pace of the dialogue. Does the dialogue occur constantly, regularly, or occasionally? Is it delivered at a rapid pace without significant breaks, comfortably exchanged between the characters, or spoken slowly or with regular breaks?
   d. Do visual edits typically occur when characters exchange lines, or are cuts made while a single actor is speaking?

2. **Effects:**
   a. Are sound effects heard in the sequence?
   b. Is there significant noise from the setting, objects, and other non-dialogue sounds? Are some effects heard more prominently than others?
   c. Do any particular effects add to the plot of the story or serve to relay specific information to the viewer?
   d. Do effects work in a particular way to give tone to the sequence or contribute to the overall sensual experience of the movie (its general feeling or poetry)?

3. **Music:**
   a. Is there any music in the sequence? If so, is it instrumental or a song? What types of instruments are used? What is the rhythm? What style or genre of music is it?
   b. Is the music at the forefront of the sound or is it in the background?
   c. How is the music used in relation to the picture? Is it used to accent or add pace to fast drama or action? Is it used to underscore the emotion of the scene? Is it used in contrast to the scene in any way?

4. **Literary and theatrical elements:**
    a. How does the sound design of the film serve the drama of the film?
    b. How does the sound work with the images of the motion picture to influence our mood or provoke emotional reactions?
    c. Sound helps to set a tone and establish style in a motion picture. In this sequence, how did that reflect any thematic elements in the story?

Writing: Promotion

One of the most common motors for the production of moving images is the promotion of products, ideas, events, places, and people. For this exercise with Chapter 3, you will have the opportunity to create a promotional project that can take on narrative or non-narrative form. In addition, you will explore sound as an important source of material. Sometimes, inspirations can come from surprising, unimagined resources. These can include sounds heard in our everyday world.

A. **Topic: brainstorming and research** – For this writing exercise, you will explore and develop the possibilities you have to devise or solicit a promotional subject. First, devise a list of possible subjects and determine the project that you will develop. This is appropriate for brainstorming alone or with a group of collaborators.

   1. **School organization or need** – Is there a particular course, organization, or other entity that might need a promotional or informative piece filmed for their use?

   2. **Business or fundraising enterprise** – Are there any clients that might need an ad to promote their commercial endeavors? A school store?

   3. **Music or the arts** – Is there a band or another artistic group that could use a short promotional subject about them? Is there a theatrical production currently in rehearsals that might need a short to promote their opening?

   4. **Public service** – Are there any current topics of note where there is a demonstrated need for public service messages? Check out ongoing competitions or upcoming competitions that are available to young filmmakers concerning the production of public service segments (for example, anti-drunk driving or driving safety, anti-dropout messages, suicide prevention, and so forth).

   5. **Sports** – Is there a need to promote attendance or participation in a particular sport?

B. **Sounds** – Now let's use sound as a catalyst for crafting a scene and message for this short.

   1. **Noise** – What noises do you associate with this topic? Are they pleasant? Can they be used in any way to interest the viewer, either through humor, action, or in another way?

   2. **Voice** – Is there a particular message that needs to be said? What type of voice would you seek to address this topic?

3. **Music** – Are there any types of music that suit this topic? Begin to create a list of possibilities to develop an approach to crafting style and setting tone in the commercial.

C. **Writing** – Draft a proposal for the project. Include the following:

1. **Objective** – The goal of the project in terms of the message that will be conveyed.

2. **Content** – A brief summary of the images and sound in the motion picture. This should be approximately five to ten sentences.

Project: Client Project

A. **Topic for Commercial** – For Writing: *Promotion*, you prepared pre-production materials for a promotional short. For this project, you will work in a group that will decide as a team which projects will be made into motion pictures.

1. As with the project in Chapter 2, the instructor will assign a group and producer.

2. Please follow the exact same guidelines that are given with the project in Chapter 2. Students will present their plans and the group will work to a consensus to approve a proposal.

3. For this project, the instructor will indicate the time that will be spent on shooting and the estimated amount of work that is expected. For example, a group with a complex project (multiple locations, actors, and setups) may complete one short, while a group with simple proposals (one location, few setups and actors) may complete two promos. Your instructor will indicate the amount of time you will be spending on this project and will approve your proposal.

4. **Approval** – All shorts must be approved by their clients, the instructor, and individuals in charge of the topic of the promo.

B. **Sound** – Devise a sound design for this project, considering the following:

1. **Music** – Is there music that exists within the scene? Is there a soundtrack for the film outside of the characters' perspective? Can music be used to help set tone, establish style, and accent or contrast the drama or comedy of the scene?

2. **Sound Effects** – Noises should be integrated into the script of the scene and can be at the core of the conflicts in the narrative. The film should include sound that is clearly recorded during production and effects that are recorded and added to the mix during post-production.

3. **Dialogue** – The script should include dialogue or voiceover or off-screen lines.

4. **Structure** – Consider all of the elements above when planning the commercial.

   a. **Opening** – How is sound used to help set a tone and establish a message?

   b. **Narrative** – How can sound be used to serve the story of the commercial? Can it help to establish pace, whether slow, regular, or fast? Can it advance important moments in the film?

    c. **End** – What sound elements can be used to help to bring a resolution? Are they comic? Dramatic? Are they loud or quiet? Abrupt or flowing?

C. **Final preparations** – As a group, create lists and schedules for the production:

    1. Locations noted scene by scene

    2. Personnel necessary for filming, including direction, camera, sound, and editing

    3. Actors and extras necessary for each scene, including group members

D. **Guidelines**

    1. The short sequences should last between **one to two** minutes. If appropriate, get approval for shorter lengths (such as a commercial of the standard length of thirty seconds) or longer (up to four minutes maximum, for example to fit a song).

    2. **Editing** – the film must display clear choices of editing, including:

        a. Lack of "dead space" in edits (unless for clear dramatic or comic reasons)

        b. Music, if used, should be employed intentionally and purposefully

        c. Titles used if appropriate during the body of promo, or added after a brief separation, such as black space

    3. **Photography** – the film must show attention to visual quality, including:

        a. Focus must be consistently sharp.

        b. Framings should be appropriate to shots and scenes—watch for head room and wasted space, unless present by design.

        c. Demonstration of compelling choice of color and/or contrasts

    4. **Evaluation** – All shorts will be evaluated according to the objectives agreed upon by the creators of the promo and the concerned individuals linked to the topic.

Report

Write a minimum of two paragraphs describing your work on Project: Class Project.

A. **Process – Please note the following:**

1. Your positions and all that you did.

2. **Requirements** – Comment on your ability to complete the projects appropriately.

   a. Were you properly prepared?

   b. Did you complete the sound work as described in the assignments?

   c. Was the edit complete with all of the appropriate visual and sound elements?

3. In what ways did the group work together effectively? What elements of the projects were possible through successful collaborative work? Give at least two examples.

4. In what ways would you like to improve production or post-production for the next project?

B. **Video Analysis** – Comment on the following elements in your evaluation:

1. Full expression of the message and quality of the structure of the commercial

2. Pacing of shots and sound

3. Mix of sound elements

4. Quality and use of dialogue

5. Overall impact of motion picture

C. **Client Analysis** – Include the critical reactions of the group for whom the commercial was made.

Glossary

Action – Passages in scripts that contain descriptions of actions, settings, and other visual elements. Also called scene directions or body copy.

Ambient sound – Production sound recorded separately from picture and without any talking or movement to preserve the noise that is present on location or a set.

Amplifier – Device used to increase the level or magnification of an electrical signal produced by a sound generally through the use of transistors or electron tubes, thus making the audio loud enough for projected listening.

Automated Dialogue Replacement (ADR) – Also referred to as Additional Dialogue Recording or dubbing or looping, ADR is the process of recording dialogue in sync with the images of a motion picture during post-production.

Boom – In audio recording, a boom is a long, retractable pole (sometimes referred to as a fishpole) to which a microphone is attached in order to be held near the source of sound in a scene.

Cardioid microphone – Type of unidirectional microphone whose sensitivity to sound is useful for vocal or speech microphones.

Casting – In moviemaking, the process of selecting actors for the roles in a film. This is generally done through auditions or meetings with a casting director or members of the production team.

Character – Fictional figures in stories, understood through the actions they perform and words they say.

Characterization – Background elements of a character that provide contextual elements about their history, situation, and personality.

Conflict – Situation of opposing needs, actions, or interests between characters or a character and a natural, manmade, or supernatural force.

Dialogue – In a screenplay, the words spoken by characters, either on-screen or off-screen.

Digital Audio Tape (DAT) – Commonly known as DAT, this digital recording and playback source is one of the first highly used digital formats for film production sound. DAT consists of small cassettes that record and play sound digitally.

Digital recording – Sound recording is the process of capturing the signals produced by the emission of sound so that they can be reproduced as closely as possible to the original source. In analog recording, the signals are captured in a continuous wave. In digital recording, audio is reproduced by a series of ones and zeroes that capture changes in the sound signal.

Dynamic range – The range of sounds from softest to loudest that a recording format or system can reproduce suitably.

Foley Effects – Noises created to synchronize with the images filmed during production, often recorded in a sound studio with a viewing system.

Hard disk recording – Digital sound recording in which the production sound track is stored directly onto a computer hard disk.

Intertitle – Printed words on the screen, usually over black, appearing in a motion picture to provide dialogue or information such as time and location.

Location – The actual physical space in which a film is set; the term is often used for any shooting site that is not in a film studio environment.

Microphone – Instrument that converts sound vibrations into electrical signals.

Nagra – Brand of professional tape recorders used for sync sound recording. The machine uses constant speed systems (first Neopilot, later Timecode) for the tape to move forward at an exact rate and allow perfect sync with motion pictures.

Objective – Goal of a character, either in a particular scene or the overall story.

Off-screen – A character, prop, or event not seen on the screen but perceived by the spectator through sound or known proximity to the scene in the frame. Used to indicate dialogue or sound coming from the physical space outside the frame.

Optical sound – Systems of reproducing sound visually, also referred to as sound-on-film, in which audio waves transformed into electric impulses produce a pattern printed on film and read by a photoelectric cell.

Phonograph – A device that can create and play sound recordings through the reproduction of sound waves. Thomas Edison invented the phonograph in the form of a cylinder and later versions include the disc phonograph or turntable.

Plot – The series of events that actually occur in the course of a story.

Production Sound Mixer – The person responsible for operating sound recording devices on the set, adjusting recording levels of microphones to attain a proper balance of sound, and maintaining recordkeeping for all audio during production.

Radio microphone – Also known as wireless mic and often in the form of a lavalier microphone, this microphone uses radio waves to transmit its signals, so it is used without a cable attaching it to the recording device.

Scene heading – In a screenplay, formatted indication of location and time of day for a new sequence. Also called a slug line.

Setting – The place and time period in which a scene or story occurs.

Shotgun microphone – Family of microphone often used by boom operators because of their highly directional sensitivity to sound.

Slate – A small rectangular board with clapsticks at the top (also called a clapperboard, clapboard, or marker) used to synchronize recorded sound with moving images and to provide technical and recordkeeping information.

SMPTE Time Code – Society of Motion Picture and Television Engineers time code is a system designed to set exact time registration and synchronize different recordings of sound and picture, by recording pulses that document individual frame numbers, seconds, minutes, and hours.

Sound effect – Other than dialogue, voice-over, and music, sound effects are all sounds created or obtained separately from the production track of synchronized audio that was captured during shooting.

Synchronous sound – Type of sound, often referred to as sync sound, that is heard exactly as its visual source moves or is seen or perceived to create that sound, such as when a person's lips move as they speak. When image and sound are exactly matched as intended, they are described as in sync, and when they are incorrectly matched, they are said to be out of sync.

Vitaphone – Sound-on-disc system developed by Western Electric and Bell Telephone Laboratories in the 1920s, which linked a turntable to the film and employed special projectors, amplifiers, and speakers.

Voice-over – Spoken dialogue or narration heard by the viewer but that is not voiced directly by a character in the scene. This includes interior monologues or thoughts of a character, narration by a character or unseen narrator, commentary such as in a documentary film, or voices imagined or remembered in the minds of characters in the story.

Wild sound – Non-synchronous sound effects, off-camera lines, and non-sync dialogue recorded during production separately from the picture

Windscreen – Device used to shield the microphone from wind or air currents or pressure. A common type is the blimp, which is a large hollow windscreen that encloses the microphone but allows sound to pass through relatively freely.

Close-Up

Behind the Scenes with Copywriter
Kevin Goff

Associate Creative Director Kevin Goff, whose credits include internationally recognized work for clients such as McDonald's, Capital One, and State Farm. (*Courtesy of Kevin Goff*)

Q What were some useful lessons you learned through your first experiences?

A There's no right answer. But there are countless wrong answers. And you'll eventually find countless examples where that's true. For example, a joke on a script that we've been laughing about for weeks, even through auditions, comes out flat when the camera starts rolling. The belly laughs are suddenly replaced by crickets. There's no explanation for it, but it doesn't really matter why it's happening. Because it's not working. And you better start writing. Fast. I highly recommend going into a shoot with a good list of prepared alternatives. (They're easier to write when you don't have the client, director, producers, and entire film crew waiting on you to be funny.) You never know–an alternative may be better than what was originally scripted. But you won't know until the shoot, or even until you start editing.

Q Can you cite an instance when you were able to find a visual solution to a storytelling issue?

A I was working on an assignment involving a movie promotion for a major restaurant chain. I needed to find a way to tell a story that linked together the restaurant chain with the motion picture, and do it in a way that would get people excited to go buy the food and go buy a movie ticket. Additionally, the spot would be running globally so I had to find a solution that didn't rely on dialogue. Not surprisingly, months went by where no one was able to sell a script. If one side liked a script, the other side didn't. It's how these promotions usually go. Eventually I sold a script that satisfied everyone. It was a purely visual comparison of the similar sensory experiences people would enjoy while watching the film and while eating the food. For example, I compared how someone watching an intense action scene in a theater might grip the arm rest of the seat their sitting in, the same way someone might grip their bag of food if they were worried someone was going to steal it.

Q How do you balance visual storytelling in your pieces with the importance of sound in establishing tone and style and in communicating key information?

A There's more than one way to tell a story. You can do it purely through visuals, without any sound. But you can also tell the same story purely through sound, without any visuals. The balance of visual and sound ultimately comes down to the story you're trying to tell and how you want to tell it. Any stimuli you choose to include, or choose to omit, communicates something to your audience. It's up to you to determine just the right combination of stimuli to communicate your story in the most impactful way.

Sound is important in every project I'm involved with. From the music and sound effects, to the dialogue and voice talent, sound is vital to the communication. Music can evoke a variety emotions, add energy- or remove it, and even set a pacing for the film. Sound effects simply help explain what you're seeing on film, adding a texture to the visual. Voice talent can be a challenge. Male or female. Old or young. And all the different voice qualities you can think of–the slightest variation of which can mean the difference between feeling authentic or fake, and getting laughs or getting crickets. It's common to audition as many as 400 or so voices just to get the right one. Because without the right voice, the spot might simply not work. Sound is a sensitive thing. It usually works or it doesn't. And you don't usually know if it works until you see it put to picture.

Q What have been some of your observations of the filmmaking process?

A Have an opinion. And have a reason for it. Because everyone has an opinion–some good and some bad. Listen with an open mind. Then listen to your gut.

Once you start shooting, anything can happen. Actors you thought could act–can't. Lines you thought were funny–aren't. You go from being ahead of schedule, to 4 shots behind. And weather that's sunny and 80, is suddenly a flash flood washing your set away. Filmmaking is a fluid process. You have to roll with the punches and find solutions- fast.

Visit the textbook website to read the entire interview with Kevin Goff.

Storytelling with Light

CHAPTER IN FOCUS

In this chapter you will:

- create a fiction motion picture, including script, pre-production elements, editing, and sound design
- investigate basic principles of motion picture photography
- evaluate the application of focus, exposure, composition, and movement in cinematography

Light on the Wall

Shadows dance upon walls, and people look at images that tell of their lives and imagined tales and dreams. At the dawn of humanity, people crawled, torches in hand, into deep caves to paint and then see images of hunters and their prey. Since then, we have returned time and again to darkened spaces to watch stories illuminated upon walls. Now, you can sit in plush seats and look up at the **light** and shadows playing as the sounds that accompany them resound in a man-made cavern. Or you watch them in a brightly lit living room, perched at a laptop, or even on your cell phones. Perhaps you are dropped into your own cavern as you plug yourself into an immersive game that envelops you in its world of moving images.

Figure 4-1 Cinematography helps to establish style and tone in the opening sequences of Charles Burnett's *Killer of Sheep. (Courtesy Milestone Film & Video/Photofest)*

- Young boys play in the dusty rubble of a railway yard in Los Angeles. They throw rocks incessantly and badger each other. The black and white of the images possesses a thickly textured light with overexposed highlights that brilliantly reflect the harsh, nearly surreal context of the scene. This look also mirrors the feel of gritty documentary films of the 1960s, lending an authenticity that makes us feel as if we have been dropped right into the neighborhood of Watts after the riots of the 1960s. (*Killer of Sheep*, 1977, directed and photographed by Charles Burnett)

- On the screen, a young man quickly winds a string around a simple rounded pyramidal top. The earth-colored tones of hand, wooden top, and twine are followed by a face pinched-up in concentration, then the top spinning perfectly onto dirt amidst old coins. Within the next few minutes, the screen will pulsate in close-ups with successively brighter colors and the rhythms of darting tops. Edits and music push and pull our attention between lingering shots of concentration, then rapid fire cuts to capture kinetic energy. The range of sizes, styles, and people we see paints a vibrant portrait of human cultures and inventive movement. (*Tops*, 1957, directed by Charles and Ray Eames)

In each of these instances, we see the work of filmmakers placed in front of us like the drawings on the cave. However, in this case it is light itself that we are looking at.

When we are studying creative occupations, we often focus on the methods and tools of the inventive process. To use this approach exclusively is shortsighted. It is vital to consider the perspectives of the people experiencing the works that are being offered. Thus, you need to investigate not only the instruments of film production, but also the experiences of motion picture viewing.

You will now consider the essence of the experience of motion pictures: *light* and the *frame* that holds it. To understand these elements, first we will study cinematography as it moved from black and white to color. Next, we will explore the history of standard screen dimensions.

Framing the Discussion

- *Can you think of a single image from a movie—in other words, a frame from a motion picture—that is memorable to you? Why does it remain strong in your memory? Now, think of the length of the entire shot. What happens during the entire shot? Is there movement within the frame? Does the frame change because of camera movement, changes in light, or other factors?*

- *Can you cite any examples in which light and dark were used successfully in a motion picture? Name two and compare and contrast them.*

- *Can you think of any examples in which color played a major role in a motion picture? Name two and compare and contrast them.*

The Essence of a Medium

Look around you right now. What is the source of the light that allows you to read the words on this page? Are you indoors? Outdoors or near an exterior light source? What kinds of light are illuminating what you can see right now? Can you see shadows?

The human eye is a very effective receptor and interpreter of light. The eyes and brain adjust instinctively to make what we see more palatable to our senses and more pleasant to watch. People tend to take this for granted. However, photographers must train themselves to be able to understand what the camera, film, or other preserving materials are able to capture and reproduce.

As you have learned, photography was invented as a result of experiments involving chemical reactions and the effects of light on different surfaces. A key issue to consider is the component of traditional photography known as **grain**. The surface impression of traditionally photographed pictures, whether for still or moving images, includes particles that register as tiny grains as they are exposed and developed. As the silver-halide crystal particles react to light and emerge they help to give a photograph or motion picture a particular texture, quality, and luminescence. The grains differ in distribution, size, and density according to film type, the light that hits the film, and how it is processed. Typically, the grains are well distributed when there is proper exposure to a particular type of film. On the other hand, the grains generally cluster together when there is too little or too much light or when films are reprinted through many generations.

Figure 4-2 Charles and Ray Eames, who headed one of the most creative and influential design and arts studios of the twentieth century, shooting one of their playful and enlightening short films, *Toccata for Toy Trains*. (*Courtesy Time & Life Pictures/ Getty Images*)

Digital Capture of Light

With digital cinematography, the recording medium does not involve chemical particles embedded in a surface, so there are no physical grains reacting to the light. Instead, the light is electronically converted into the binary code known as **bits**. Computers function using strings of 0s and 1s , and digital photography works in the same way.

As light passes through the lens and into the body of the camera, it strikes a photographic **sensor** that contains a light-sensitive grid that registers light in **pixels**. Each pixel contains a single measurement of the light's brightness and color at that exact spot, with the number of bits per pixel determining the detail of that information. As a result, the quality of a digital image depends on the number of pixels making up the frame and the number of bits per pixel. The quantity of pixels is measured in width by height (such as

Figure 4-3 Light, darkness, and color at night, photographed on 35mm slide. *(Courtesy http://www.farleyfilm.com)*

Figure 4-4 Composition, light, darkness, and color values create a cinematically enticing arrangement on a 35mm slide. The viewer is compelled to want to know what is going to happen here. *(Courtesy http://www.farleyfilm.com)*

2048 × 1536 for 2K professional cameras), which indicates to the filmmaker the amount of visual information that will be recorded, and as a result the ability of the camera to record fine detail for an image that will be projected on a large cinema screen or shown on a television screen or computer monitor. The pixels that form the image are distributed uniformly across the face of the sensor, but if the sensor encounters difficulty in registering the light or if there is misreading of the electronic information, this causes areas of poor image quality known as **noise**.

Figure 4-5 Paris at sunset in 35mm film. *(Courtesy of Carl Casinghino)*

Achieving the Right Look

There are many factors that affect the visual qualities and feel of the photographed image, and the control of film grain or pixel quality is one of the primary considerations of a **cinematographer**. As you study various motion pictures and shoot your own movies, consider the visual qualities of different kinds of photography and of the work of various cinematographers. Digital and film-based cinematography offer a variety of different opportunities and challenges to filmmakers. Thus, when considering the needs and intentions for a particular motion picture project, it is vital to evaluate the visual attributes and qualities of the finished product that are possible with a chosen set of tools and materials. For Internet streaming video, broadcast media, and gaming platforms, digital image capture and generation have led to an explosion of new content and have established fresh modes of motion picture usage.

The different "looks" of film seen in feature movies have been an important part of the artistry and aesthetic experience of theatrical movies and some television shows. Achieving the proper look is a major consideration of filmmakers, and this includes effects of texture, depth, and luminosity in cinematography. With some digital cinematography, a properly exposed image can look so clean that it appears flat and lacks the feel to which moviegoers are accustomed, while low light situations can create significant amounts of noise that make the image look muddy or snowy. The top objective of manufacturers of professional digital cameras (such as Sony, RED, Thomson, and **Panavision**) has been to develop sensors that compete with the image quality of **film stock**.

Fundamentals of Cinematography

The camera, lens, and recording medium are used to capture the light of the scene that they are facing. Let us examine the key factors that determine the parameters and qualities of the images that are recorded by the camera.

The Lens

The lens mounted on the camera is a key instrument in determining the frame the filmmakers wish to photograph. The relative size of the frame in relation to the field of view in front of the camera is affected by the **focal length** of the lens. Focal length is the measurement in millimeters that indicates the type of a particular lens, such as 16mm, 25mm, 50mm, or 150mm. Focal length is measured inside the body of the lens: It is the length from the rear nodal point of the lens (where light is being sent back by refraction) to the film plane when the lens is focused at infinity. Lenses with small focal lengths are referred to as wide-angle, while large focal length lenses are referred to as long-focus, including telephoto lenses. A lens that duplicates the general perspective of the human eye and falls between wide and long lenses is called a **normal lens**.

Essentially, focal length is what determines what kind of shot will be photographed. Before the invention of the **zoom lens**, all lenses were **prime lenses**, which have a fixed focal length (such as 25mm, 50mm, 150mm, and so forth) and which are still used today because of their extreme sharpness and **aperture** range. With a **zoom lens** such as the one found on consumer digital cameras, you can change your focal length

Figure 4-6 Image photographed with a long lens: Note that the trees and fence at left and right and the people in the background are out of focus, while the principal actor is in focus. From *Side Streets* directed by Tony Gerber, photo by Seth Rubin. *(Courtesy Market Road Films)*

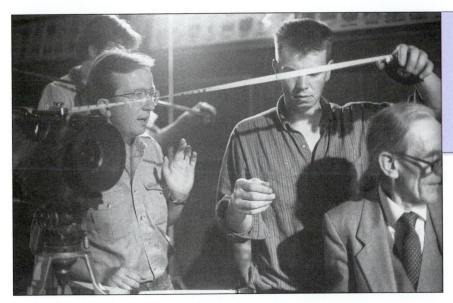

Figure 4-7 Assistant camera Aegir Gudmundsson measures focus in the feature film *Of Men and Angels*, directed by William Farley. *(Photo by Gregg Mancuso, Courtesy of http://www.farleyfilm. com)*

to move from a wide to a telephoto shot. In other words, you can "zoom in" or "zoom out."

A tool of cinematographers that complements lenses is the filter. Glass filters can be placed in front of the lens to alter the light that reaches the camera. Filters can cut light without affecting colors, reduce light in certain areas of the frame, polarize light to help with skies, change the colors of a scene, or induce many other visual effects.

As seen previously, the core task of the cinematographer is to control the quality of the light that is being recorded. There are three basic parameters that shape the essential properties of the moving image: **focus**, **exposure**, and **sensitivity**.

Factor One: Focus

First, focus is the point at which light rays converge so an image or view appears sharp with a normally functioning eye or lens. A lens must be adjusted—either manually or automatically—to achieve a focused view of the subjects that are at a particular distance from the camera. High-quality lenses typically have a calibrated focusing ring that is turned directly or remotely to match the distance from the camera that is intended to be in focus.

For best precision, the distance is measured from the **film plane** (just behind the lens) to the desired point of focus in the shot (often precisely to the eye of the main character). Digital cameras often have an automatic focus feature, in which the camera determines the focusing distance of the subject at the center of the frame. The choice of lens and film stock or sensor used to record the light affect the sharp **definition** of the image, generally referred to as the quality of **resolution** in digital photography.

Figure 4-8 Actress Aunjanue Ellis is in focus while the bright background outside is out of focus in this still from *Side Streets*. *(Photo by Seth Rubin, Courtesy Market Road Films)*

Factor Two: Exposure

Exposure is the process of allowing light to make contact with a film negative or other light-sensitive recording surface for a specific amount of time. Two primary features affect the amount and quality of light necessary to produce a visible image. One feature—the aperture—is the adjustable opening that allows the light to enter the lens. The other feature—**shutter speed**—is the amount of time that the opening admits the light into the camera before closing.

Setting the Iris

Aperture is the opening in the lens regulated by the lens **iris** (or diaphragm iris) to allow a specific amount of light to pass through the lens. To admit more or less light by increasing or reducing the aperture of the lens, the iris is adjusted in precise measurements known as **f-stops**.

The f-stop is a number that expresses the relationship between the focal length and the iris of a lens (from the optical concept of f-number). These numbers make up a logarithmic scale because each single step made to open the lens by one f-stop *doubles* the amount of light passing through the lens.

To understand this, think of a flashlight being used to light up a pitch-black cellar. If you turn on a second flashlight, you double the amount of light in the space. To increase the light by the same *proportion* as when you lit the second flashlight, you will need to turn on two more flashlights, or double the amount again. If you want to increase the light by the same proportion again, now you will need to turn on four more flashlights. Many of the principles of light and photography work on concepts of logarithms such as this example.

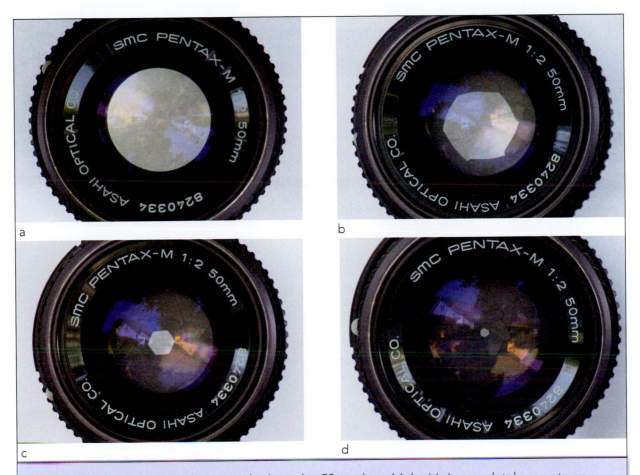

Figure 4-9 Here, we are looking straight through a 50 mm lens: (a) the iris is completely open to an f-stop of 2.0 for this lens. (b) the aperture is reduced one stop to 2.8 (c) the aperture is reduce two more stops to 5.6. (d) the aperture only allows the small patch of white to be seen behind the lens when it is set at f/22. Regulating the size of the aperture on a lens is one way to control exposure.

The standard range of f-stops is: 1, 1.4, 2, 2.8, 4, 5.6, 8, 11, 16, and 22. Each higher f-stop cuts the light by one half, and they are typically used with increments of one-half or one-third between each standard f-stop number. A low f-stop corresponds to a greater amount of light being allowed to pass through the lens, while a high f-stop corresponds to a reduced amount of light passing through the lens. Thus, in a dimly-lit scene, the f-stop might be 2.8, while a brightly lit exterior could have an f-stop of 22.

Shutter Speed and Frames per Second

Shutter speed is the length of time that the shutter on the camera is open to allow light to pass into the camera and onto the light-sensitive surface. On a camera, the standard shutter blade is a semi-circle shape so that as it rotates it exposes then blocks the film **gate** to control the light passing through to the surface of the advancing film. Normal camera speed for

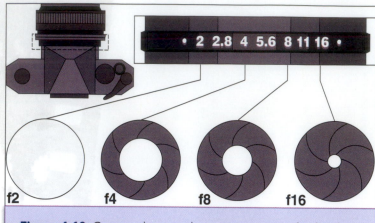

Figure 4-10 Camera, lens, and aperture settings for f/2, f/4, f/8, and f/16.

motion picture photography in the United States is 24 **frames per second** (fps), so that means a camera running at normal speed exposes 24 frames each second (for video or television, it is approximately 30 fps). Since the rotating shutter surface covers the opening for half of the time that frame is moving past the camera gate, the exposure time of each frame is actually 1/48 of a second.

When cinematographers want to shoot for slow motion or fast motion effects, they can alter the rate of frames per second. For slow motion, the rate of frames per second is increased, because when that footage is played back at the normal rate, it will appear slow. In other words, normally a film camera will shoot 24 frames per second. If cinematographers increase it to 48 frames per second, in each second they will record 48 frames. When the images are played back at the normal rate of 24 frames per second, they will take twice as long to be seen, so what took one second to happen in reality will take two seconds in the movie. Everything moves in slow motion. To achieve fast motion, the camera is slowed down, and then when the moving images are run back at a normal rate, everything is moving quickly. This is also the basis of time-lapse photography.

Let us return to shutter speed. A cinematographer can also have the *film* run through the camera at a normal rate of frames per second while the *shutter speed* is altered, which causes different optical effects depending on the shutter and its speed. There are a variety of types of shutter design, but the important issue is its opening in degrees. A high shutter speed causes motion to take on such sharpness that "the resulting footage takes on the animated stuttering quality of a flip book because there is not enough blur in the 24 still frames to fool your brain into imagining that you are seeing fluid motion," according to cinematographer Adam Keker. This effect was used throughout the groundbreaking D-Day beach landing sequence of *Saving Private Ryan* (1998, directed by Steven Spielberg, cinematography by Janusz Kaminski). Slow shutter speeds can be used to create a blurry, impressionistic effect or they can cause such effects as seeing rain falling in daylight when the drops would have been transparent using a normal shutter speed (of 1/48 of a second).

Factor Three: Sensitivity

The third basic parameter affecting cinematography—sensitivity—is an expression of the varying reactions of different types of light-sensitive recording materials with exposure to light. Film stocks and photography supplies are materials produced by chemically developed substances and processes, and

Figure 4-11 Shot from the D-Day beach landing scene of *Saving Private Ryan*. *(Courtesy Paramount / Photofest)*

Figure 4-12 Hallway sequence that captures low light scene in *Side Streets* with cinematography by Russell Lee Fine. *(Photo by Seth Rubin, Courtesy Market Road Films)*

there are many different ways in which light-sensitive products react to light. The sensitivity to light of a particular emulsion or other photographic surface is expressed by **ISO rating** and **exposure index (EI)** values. Film speed ratings, determined by official standards and referred to by such terms as ISO (International Standardization Organization) or the older ASA (American Standards Association) index, are values that measure the sensitivity of a particular film stock or photographic medium and are used to determine the appropriate exposure settings (f-stop and shutter speed).

A film stock that is more sensitive to light is described as *faster* than another stock, although with higher speed types of film, the grain is increased and sharp definition is reduced. There is a tradeoff between sharpness and sensitivity to light. However, this is an area of cinematography that has advanced enormously in the late twentieth and early twenty-first century: Film stocks have increased significantly in their speed while retaining superior grain structure. This is yet another way in which technology has had an enormous impact on the content of motion pictures. Filmmakers have more options to shoot with less light, which means they can move about more easily and shoot in more locations such as dark places that were previously impossible to capture adequately.

With digital cinematography, sensitivity is determined by digital cameras and their sensors, which are the source of the ability to capture and reproduce light. This sensitivity can be increased by adjusting the gain, which is the amplitude of the light signal on the camera. The actual sensitivity of the sensor is not being increased, but the camera is making digital adjustments to alter the light of the image. As with film stocks, as gain is increased, definition is decreased and the image begins to lose quality of **contrast** and color values. On the other hand, increasing the gain and slowing the shutter speed can be used to shoot in extremely dark situations, such as on a dark street at night.

The Cinematographer

Throughout the history of motion pictures, filmmakers have worked to understand the limitations and explore the possibilities of cinematography. As you have discovered, they developed the capacity of the camera and lens to depict subjects both near and far, to capture movement, and to move in front of and around a subject. In visual storytelling, the selection, quality, and expressiveness of the images are generated through technical and artistic challenges. Ellen Kuras, the cinematographer of such feature films as *Be Kind Rewind*, *Eternal Sunshine of the Spotless Mind*, and *Bamboozled*, explains:

> I think that we can't forget that being a cinematographer is not only about taking a camera and photographing a scene. It really is about the ideas and the vision behind what you say . . . I think that a lot of people think of cinematography as a craft only, and once you've mastered the camera and the technical that you can become a cinematographer . . . for me, the material and what I want to say about the material is what motivates me and has motivated me to become a cinematographer.

- Directors will often review the previous work of cinematographers when considering hiring them for a production. For the black-and-white film, *Sweet Smell of Success* (1957), director Alexander Mackendrick sought the collaboration of cinematographer James Wong Howe because "his hard-edged approach would be ideal for this particular subject." Howe, a Chinese native raised in America, was an innovative cinematographer who was able to work in a great

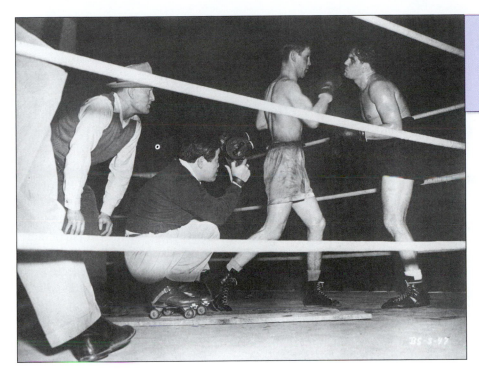

Figure 4-13 James Wong Howe shooting a boxing scene from *Body and Soul* on roller skates. *(Courtesy United Artists/Photofest)*

Figure 4-14 Production design, performances, and storytelling values are all enhanced by the cinematography of Emmanuel Lubezki in *A Little Princess*, seen in this still featuring Vanessa Lee Chester and Liesel Matthews. *(Courtesy Warner Bros./Photofest)*

range of styles, like many successful motion picture photographers. Right from the opening of *Sweet Smell of Success*, the viewer can perceive Howe's ability to light areas of kinetic activity and control strong contrasts of dark and light with characters moving between interiors and exteriors.

- In *A Little Princess* (1995), Alfonso Cuarón appointed his habitual collaborator Emmanuel Lubezki to illuminate visual schemes that balance the reality of a young girl's situation at a boarding school during World War One with fairy-tale qualities. The cinematography consistently uses the motivated light of large school windows, fireplaces, and glass fixtures to provide subtle illumination of faces and interiors. Lubezki had to meet the challenges of the color combinations that help to create the tone of the movie, particularly the difficulty of creating agreeable skin and wood tones alongside prominent uses of green in the production design. The execution of expressive lighting, resourceful framing, and well-designed and well-timed camera movement combines to create a world that achieves deep resonance through the quality of its images.

- In *Los Olvidados* (1950), director Luis Buñuel and cinematographer Gabriel Figueroa capture the bright sun and dusty streets of Mexico City, and the film powerfully uses the contrast of bright and dark in both exteriors and interiors to depict the harsh forces of the world inhabited by these characters. The brightness of a dusty path, the faces of children stuck in shadows as they prepare to commit aggression, the pathetic beggar being hit shockingly in the face with dark mud,

Figure 4-15 The boys attacking the blind beggar in the brightly lit exterior photographed by Gabriel Figueroa of *Los Olvidados*. *(Courtesy Heraut Films/ Photofest)*

Figure 4-16
Cinematographer Tilman
Büttner with Steadicam and
director Aleksandr Sokurov
at right filming *Russian Ark.*
*(Courtesy Wellspring Media/
Photofest)*

all these elements combine to paint the portrait of a brutal daylight attack. In night scenes, Figueroa creates pools of light to depict the interior of the family's house, and the lighting of the characters' faces allows for a powerful range of expressiveness and strength of emotion.

- For their film *Russian Ark* (2002), Aleksandr Sokurov and cinematographer Tilman Büttner developed a new system of digital photography in order to shoot an entire feature length film using one shot with a camera traveling through the rooms and courtyards of the Hermitage Museum. This astonishing feat was envisioned by Sokurov to create a portrait of Russian history that uses the flowing perspective of the camera to orchestrate this voyage like the choreography of the dance. In fact, it is a grand ballroom dance that serves as a majestic set piece to culminate the film.

Selecting and Manipulating Focus

The cinematographers of these examples all had to consider focus, exposure, and light sensitivity of the recording medium in order to capture the illumination of the scenes that they were photographing. They also had to select tools appropriate to their work. When you use particular lenses and cameras, you will see that focus, exposure, and sensitivity can affect each other significantly. A fundamental example of this is **depth of field**.

Depth of Field

Depth of field is the range of the image that is in focus for a specific shot. Imagine that you are photographing an actor. Your camera is on a tripod and you measure the distance between the film plane and the exact spot of the actor, which is five feet. You adjust the lens so that everything that is five feet from the camera is in exact focus. This is the **plane of focus**. The depth of field is the space in front of and behind that plane that is also in focus.

In a particular situation, the depth that is in focus may be one foot in front of the person and two feet behind the person (since one third of the full depth is always in front of the focus point and two thirds behind that point). Thus, everything that is four feet from the camera to seven feet from the camera will be in focus. This range of what is known as "acceptable focus" is the depth of field for that shot.

In fact, depth of field can also be understood in relation to the function of your eyes. Hold your finger directly in front of your face. If you look at a distant object or surface—such as a wall—your view of your finger will be out of focus. If you shift your focus to your finger, the view of the distant object or surface will now be blurry. You are not able to keep both objects or surfaces in focus at the same time because the natural depth of field of your eyes is not deep enough to do this.

Pulling Focus

Depth of field is affected by a number of factors including type of film stock used, distance between camera and subject, and f-stop setting on the lens. The focal length of the lens is important: a wider lens has a greater depth of field and a long lens has a smaller depth of field. This is why telephoto lenses are used to shoot a distant person on a street in sharp focus with blurry-looking crowds in front and behind the character.

Figure 4-17 In this tight shot, the cinematographer takes advantage of a shallow depth of field. (*Courtesy Kendelyn Ouellette*)

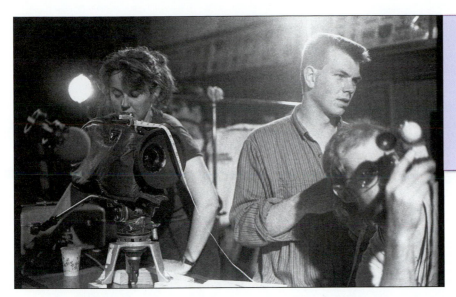

Figure 4-18 Gaffer Eric Blum measuring the light using an incident light meter for a scene in *Of Men and Angels,* while Director of Photography Kathleen Beeler stands behind the camera. *(Photo by Gregg Mancuso, Courtesy http:// www.farleyfilm.com)*

For cinematographers, one of the most important elements of their artistry is the use of selective focus and the creation of particular depths of field for different shots and sequences. By focusing on a particular plane in a shot, the filmmakers can draw the attention of the viewer to particular subjects or areas of importance in a shot. As characters move during a shot, an assistant to the cinematographer will change the focus setting on the lens so the actor will remain in focus. As described in Chapter 1, this is called a **focus pull**. The camera crew can also administer a focus pull to draw our attention elsewhere. This will shift sharpness to a particular element, leaving a softer-edged or textured look to another subject or visual feature. These are all important considerations when deciding on the recording medium and the tools that will be used by a cinematographer.

Measuring and Controlling Light

When cinematographers prepare to photograph a shot, they may use a **light meter** to measure the light that is on the subjects of the shot or they may use measurements available through a digital viewfinder. Cinematographers can face the source of illumination and use an **incident light meter** to measure the light source or they can measure the light as it reflects off the scene with **reflected light meters** (which include the **spot meter**). Often, the amount of light in various areas of the shot will be different. In order to achieve the proper exposure for the shot, cinematographers must use their skills to introduce and measure the desired amount of light throughout the frame, which is gauged in **foot-candles**. From the information about the amount of light on the scene (directly expressed as foot-candles), cinematographers will have to set the lens and camera for proper exposure. When reading light meters, cinematographers have typically accessed measurements in foot-candles or f-stops.

Figure 4-19
Cinematographer Sven Nykvist looking through a spot meter with director Andrei Tarkovsky next to the camera on *The Sacrifice*. *(Courtesy Lars-Olof Löthwall)*

When there is a low f-stop, which opens up the aperture of the lens, there will be a smaller depth of field than when there is a high f-stop, in which the aperture of the lens is closed to allow less light. For example, when shooting outside on a bright day, a photographer would probably need to set the lens to a high f-stop so that the image would not be overexposed. Subsequently, there would be a relatively high depth of field to the shot. It is primarily through lighting that cinematographers can control the amount and quality of light on a scene, and thus also the f-stop used and depth of field for focus.

These are the rudiments that determine the primary technical considerations of photography. The artistic challenges of cinematography revolve around the use and creation of light, shadow, and color, and the placement and movement of the camera and the elements present in the frame. The technical skills of cinematographers allow them to create the images that most fully express the intentions of the originators of the motion picture.

Cinematography in Black and White

During the first decades of the cinema, cinematographers developed many approaches to the creative depiction of subjects. Black-and-white photography affords a wonderful range of expressive possibilities. Even before considering the introduction of color, the use and manipulation of light on the screen involves the mastery of all of the central aspects of photography we have discussed, and the search for artistic originality using these basic elements continues to this day.

First, consider exposure. With black and white film, there are many avenues to explore in the use of contrast between light and dark and the palate of grays

Figure 4-20 Still from *Touch of Evil*, directed by Orson Welles with cinematography by Russell Metty, noted for its intense contrasts between light and dark. *(Courtesy Universal/Photofest)*

Figure 4-21 Man and baby in *Lazybones* (directed by Frank Borzage, 1925) are in sharp definition with background in soft focus. *(Courtesy Fox/Photofest)*

that can register with quality photography. Cinematographers can use deep blacks and bright highlights to create contrast in images, or they can strive for low contrast to employ the full range of grays and bring out the nuances of light on subjects. The key parameters are in the sensitivity of the recording medium (such as film stock or digital sensor) and the quality of the exposure, which is typically a result of the talent and work of cinematographers and camera and lighting crews.

Next, focus is a key concern. The application of focus has been employed in many ways. Some cinematographers have shot for highly selective sharpness on key subjects with other elements registering in soft focus (either slightly or very blurry), while other filmmakers have worked to create shots that have an extremely deep range of focus, primarily through lighting for a high depth of field.

Painting with Light

When we look at certain paintings, we notice that what might look like a blotch when observed up close looks like an easily recognizable flower at a comfortable distance. Painters from Rembrandt to the French Impressionists to contemporary cartoonists have demonstrated that the properly applied suggestion of an image, if rendered appropriately, can provide enough detail to register the subject, and the overall effect can be perceived in pleasing and aesthetically satisfying ways. The same can be true of the use of out-of-focus planes in a shot, which have been seen in cinematography from its inception to today. For example, in a number of silent and sound films by director

Figure 4-22 Janet Gaynor and Charles Farrell in Frank Borzage's *Seventh Heaven*. *(Courtesy Fox/Photofest)*

Frank Borzage, characters stand in sharp focus while backgrounds register in less detail, occasionally shimmering in a striking light. In certain sequences, the settings—whether beside a river, a snow-covered train station, or cobblestone Paris streets—provide a painterly backdrop to stories that have been described as depicting "souls made great through love and adversity."

Razor sharp focus in depth has been another stylistic tool of cinematography. In the 1930s and 1940s , cinematographer Gregg Toland developed a style that capitalized on the possibilities of increased depth of field. Through his innovative use of film stocks, lighting, and pre-production work, Toland's cinematography enhanced the narrative force and visual impact of many films, including *Citizen Kane*, directed by Orson Welles, and *Little Foxes*, directed by William Wyler. In key sequences in these films, characters in both the foreground and background are seen in sharp focus, providing a striking visual feel to the film and allowing a dramatic approach that fed off this high depth of field.

Cinematographers have employed various tools to extend their abilities to manipulate focus. For example, a device that is designed like a filter but functions as a lens element to allow for close focus is a **diopter**. A diopter that is cut so that it does not stand in front of the entire lens is called a split diopter. Describing his work on the film *All the President's Men*, cinematographer Gordon Willis explains, "If you have someone very close to the camera and somebody who is way upstage of the camera, by using a diopter it enables you to carry the focus from this very close subject to a subject that is further upstage...There's one shot of [actor Robert] Redford on the telephone, a zoom shot actually, that took place over a two- or three-minute period." The filmmakers wanted Redford's character—Bob Woodward—talking on

VIEWFINDER

"Most directors from my observation take much too much time looking into the camera for the framing and forget the essential part which is the lighting."

–Jacques Tourneur–

(Director of dozens of features, including *Cat People* (1942), *I Walked with a Zombie* (1943), and *Out of the Past* (1947))

the phone in the foreground and a television in the background both clearly in focus. For this shot and others in the film, Gordon Willis achieved this effect through a complicated system of a split diopter mounted on a precisely calibrated bar.

Moving the Camera

Naturally, even in the first decades of cinema, not all of the issues of photography revolved around exposure and focus. While the frame of the cinema was eventually set at a standard 1.33:1 **aspect ratio** and photography was in black and white, there were other matters to consider, particularly movement. Filmmakers have exploited the expressive and dramatic possibilities of camera movement from early in film history. Dollies were created by film crews, and inventive solutions were continually devised to move the camera around. Through movement, the camera could place the spectator in the middle of the action, reveal certain elements of the scene, and offer a changing perspective to the sequence. A common source of camera displacement at that time employed a familiar component of the first projected films: train tracks. Dollies mounted on tracks were used to move cameras during the silent era of the cinema, and they are still in use by camera crews today.

One of the most important attributes of filmmakers has always been innovation and hands-on improvisation with materials. On set, devising inventive solutions to difficult or exceptional situations has always been a hallmark of film production. Whether involving setting lights, moving the camera, or placing microphones, creative and unique problem solving is essential to successful filmmaking. Here is director Allan Dwan explaining the first use of a dolly in 1915:

> Well, we got a farm scraper and we scraped the street flat, got all the bumps out. And then we softened the tires so they wouldn't joggle,

Figure 4-24 Tracking shot from Andrei Tarkovsky's *The Sacrifice* with Sven Nykvist at the camera. *(Courtesy Lars-Olof Löthwall)*

we locked the springs and fastened the camera on securely with a few two-by-fours, got it well wired down so it wasn't bobbley, and it worked great.

As discussed in Chapter 1, many ways to move the camera have been developed and used by filmmakers, including independently-moving dollies, cranes, Steadicam rigs, and handheld techniques.

From Black and White to Color

There are many processes at work to produce the qualities of the light that we perceive. The production of color in the light spectrum is a complex sequence in which luminescence, translucence, and many other properties take part. To understand some of the fundamental properties of color photography, let us consider one simple manner in which we see color.

As light hits certain substances in front of us and bounces off of them to reach our eyes, some of it is composed of wavelengths that are formed through the reaction with the **pigments** of these substances. These wavelengths correspond to the color spectrum of visible light. As the light passes through our eyes, it interacts with cones, a type of cell at the rear of the eye. These cones determine the ways in which our eyes perceive color. Each cone is sensitive to one of three parts of the spectrum: red, green, or blue.

Just as the cones are each sensitive to one of three parts of the spectrum, the **primary colors** from which all color combinations are generated emanate from this trio of hues. All of the colors that we perceive between the opposites of white and black are made up of combinations of red, green, and blue. We can look at this from the perspective of colors being added together to produce certain hues, in which they are combinations of red, green, and blue.

When we consider the pigmentation of different types of matter, we observe that the pigment of a substance determines its absorption of a distinct color, while the opposing color of the spectrum is reflected, resulting in the color that we see. Colors are essentially being "taken away," so this is known as a subtractive process. Because the subtractive process works in the opposite manner to the primary colors being added together, the system uses their negatives, which are cyan, yellow, and magenta.

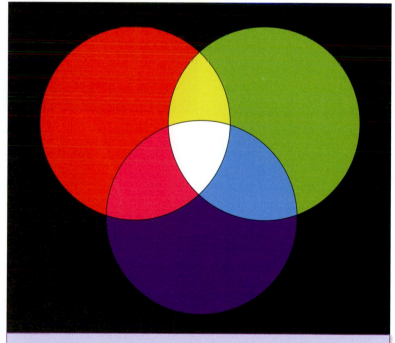

Figure 4-25 Color wheel: primary colors are red, green, and blue, with their complements opposite each one on the color wheel: cyan, magenta, and yellow.

Color photography originates from the principles that are observed in the functions of human eyesight and the properties of the color spectrum. As they experimented with color photography, scientists understood that the full range of colors in the spectrum could be duplicated through combinations of red, green, and blue or their opposites, cyan, magenta, and yellow.

Technicolor and the Three-Strip System

Films in the first decades of the cinema used hand tinting of frames or dyeing of sections of the roll, including the Edison company's *Annabella's Dance*, Méliès's *A Trip to the Moon*, and many features of the 1920s that used tints for particular scenes, whether red for fire or blue for moonlight.

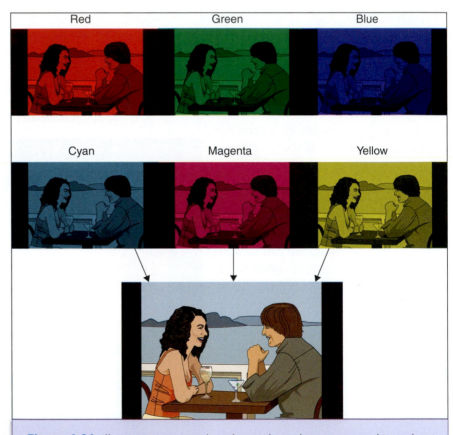

Figure 4-26 Illustration image that shows the colors separated into the three primary hues of red, green, and blue. With the Technicolor system, there would have been three negatives of cyan, magenta, and yellow that would combine in the positive print to produce a full-color image.

These early uses added some color to black and white moving images, but true color soon became a goal of some motion picture technicians. Additive color systems were created in the first years of the twentieth century, including Kinemacolor in England and Dufaycolor in France, but these processes required too much light through the filters in which primary colors were added together to produce the full spectrum of colors.

The color system that first took hold on the industry was a subtractive system known as Technicolor. In the three-strip Technicolor process, separate rolls of negative pass through a complex camera setup that split the light so that it can be recorded onto three rolls of film that are sensitive to either red, green, or blue. The three film negatives, which are in cyan, magenta, and yellow, are combined to produce a single positive print in full color. Use of this process required quite a significant amount of technical mastery and the reactions of the celluloid to particular hues and saturations of color demanded rigorous oversight.

The results could be quite brilliant, as one can see in some of the most notable color films from the 1930s and 1940s , including Disney's *Silly Symphonies, Snow White*, and *Pinocchio*, and two well-known Metro-Goldwyn-Mayer classics directed by Victor Fleming in 1939, *The Wizard of Oz* and *Gone with the Wind.* The vibrant tones of *Robin Hood*, directed by Michael Curtiz in 1938, perfectly match the robust energy of the action and romance in the movie. *Meet Me In Saint Louis* (1944) and *Gigi* (1958), directed by Vincente Minnelli, are noted as landmarks for their uses of color to add resonance to the drama and emotions of their stories and to bring their settings vividly to life.

Figure 4-27 Hermione Gingold, Louis Jourdan, and Leslie Caron in *Gigi*, directed by Vincente Minnelli with Technicolor cinematography by Joseph Ruttenberg. *(Courtesy MGM/Photofest)*

Figure 4-28 Cinematographer Jack Cardiff and camera operator Geoffrey Unsworth with the enormous Technicolor camera used to shoot *A Matter of Life and Death*, directed by Michael Powell and written by Emeric Pressburger. Note the dolly, the large studio lamp on wheels, and the apple box (a useful item on movie sets) on which Unsworth is standing. *(Courtesy Universal Pictures/Photofest)*

However, just as the transition to sound was made very difficult because of the unwieldiness of the equipment necessary for blocking the sound of the camera and recording audio properly, the use of a three-strip system was cumbersome and costly. It was clear that a system of one strip of film would lessen the need for highly specialized equipment and exacting laboratory processing.

Color Photography in Contemporary Motion Pictures

In the early 1950s, Eastman Kodak began to introduce color motion picture film stocks that ran through the camera with only one negative. This meant that they could be used in a regular camera and would allow for much easier oversight by the film crew. Over the years, many new stocks by Eastman Kodak, Fuji, Agfa, and other laboratories were introduced that improved on speed, sensitivity, and grain quality. However, it is important to note that Eastman color and other similar film stocks used from the 1950s to the mid-1980s have proven to be quite unstable and prone to fading. For many motion pictures, image degradation over years of storage has been significant, and the salvaging of movies shot on these stocks has been one of the most important endeavors of film preservation.

Control and use of color during shooting has been a principal task of filmmakers using color film since its entrance into the mainstream in the 1930s. With black-and-white film, differences between objects are visible when they register as contrasting hues of gray, just as Méliès discovered in his set designs and backdrops (discussed in Chapter 8). For example, shades of red and green can easily photograph as exactly the same in black and white. Now, cinematographic composition was changed significantly by the introduction of color into the image.

In addition, **color temperature** was now vital for cinematographers to consider. With black and white, the light source did not matter; it was only the illumination. With color photography, the source of light greatly affects the image. For example, sunlight, tungsten light, or fluorescent light generate completely different wavelengths and resulting color values. With digital cinematography, this is dealt with through the use of **white balance**, in which the camera uses the standard of a white card to automatically adjust its internal settings for proper color temperature with the light of that scene. To do this, the camera operator frames a perfectly white surface lit by the primary light source of the scene and uses the camera controls to set white balance. Once this is done, the sensor knows how to capture the light.

Figure 4-29 Daylight scene in digital color with dramatic focus in shadow. *(Courtesy of Carl Casinghino)*

Exposing Colors

With the introduction of color, cinematographers had to deal with not only the parameters discussed earlier, but also with the task of matching colors from shot to shot (particularly blue skies, often difficult to control!). Naturally, there are also the artistic choices of the use of color, which are made through the concerned members of a film production, including the director, cinematographer, production designer, costume designer, and any other person introducing color into the image.

In fact, one factor introducing colors into the image is the actors. One of the most important concerns for laboratories is the proper registration of the full range of human skin tones. Color film is the result of chemical compounds and interactions tested for favored results, and it was designed for greatest sensitivity to peach-toned color values. Another challenge to cinematographers is to use the particular qualities of film stocks and digital sensors to find the proper exposure, balancing, and consistency of skin tones between the various actors of a motion picture. Both within shots and throughout sequences, the skin tones are expected to be photographed appropriately according to the visual style of the motion picture.

Digital Color

You will remember that in digital photography, the image is made up of pixels that have a brightness value and a color value. Each pixel has three numbers assigned to it corresponding to the red, green, and blue to make a single distinct hue. The number of bits per pixel determines the number of possible color choices there are for that single pixel. For a 24-bit image

Figure 4-30 Working for balanced exposure of color skin tones in digital photography. *(Courtesy Kendelyn Ouellette)*

(in which each of the three primary colors has eight bits of information), each individual pixel can contain one of nearly 17 million colors, since the number is calculated as 2^{24}.

As film stocks and digital sensors have become more sensitive and faster, thus requiring less light for proper exposure, filmmakers have been freed up

Figure 4-31 A frame from *Immersion*, a short directed by Richard Levien and photographed by Frazer Bradshaw on the RED digital cinema camera. Shooting with untrained child actors, the filmmakers capitalized on the ability to run multiple takes without using a slate, which allowed for more natural performances from the actors. Richard Levien explains, "Using film negative with this technique would have been prohibitively expensive." *(Courtesy Richard Levien/Frazer Bradshaw)*

to shoot with less light and smaller crews. A number of films and television shows of the early twenty-first century have capitalized on this accessibility and have been made quickly and with smaller budgets than would have been previously possible. This includes many comedies such as *The Office* and even complicated dramatic productions such as *Battlestar Galactica* (executive produced by Ron Moore and David Eick).

Screen Dimensions

Now we will examine the last key consideration of the motion picture viewing experience: the screen itself. Earlier, we discussed the importance of focal length in lenses to determine the relative width of the image being photographed in relation to its distance from the camera. When considering the size of the field viewed by the lens and camera, it is essential to consider the size of the frame on which the image is being recorded.

Motion pictures are recorded onto frames that have two dimensions: width and height. The first motion picture images filmed by Edison and Lumière show the same relationship of width to height that is seen on traditional televisions and personal computers: 1.33 to 1. In other words, the rectangle that constitutes the frame of motion pictures is one-third wider than it is tall, which is expressed as a 4:3 aspect ratio for television. There are both practical and aesthetic reasons for the establishment of this screen ratio, among them the fact that human eyesight is experienced naturally with more width (perpendicular vision) than height. After all, our eyes are side by side, so we can take in and enjoy more comfortably a moving image on a screen that is wider than it is tall.

Framing the Discussion

- *Do you know of any examples when aspect ratio was used to excellent effect in a motion picture? Consider screen dimensions of height and width to find two examples and compare and contrast them.*

- *Think of a movie you have seen within the last month. Try to remember the shots that made up the first sequence of the film. How were colors used in the shots of this sequence? Were there strong primary colors, or hues muted towards black, white and gray, or soft color tones? Did the color scheme of the opening continue through the film? Was there a distinct shift in the movie in the use of color? Were there any particular patterns you could see in the use of color in different sections or sequences of the film? Were these uses repeated?*

- *Now think of a dramatic climax to a movie that you have seen recently. What colors stand out for you when you remember this sequence or section of the film? Does the use of color in this movie seem important to you? How does it contribute to the visual style of the movie? Are any of the uses of color in this climax employed throughout the film or echoed in any other sequences or parts of the movie?*

Figure 4-32 Frame from *The River*, directed by Jean Renoir with Technicolor cinematography in the 1.33:1 format by Claude Renoir. A master of storytelling in both black and white and color, many of Jean Renoir's films have been cited among the greatest films ever made by critics, festival panels, and fellow filmmakers. *(Courtesy UA/Photofest)*

When optical sound was introduced to film, the width of the image was reduced to make room for the track of sound. This made the image nearly square, and people reacted to this change negatively. As a result, the Academy of Motion Picture Arts and Sciences established a practice of masking the top and bottom of the frame to achieve the screen ratio of 1.33:1. This became an international standard that is known as the "Academy aperture."

A Wider Screen

This remained the norm for two decades until economic forces compelled the film industry to adjust to a sharp downturn in the number of moviegoers. In a few short years, box office receipts plummeted because of changing lifestyle patterns of post-World War II societies and the arrival of a new motion picture phenomenon: television. To draw viewers back to movie theaters, studios and cinemas capitalized on a factor that television could not deliver: Since they already represented the "big screen," why not make it even bigger? Studios developed lenses for shooting and projection that augmented the width of the screen to allow for increased spectacle and a more overwhelming moviegoing experience.

The first feature film using the CinemaScope aspect ratio to be shot in Hollywood was *The Robe*, released in 1953. This system, based on an **anamorphic** distorting lens invented by Chrétien in France in the 1920s, actually squeezes the image onto a frame using the standard aspect ratio, and this frame is then "unsqueezed" in projection by a special lens. Without

Figure 4-33 Widescreen aspect ratio (2.35:1) in *Star Wars: Revenge of the Sith*, directed by George Lucas. *(Courtesy Lucasfilm Ltd./Photofest)*

the special lens, the image looks distorted. With the lens, **CinemaScope** and processes such as VistaVision and Panavision films typically project between an aspect ratio of 2.2:1 to 2.55:1.

As you may guess from the perspective of a television- and movie-viewer of the twenty-first century, widescreen has been a success. The first productions in the 1950s were a hit, and by the latter part of that decade, the widescreen format had become conventional for big screen movies. By the end of the twentieth century, the standard aspect ratios of movies were 1.85:1 in the United States and 1.66:1 in Europe, with widescreen movies being shot at 2.40:1. Many other film systems have been developed, including IMAX, 3-D technologies, and 360° viewing systems.

Aspect ratio also has an enormous impact on a film. The depiction of individual characters, landscapes, or groups of subjects is shaped by the manner in which they are framed, and the dimensions of that frame are determined by the aspect ratio in which the film is being shot. During the first decade of CinemaScope and similar processes, some filmmakers embraced the new dimensions of the screen and exploited them fully, using the wider view to increase the horizontal information portrayed in a shot. Others saw the wide perspective as not conducive for photographing people, describing it as suited for depicting mountain slopes or funerals. The key decisions remain with the importance of establishing the needs, stylistic desires, and technical considerations of a motion picture project. What any filmmaker must ask is: "What is the frame most suited to what I need to express, to the story that I am going to tell, or to the message I am going to convey visually?" In the meantime, producers will also ask: "What is the frame that the audience wants to see?"

Managing the Ratio

When applied to television sets that are physically bounded by their 1.33:1 ratio screens, the wider aspect ratio posed a problem. Initially, movies were cut to fit into the bounds of the screen. Thus, for many decades, many films being projected on television would not show a significant portion of the true image of the film. Eventually, this corruption of the actual creation of the filmmakers was compensated by black bars that mask the screen to duplicate the authentic aspect ratio of the movie and to allow the entire true image to be seen.

The most significant twenty-first century development in the evolution of aspect ratios has been to alter the standard size of the television set. A half-century ago, the movie industry responded to pressure from the newly emergent television phenomenon by making its screen bigger. Fifty years later, the opposite effect has occurred. First, the significant increase in overall television size, improvements in stereo surround sound, and the sale of movies through the medium of DVDs and BluRays transformed living rooms into a reduced version of the movie theater. Next, technical developments such as high-definition television, or HDTV, increased the sharpness of television viewing, and along with these innovations came a push for a widened aspect ratio. Now, it is television that has made its screens bigger with the advent of 16:9 aspect ratio high-definition home theater monitors, which have become an international standard.

Not only has the moviegoing experience been shrunk to the living room (or bedroom or bathroom or family minivan), but motion pictures are being

Figure 4-34 Watching motion pictures on a tiny screen. *(Courtesy Kendelyn Ouellette)*

Figure 4-35 Shooting *The Four Horsemen of the Apocalypse*, directed by Vincente Minnelli (leaning on rail) with cinematography by Milton Krasner. *(Courtesy Roger Viollet/Getty Images)*

experienced through increasingly smaller formats, from laptops to cellular phones. These media are stimulating new communicative strategies designed to take advantage of these formats. What are the most appropriate ways to create moving images the size of a postage stamp? What compositions, colors, and movements work well in these formats? Internet platforms, new 3-D polarizing technologies, and unforeseen developments are sure to present appealing creative challenges to future filmmakers.

Naturally, directors, cinematographers, and other motion picture creators who have worked to achieve desired framing, exposure, focus, hue, and visual style must wonder how much of their intent and vision are being experienced in such circumstances. After all, *Lawrence of Arabia* (1962) and *The Empire Strikes Back* (1980) seem to lose a little something when watched on an iPhone.

It's a Wrap!

In the first four chapters of this book, we have explored the fundamentals of motion pictures as they have been made and experienced: the establishment of motion picture language, application of sound elements with moving images, and use of cameras and lenses for cinematography. Having formed a basic understanding of these key elements to motion pictures, it is time to undertake a complete project for which you will be individually responsible. Along with the critical thinking activities of the unit, there are original writing and producing projects that will allow you to use light and sound to communicate on a moving image screen.

As you prepare to create your script and other production materials, pay attention to the possible inspirations around you. Listen. Observe. The people, objects, life, and places that surround you can be vital sources of creative stimulation. The worlds that we create and see on our screens are born through the depiction and inventive interpretation of our surroundings aided by the activity of our imaginations. Through the cinema, these worlds can move, speak, and play for us.

VIEWFINDER

"When time is short and every decision seems hurried, the combination of preparation and experience will get you through the storm. And I'm not talking about just getting the shot. I'm talking about doing beautiful, challenging work that everyone on the film can be proud of."

–Lisa Rinzler–

(Cinematographer whose credits include *Menace II Society* (1993), *Dead Presidents* (1995), *and Pollock* (1999))

Analysis: Examining the Image

As you view motion pictures, keep these questions in mind:

- **How** is cinematography used to help to indicate an initial reaction to the motion picture? How are visual cues used to tell viewers about what they are about to see?

- **How** do key visual aspects of the film—framing, exposure, contrast, color, movement—affect the portrayal of the people, places, and events of the story?

- **How** does the image help to set the style and tone of the movie in order to tell a story effectively or convey emotions and messages?

Expressive Values of Moving Images

You will watch a selection of short movies, including *Lucky* by Nash Edgerton (see included DVD), to answer these questions in discussion or writing:

1. **Focusing on Light**: How does the impact of light, color, and texture of the image help to set a tone with the movie? Consider the following:

   a. Use of focus and depth of field to establish style and communicate

   b. Qualities of brightness and darkness in the images

   c. Use of color in the frame

   d. Recording medium (film, digital, and so forth) and overall look of the images

2. **The Frame:** How does the framing and movement of shots and sequences serve the drama or visual artistry of the story? Consider the following:

   a. Screen aspect ratio and impact of the dimensions of the frame

   b. Movement of the camera

   c. Choices in composition and use of depth in framing

3. **Visual Style:** Describe the overall effect of visual style in the motion picture. You may also imagine a contrasting approach to the cinematography and include a description of the effect of such a visual scheme on the finished movie.

Writing: Script for a Short Film

For Unit 4, you will have an opportunity to write, direct, and produce your own complete short film. You will be applying principles investigated in earlier units, including such concepts as visual communication, story structure, character development, and use of sound.

A. **Final Goal** – For this unit, your objective is to produce a short film, preferably between five and twelve minutes in length. In order to prepare for this exercise, you need to produce a script for the film, as well as pre-production materials such as a shot list, floor plans, storyboards, and schedules.

B. **The Writing Process** – There are many ways in which we are inspired to create. Some people are highly self-motivated for creative endeavors and require little guidance or prompting to give communicable shape to their inspirations. In the present situation, you may already have a well-developed idea for this project. Perhaps you have created characters or scenes in earlier units that you can use to develop a complete short film. If this is the case, you may already be ready to complete character descriptions and write the first draft of the script. Later, we will discuss the importance of effective rewriting.

C. **Writing Prompts** – For others, it may be necessary to have clear guidance and an abundance of examples. Here is a series of ideas to help generate story material and to stimulate your desire to communicate through motion pictures. One of these brainstorming prompts might function as a starting point for you to create a central character or characters with appropriate objectives and backgrounds. From that point, you can develop a story structure and narrative culminating in a completed script.

D. **Image** – In writing activities for this class, you may have written a series of descriptions of images that you saw during the course of a day or over a few days. Sometimes there are particular images or visual sequences that resonate with us. Something we see or imagine that sticks in the mind. Whether the image is from writing activities that you have completed for this class or whether it comes from another source, there may be one that seems interesting or powerful to you. Where is it? Who or what is in the image? What happens before this image, and what happens next?

   1. **Memory of Conflict** – Similar to the last prompt, you may have a particular image in which two people are in conflict that forms a strong memory for you. Is there a particular single image that stays with you, or does it seem to move? Who is involved? What is the source of their conflict?

   2. **Memory of Place** – Similar to the last prompt, you may have a particular image that forms a strong memory for you of a place. Why is an image of this place seen clearly in

your mind? Can you see an event taking place here? Who is involved?

3. **Text** – Have you been inspired, moved, or provoked by a story you have read? What was it about that story that stays with you the most? A detail or event from a story can incite us to think of an original response to its themes, events, and other storytelling elements (setting, characters, style, and so forth). For this exercise, generating an original story is recommended. Adaptations will be discussed as an option later in the book.

E. **Preparations for Script Writing** – Once you have generated ideas, it is helpful to determine the characters and create descriptions as we have done in Units 2 and 3. Next, it can be useful to devise a narrative structure for the stories.

1. What is the initial setting of the story? How do we establish the situation of the central character or characters?

2. What is the character trying to accomplish?

3. What complicates or hinders the achievement of that desire?

4. As the basic elements of the story are established, a series of actions can begin to take shape. What actions do we witness in the course of the story?

F. **Script Writing** – Return to the screenplay format introduction in Chapter 3 for guidelines. You should produce a screenplay of four to ten pages for this assignment. Remember that one page of script is roughly equivalent to one minute of screen time, but if there is little dialogue on the page, this tends to stretch out the screen time. Thus, a script with significant body copy will most likely produce a film longer than the actual number of pages.

G. **Revising** – It is essential to rewrite your script to refine your writing and fully develop the potential of the blueprint for your film.

1. First, obtain feedback from appropriate readers, such as teachers or collaborators. When getting responses to your script, elicit views on the following issues, whether in writing or in discussion:

   a. Does the beginning of the script make you want to continue the story to find out what happens?

   b. What do you find interesting about the characters?

   c. How do you visualize the characters? If you do not have a clear impression of the characters, why is this the case?

   d. Are you surprised by any of the events of the script? If not, why?

   e. Do you find yourself visualizing the events of the story clearly?

      f. Do you see particular places when you read the script?

      g. Are you satisfied with the ending? If not, does it provoke your mind so that you continue to ponder the events in a contemplative way? If not, why?

2. Next, work on rewriting the script. Make sure to save copies of each draft separately and note the number of the draft on the title page.

      a. It is important to take notes from the feedback you have received. Another useful step is to write a journal entry in which you draft your own evaluation of the script and your current assessment of it.

      b. As stated in earlier writing assignments, reading text out loud can help the analytical process significantly. If it is possible to get actors or peers to perform a reading of the script, this can be extremely helpful, particularly in working on dialogue.

H. Final Draft – Once you arrive at a version of the script that satisfies your vision of the film—or at least you feel that you simply *need to make this movie now*—you will make copies of your script to share with your actors and crew. Here is your shooting script! This is your blueprint for the film, the copy from which you plan your entire project. With it, you can create a shot list, storyboards, floor plans, and the schedule for your production.

Exercise: Using Light to Tell a Story

For Writing 4, you created a script for your first major individual project. Exercise 4 is the point at which you take those plans and transform them to light upon a screen. After you are satisfied with the writing of the script—or at least you have arrived at the date when you need to begin shooting (hopefully not the day before the deadline to hand in the film; after all, you still need to edit!)—it is standard practice to prepare for the production phase of the motion picture. For this exercise, the following steps are recommended for pre-production:

A. **Location Scouting** – To determine and visit locations before the shoot is instrumental to the success of a motion picture. If the cinematographer and director are familiar with the space in which they will be working, it helps in both completing pre-production and making decisions during production.

B. **Shot List** – Using your script, plan sequences of shots to tell your story. For the numbering of shots in relation to your script, follow the pattern of Number/Letter for Scene/Shot. So the first planned shot of the film is 1a. If there is another shot that corresponds to scene 1 from the script, it will be shot 1b. When the script moves to scene 2, you begin with shot 2a. Use the shot descriptions from unit 1 along with necessary information such as movement and characters in the frame.

C. **Floor Plans** – With floor plans, shots, characters, and key spatial information are indicated in a bird's-eye view of the scene. These are quite useful for a cinematographer to map the camera positions and devise a plan for shooting each sequence. Use the shot list to identify shots alongside camera angle indications.

D. **Storyboards** – These visual preparations are the most famous pre-production tool and can range from very simple line drawings and stick figures to detailed, comic-book-like sequences that map out the film shot by shot. They are useful for a director to communicate with the cinematographer and other collaborators, and they can serve as a reference when various possibilities for shooting are explored during production.

E. **Scheduling** – Finally, and perhaps most importantly, is scheduling. You need to get the crew and actors to the shoot—and all at the same time!

   1. Personnel list
   2. Locations
   3. Shooting dates
   4. Editing schedule

F. **Final Product Guidelines**

   1. **Length** – Completed short is between five to twelve minutes.
   2. **Editor** – Editing must be completed by the director.
   3. **Titles** – There must be credits to the film, whether generated using an editing program or through direct means during filming.

Report

A. **Exercise Work** – Write a minimum of two paragraphs describing your work on Exercise 4. Please note the following:

1. **Requirements** – Comment on your ability to complete the projects appropriately.

   a. Were you properly prepared?

   b. How did you apply learning of visual components of filmmaking in your work?

   c. Was the edit complete with appropriate visual and sound elements? Explain key decisions in the two fundamental areas of motion picture production.

2. In what ways did the production progress effectively? What difficulties did you encounter? Give at least two examples.

3. What were your most satisfying moments from this process?

B. **Video Analysis** – Comment on the following elements in your evaluation:

1. Establishment of characters and context for the story at the opening of the film

2. Use of character actions to establish the narrative of the story. If appropriate, indicate use of character perspectives or other means to establish narrative.

3. Use of the camera in effectively communicating the story visually, including quality of focus, control of lighting, and selection of shots

4. Pacing of shots and sound

5. Quality and use of sound design, including dialogue

6. Overall delivery of content intended by the script and other preparations by the filmmaker. How effective was the movie in achieving the goals you established for it?

Glossary

Anamorphic – A lens that distorts the image by squeezing it (to the standard aspect ratio of 1.33:1) so that the picture can be unsqueezed by another lens during projection to achieve a widescreen aspect ratio.

Aperture – Inside the body of the photographic lens, the opening typically regulated by an interlocking system of metallic leaves.

Aspect ratio – The ratio of width to height of a motion picture screen. Standard ratios are 1.33:1 (early film and standard TV ratio, also known as 4:3); 1.85:1 (American theatrical standard), and 2.40:1 (Panavision widescreen standard).

Bit – One binary digit, which is a zero or a one. Bits are strings of digital information registered as 0s and 1s. 8 bits = 1 byte; 1024 bytes = 1 kilobyte; 1024 KB = 1 megabyte; 1024 MB = 1 gigabyte.

CinemaScope – An anamorphic cinematographic process using lenses which produced films in aspect ratios from 2.35:1 to 2.55:1.

Cinematographer – Individual in charge of motion picture photography, particularly the choices of equipment and photographic media, lighting of the scenes, and framings and movements of the camera. Also known as Director of Photography (DP); although there may be distinctions made when there is a separate camera operator, the individual responsible for cinematography is referred to using both terms.

Color temperature – Measurement of light rays along the color spectrum to determine the inherent color value of a light source. Used in cinematography to insure accurate depiction of color or as a tool in the manipulation of color.

Contrast – The difference between the brightest and darkest points in a picture. A high contrast image features little gradation between light and dark and sharp whites and blacks, while a low contrast image contains significant gradation.

Definition – The definition of film emulsion or another recording medium expresses its graininess and ability to depict sharp edges and fine detail.

Depth of field – Depth of field is the portion of the image that appears in focus as measured by the points at a distance in front of the camera.

Diopter – One-element lens, designed like a filter, used to enable close focusing with the camera lens, generally for extreme close-ups. A split diopter covers part of the lens for dual planes of focus.

Exposure – The process of allowing light to make contact with film negative or other light-sensitive recording surface for a specific length of time.

Exposure Index (EI) – A value determined to rate the sensitivity of film stock or photographic media in order to set the appropriate exposure.

Film plane – The plane at which the film is held for exposure by the camera.

Film stock – Unexposed photographic film characterized by its gauge (such as 8mm, 16mm, 35mm, or 70mm), type (black and white or color, along with other factors), light and color sensitivities (such as ISO and color temperature ratings), physical characteristics (such as length), and brand (Eastman Kodak, Fuji, and so forth).

Focal length – Measurement that defines the type of a particular lens, such as 16mm, 25mm, 50mm, or 150mm, typically determined inside the body of the lens: it is the length from the rear nodal point of the lens (where light is being sent back by refraction) to the film plane when the lens is focused at infinity.

Focus – In optics, focus is the point at which light rays converge so the image appears sharp when viewing it. A lens must be adjusted—either manually or automatically—to achieve a focused view of subjects at a particular distance.

Focus pull – A change in the focus plane during a shot. At the beginning of a take, the lens will be set at a distance (for example, at five feet), and during the shot this can be changed manually or remotely to another distance to follow an actor, adjust with a camera move, or shift visual information and attention.

Foot-candle – Unit of measurement of light that equals the illuminating intensity from one candle falling on one square foot of surface at a distance of one foot.

Frames per second – The rate at which individual frames are advanced per second through a camera, projector, or other moving image device. For American motion picture photography, the projection standard is 24 fps and for television, it is 29.97 fps (rounded to 30).

F-stop – Number that is measured by dividing the focal length of a lens by the effective diameter of its aperture and is used for setting the iris. The standard range of f-stops is: 1, 1.4, 2, 2.8, 4, 5.6, 8, 11, 16, and 22, in which each higher value in this logarithmic scale cuts the light by one half. An f-stop number can also be understood as the denominator of a fraction in which the focal length of the lens is the numerator, the solution for which equals the aperture diameter. F-stop is also known as relative aperture.

Gate – The opening on the camera behind the lens through which light passes onto the film which rests on a metal plate that forms the back of the gate.

Grain – Granular texture in negatives that emerges as a result of clumping of silver-halide particles during processing, viewable under magnification.

Incident light meter – Light meter that measures the intensity of light falling on the precise spot where the meter is turned to the source.

Iris – In the eye, the iris is the membrane suspended between the cornea and the lens and is perforated by the pupil. In photography, the iris diaphragm is composed of metal elements that open and close to let in more or less light.

ISO rating – From the International Standardization Organization, scale for measuring the sensitivity of film to light. Commonly described as the film speed, in which a slow film requires more significant exposure (either more time or more relative light) and a fast film less light for the same quality of exposure.

Light – Visible light is a form of electromagnetic radiation that the human eye can perceive. The spectrum of visible light lies in a relatively small band of wavelengths that register as a series of colors such as those seen in a rainbow.

Light Meter – An instrument used for measuring the intensity of light on a scene.

Noise – Areas of incorrect detail reproduction in a digital image caused by sensor chip misreadings or the inability of the camera to process visual information due to problems in exposure.

Normal lens – A lens whose perspective offers a close approximation of human eyesight for a particular type of film. For 16mm film, a 25mm lens is considered a "normal" lens and for 35mm film, a 50mm lens is considered "normal."

Panavision – Term for widescreen aspect ratios achieved by cameras and processes developed by the Panavision company, particularly 1.85:1, which has become an American standard and 2.2:1, known as Widescreen Panavision.

Pigment – The color of non-luminous matter determined by the absorption of a certain wavelength of the spectrum and the reflection of its opposing color value when exposed to white light, resulting in what is seen.

Pixel – Term adapted from "picture element" that is actually a tiny square in a digital image. It represents a single light intensity and color value (measured in red, green, and blue components) among over 16 million possible colors.

Plane of focus – This term from geometry is commonly used in filmmaking to define the area at a specific distance from the camera that appears in sharp focus.

Primary colors – In photography, red, green, and blue are the primary additive colors that combine to create white light, and the primary negative colors, used in subtractive systems, are cyan, magenta, and yellow.

Prime lens – A lens with a single focal length (a 25mm lens, a 50mm lens, and so forth).

Reflected light meter – A light meter that measures the light that is reflecting from the subject, one version of which is the spot meter.

Resolution – The ability of the recording medium to register fine detail, measured in digital images by the pixels per inch and quality of the sensor.

Sensitivity – The capacity of emulsion in a strip of photographic film or of a photographic sensor to react to light, measured by the EI/ISO rating of the film or recording medium. Also referred to as the speed of a film stock.

Sensor – Located inside the body of a digital camera, a sensor contains a light-sensitive grid that registers (in pixels) the light coming in through the camera's lens.

Shutter speed – The amount of time that the shutter remains open to admit light into the camera before closing.

Spot meter – A reflected light meter used to measure the reflected light at select spots on a scene. The user holds it up to the eye and looks through the viewfinder at the precise spot on the scene that is being measured for its illumination.

White balance – Sensor system used for adjusting the camera to the appropriate color temperature setting in response to the light illuminating the scene.

Zoom lens – Lens with variable focal length at a specific range, which allows for rapid subject magnification. Zoom lenses are included on virtually all consumer digital cameras so the user can change the focal length of the lens easily.

Close-Up

Behind the Scenes with Cinematographer
Hiro Narita

Cinematographer Hiro Narita, whose extensive credits include Never Cry Wolf; Honey, I Shrunk the Kids; Star Trek VI; The Rocketeer; James and the Giant Peach; *and the pilot for* The Gilmore Girls. *(Courtesy of Hiro Narita)*

Q How did you begin working in movies?

A I went to art school and at the time I wasn't thinking of getting into film. For the first ten years I worked as a graphic designer, and then by chance I got involved in helping filmmakers design movie posters and so forth. And then that led to, "Can you take some stills?" And then to, "Are you interested in shooting a documentary for me?" In fact, I was almost 30 when I made the shift into cinematography. And it was not easy to make a living, just proclaiming yourself a cinematographer. I learned a lot from old master gaffers. They really taught me. I knew what looked beautiful to my eyes, but I didn't know how to get it. So the old lighting masters would say, "If you use a 5K here and diffuse it, this is the kind of quality you get." I learned most of my trade on the job.

Q How did you move on from those initial steps and what lessons did you learn?

A I started to do some corporate slide shows, and that led to corporate identity films, and that led to more legitimate documentary films – not selling products, but selling personalities or ideas, telling stories or capturing emotions with moving images. That really was fascinating to me. I had to catch up with the technology, of course – I was always a few years behind the technology. But if you have the desire to tell visual stories, the equipment is just a tool. I was constantly learning.

I think it's the human story that I wanted to tell. I was asked to film a documentary on children with leukemia. Just to see these young kids telling their experiences to the camera – brave souls, you know – just to see those images of people was much more fascinating to me than shooting beautiful shoes or plastic-piping. Though to sell that, I'm sure it takes a talented advertising mind and some people are really great at it.

One of the first things I learned was how to establish relationships with actors, to respect and appreciate what they do. Even today I see directors treating actors like props. That's the worst thing you can do. Experienced directors know how to deal with actors, how to deal with their psychology and they know how to turn them around to perform for *you*, the audience. You have to let the actors feel that they're making a contribution rather than just being told what to do. Young directors tend to say, "Well, this is *my* film, and I'm not getting it, I'm not getting it!" It really exhausts actors. Not to disagree with some great actors who have some incredible arguments and discussions before the camera rolls. Understanding the different types of actors, and learning how to communicate with actors so that they feel comfortable, is very important.

Q How do you work with directors and actors to balance lighting and movement?

A The cameraman is not the person who decides the actors' movements. We participate. There are some directors who are more open to suggestions, but surprisingly some directors don't want to hear any of it. Some directors are very visually oriented and they do express it, they say, "I'd like to see this scene lit only by the table lamp, no other light, very moody." And if the director has such a strong feeling, then sure, let's start with that and see what happens. When I first read the script and interpret the scene and form a visual idea, I'm always telling myself, "This is only the beginning. Don't force that initial idea." I think it is important when you are a cameraman to *discover*. Some of the most interesting stuff that I see on the screen, I'm not convinced that the cameraman preconceived that imagery. He or she discovered it as the scene unfolded.

Visual style changes, from fresco to oil to watercolor, but story hasn't changed that much. It may go through a few more changes. I think it is important for young filmmakers not to separate the craft of editing, acting, cinematography and all those things for the time being. The more I work in the business, I see that they are all connected. As much as I admire "Academy Award winning cinematography," you can't take over the story. When the marriage between everything works out, then it's a success.

Visit the textbook website to read the entire interview with Hiro Narita.

Personal Expression and Studio Production

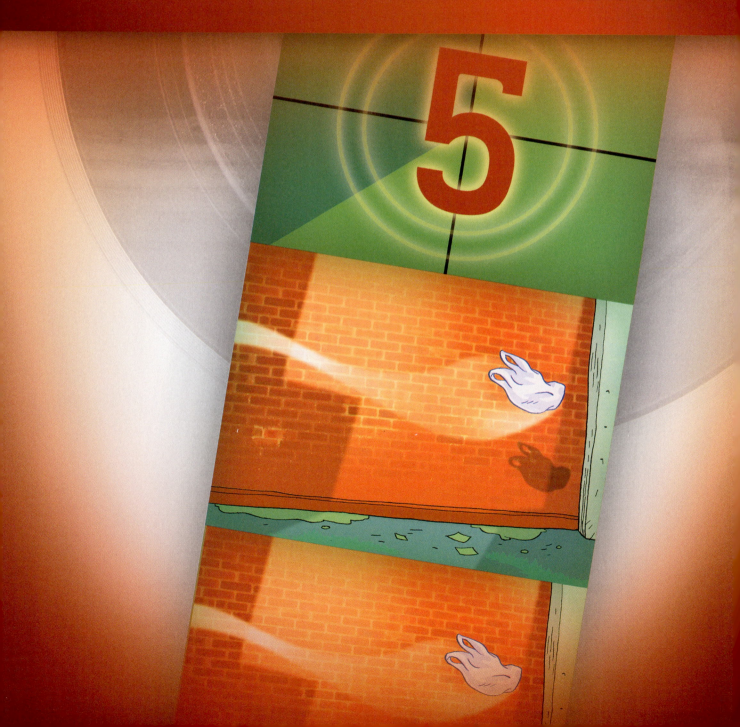

CHAPTER IN FOCUS

In this chapter you will:

- create a portrait of a person or a place
- compare and contrast who makes movies and why they are made
- classify and evaluate ways that moving images communicate stories and ideas

Of Media and Messages

What types of moving images have you seen during the past few days? Did you see a short film or feature or show that told a story? Did you see a motion picture that showed a series of images designed to illustrate an idea, to persuade the viewer in a particular way, to express a feeling, or simply to show visuals without a narrative? These may have been moving images playing in the background of a room or on a digital screen or through an advertisement. Or did you see moving images that linked you to friends or that you made together and then shared with other people?

As discussed in Chapter 2 of this text, the first motion pictures introduced two particular forms for motion pictures: the documentation of real events through recorded light and the depiction of actions through a staged filming. Essentially, the roots of documentary and fiction films were set in their most elemental of forms.

As you answered these questions, most likely when you thought of some examples of motion pictures you have seen recently, you probably had a clear understanding of their basic formats and central goals. If the examples were feature films or television shows, there are standard contexts

Framing the Discussion

- *Have you seen a story-based motion picture recently? What are the key ways in which the moving images first established that they would be telling a story?*

- *Have you seen moving images recently that documented reality? What value did you see in the images? Did they preserve any moments that were significant?*

- *Have you seen any moving images within the past few days that do not tell a story? What were they? How did you react to them? Afterwards, did you think about them very much?*

- *With the previous moving images described, do you know who was responsible for their creation? Why were they made?*

and expectations set up for viewers of these formats, including their length, whether approximately two hours or in highly chopped up and interrupted segments that add up to thirty or sixty minutes. In terms of their objectives, they are often introduced by the clearly defined type of movie or show, whether a comedy, thriller, romantic tale, or action-oriented motion picture.

These formats, in particular the "Hollywood movie" or "American TV show," are familiar to people throughout the world. They have been commonly used in the production and dissemination of narrative motion pictures for decades. However, they are probably not the only examples of moving images you mentioned in your answers to the previous set of questions. Did you mention commercials? Visual sequences made to accompany music? Short subjects or snippets you may have seen streaming on the Web? Games? Some of the forms are more difficult to define and do not fall into a clear category. Moving images assume a variety of arrangements and use diverse communicative strategies.

In this unit, we will survey key forms of motion pictures and sources of moving image production from the beginnings of the cinema to the present. In order to organize our analysis, we need to ask simple questions about motion pictures:

- Who makes movies?
- Who controls their production and distribution to audiences?
- Why are they made?
- How are they used?
- How do we understand them?

Figure 5-1 Moving images play on an extensive variety of screens today, from movie theaters to televisions to computers, digital players, and phones. *(Courtesy of Kendelyn Ouellette)*

The Motion Picture Business

To consider these questions, we will organize our investigation into two key domains. The first inquiry is about the creation and dissemination of motion pictures, or "Who makes motion pictures and how do we get to see them?" In the second part, you will explore key types of motion pictures.

The first motion pictures were produced by a handful of entrepreneurs and artisans who were interested in the creative and economic possibilities offered by this nascent medium. For a number of years, the distribution of films stemmed from this relatively small number of producers who were willing to invest in the sets, equipment, materials, and processes of cinematic production. The creation of motion pictures quickly developed a rhythm similar to industrial production, with shorts being released and distributed continuously by such companies as Biograph in the United States and Pathé in France. In the early years of the cinema, the creation of many of the shorts followed an assembly-line mentality—produce them as quickly and as cheaply as possible—and with the technical limitations of the early cinema, creative innovation was severely hampered.

The difficulty in establishing strong storytelling is very obvious when we watch movies from the first decade of the twentieth century. Many movies appear so flat and stagy, with figures that look like they are stuck in a shoebox! However, as we learned earlier, certain filmmakers devised imaginative solutions in order to use the camera as a tool for actively establishing visual narrative. Through simple but important innovations in camera perspective

Figure 5-2 Studio productions helped to bring more spectacular visuals and enhanced camera perspectives for filmmakers, as seen in this large Roman set on the back lot of Paragon studios in New Jersey in 1917. *(Courtesy Fort Lee Library)*

and editing, the communicative and artistic potential of motion pictures began to emerge.

By the 1920s, a number of tendencies could be seen in motion picture production. In the United States, moviemaking studios had developed systems of production that followed an industrial model. The simple outfits that churned out early silent movies evolved into highly structured businesses that organized the filmmaking process into a series of units. Different personnel would be responsible for a particular aspect of **pre-production**, **production**, or **post-production**. These **studios** financed and executed the making of motion pictures and then distributed them across the country and internationally. During this time, these film studios often also controlled distribution through the ownership of theater chains, but this practice was later deemed monopolistic and was curtailed by the legal system.

The Industrial Model

The studios sought to organize film production following examples seen in the industrial world. Companies such as MGM, Paramount, Twentieth Century-Fox, Warner Brothers, Columbia, and Universal also effectively "owned" the careers of the people who worked on the production of their films. Typically, production heads oversaw the selection and **development** of projects, and many aspects of creative control were kept from the personnel most responsible for the artistic decisions during the making of motion pictures, particularly writers, directors, and editors. In Europe, although there were major production studios as well, many filmmakers sought outside financing to develop individual projects or they nurtured personal initiatives with a small production team. Production personnel often worked as independent professionals hired for a particular project.

During the 1960s in the United States, the studio system that controlled company personnel and most aspects of production began to collapse. Shifts in production organization were paralleled by major changes in filmmaking content and styles. These transformations in the motion picture world can be seen in many movies of the late 1960s and 1970s and reflect the cultural and societal upheavals across the globe during that time. Film studios began to drop their in-house production lines and started to supervise the development of motion pictures in a way in which producers managed individual projects in a more independent fashion, although executives continued to retain control over **final cuts** of movies as a standard procedure.

Today, when writers and directors have an original idea for a motion picture, they will often seek out funding from studios or independent producers. To do this, they will set up **pitch** meetings to convince investors of the interest of their project. Those doing the pitch need to convey the original idea's audience appeal, unique elements, and box office potential. A pitch is one of the most common forms of salesmanship in motion picture development, and it has similar roots in the history of entrepreneurial investment, in which a businessperson seeks funding for a new project or product.

Figure 5-3 Tim Robbins plays studio executive Griffin Mill in *The Player*, a satire on the Hollywood studio system written by Michael Tolkin and directed by Robert Altman. *(Courtesy Fine Line Features/ Photofest)*

By the middle of the twentieth century, equipment and materials were developed and made available so that consumers could also create motion pictures for personal use. Although professional moviemaking tools and methods remained almost completely separate from those of amateurs for most of film history, the development of more inexpensive cameras and more widely available film stocks and other recording media allowed more widespread creation of motion pictures by small-scale outfits, independent collectives, and individual artists. Associated shifts in production have been taking place ever since and have accelerated extensively with the advent and rapid growth of digital media.

Reaching the Audience

The conditions of production have been the most central factor of the creation of motion pictures since the birth of the cinema. The next step in the complete chain of motion picture creation is the point at which a movie reaches an audience. The ability of a movie to reach an audience is fundamental to its existence, and the capacity of moviemakers to access viewers stems from their power to assure widespread distribution of their feature film, short, commercial, or other type of motion picture.

At first, motion pictures were briefly seen in **Nickelodeons** and soon after in movie theaters. Cinemas then became the exclusive site for the experience of viewing motion pictures for nearly half a century. At the core of the development of film studios was the building and running of movie theaters across the country and the world as well as the creation of systems for printing and shipping reels of film to exacting deadlines. As you learned during the discussion of the integration of sound, the infrastructure of film distribution and the relationships of film producers with projection venues (primarily consisting of chains of theaters) have a great effect on the survival of motion pictures. If a movie is made, it still needs to get to the audience. And potential viewers need to know about it.

As moviegoing audiences grew during the first decades of the twentieth century, the success of the moviemaking industry led to the construction of theaters that vied for the interest of the public. Cinemas grew throughout the United States and across the world, becoming as large and ornate as the ticket sales of the local population could support. As receipts for movies flourished and waned over the decades, sizes and types of moviegoing venues shifted with these fluctuations. In addition, the growth and subsequent decline of independent distributors and cinemas have had a strong effect on the varieties and sources of movies reaching the general public.

Another important factor in the diversity of films able to reach audiences across the world is the role of film foundations, museums, and other cultural institutions that are involved with motion picture projection, preservation, and education. These organizations have provided an outlet for certain movies, particularly foreign films and those with smaller distribution budgets and less access to major publicity campaigns, to become widely seen and even to acquire a respected status among viewers. Forward-thinking institutions such as the Cinémathèque Française in Paris, the Museum of Modern Art in New York, and the British Film Institute have fulfilled vital roles in establishing motion pictures as an important art form and in archiving a wide variety of films. Finally, the international film festival circuit has become a conduit for films to achieve recognition and to secure substantial circulation through the initial exposure to critics and audiences that can lead to distribution deals.

Figure 5-4 The Cinémathèque Française in Paris, designed by Frank Gehry. (*Courtesy Laurent Carmé*)

Films in the early 2000s that have reached wide audiences in unique ways include *Donnie Darko, Juno,* and *Paranormal Activity.*

Evolving Media

At the midpoint of the twentieth century, the development of a new mode of widespread diffusion of moving images offered a major new media outlet: television. As we discussed in the last unit, this presented new possibilities for motion pictures while posing a challenge to the business practices and prospects of film production for the big screen. Television prompted new types of formats and uses of motion pictures, such as recurring dramatic shows that evolved from the serial format. Moreover, one of television's most revolutionary developments would have an enormous impact on future societies across the world: the commercial.

Yet again, economics and motion picture production were completely intertwined. Advertising became the key financial support to the new medium of television, and commercials developed their own traditions of visual impact, narrative, thematic effect, and social commentary in the world of the moving image. Concurrently during the 1950s, there was tremendous growth in new motion picture formats outside of the traditional shorts, feature films, and newsreel images of the movie theater. Industrial shorts and educational films began to be an important source of motion picture production.

Within the past few decades, recorded media have allowed viewers to watch personal copies of motion pictures, first on magnetic tape videocassettes, then on digital discs, and finally on digitized files read and shown through computer programs. These media sources have in turn opened up new viewing

Figure 5-5 Megan Fox (as Carla) and Lindsay Lohan (as Lola) in a video-game dance off from *Confessions of a Teenage Drama Queen,* directed by Sara Sugarman. *(Courtesy Disney/Photofest)*

platforms. Personal computer screens and digital projectors have become common presentation sources for moving images.

In fact, many viewers are experiencing motion pictures solely through the format of a personal copy on a playable disc or digital file. This has led to renewed interest in a wide array of moving images and a burst in preservation of films from many periods. Most surprisingly, silent films have generated exceptional interest, as well as television shows and motion pictures that had previously been rather inaccessible and unknown by the general public, including films of the **avant-garde**. For filmmakers of the twenty-first century, digital formats such as the DVD and BluRay offer a variety of new creative outlets in addition to being used as resources for viewing motion pictures created as theatrical features and television series.

One of the most pervasive sources of moving images in the twenty-first century is the video game. While early video game images did not reflect the three-dimensional approach similar to feature films and television shows, by the turn of the century CGI was used to create visuals modeled after live-action cinematography. Story development and interactive communities have helped to raise revenue of this industry to match or surpass earnings in other motion picture media. With some games, users are able to create avatars—representations of themselves—to interact virtually with a world entirely constructed of moving images.

Let us return to our questions of "Who makes movies?" and "How do they reach audiences?" Here is a review of key sources of motion picture creation and their access to audiences:

- Major film companies with a high degree of corporate structure. With these firms, ultimate production control often rests with executives who oversee finances of the corporation, as seen in the major Hollywood studios and television networks.

- Independent, small-scale production units designed to produce single motion pictures. Such groups solicit financing for their project and develop contracts that allow for widely varying control of the final state of the motion picture. They typically seek the largest audience possible, so they work with formalized distribution networks and must negotiate or work with a major film studio that acts as the distributor of the motion picture.

- Single, independent artists or artistic collectives who create motion pictures in ways similar to other art forms such as painting, dance, and music. These highly personal or collaborative creations typically are supported by and experienced in independent art cinemas and film societies, museums, and non-profit cultural institutions.

- Production generated directly from commercial requisitions and commands, such as with advertising and promotional materials, educational missions, and industrial projects.

- Production of moving images for interactive formats such as computer games and simulation scenarios.
- Creation of amateur motion pictures for non-commercial uses by families, friends, or small groups, similar to traditions of family photography, personalized journals, and letter writing.

Making Motion Pictures

You have just reviewed some of the most important *situations* of people generating moving images. Now you will read about a selection of filmmakers who illustrate the diversity and varied approaches seen in motion picture production.

Early Pioneers

In the early years of the cinema, many filmmakers controlled the entire process of moviemaking right up through the exhibition of their films. ***Alice Guy Blaché*** was working as a secretary for Gaumont studios in the 1890s when she stepped behind the camera to direct *La Fée aux Choux (The Cabbage Fairy)*. Guy Blaché went on to lead an innovative and bold career during which she founded, designed, and ran a major production studio—Solax Films—and directed hundreds of movies both in the United States and in France.

Another of the most important early cinematic entrepreneurs is ***Oscar Micheaux***. Micheaux was an epitome of canny moviemaking flair. As a black filmmaker, he created and assured the distribution of films that existed

Figure 5-6 Alice Guy Blaché directing a Solax production in 1915 with camera operator Leo Rossi at left. *(Courtesy Fort Lee Library)*

Figure 5-7 Oscar Micheaux, writer and director of dozens of feature films. *(Courtesy Photofest)*

primarily on their own exhibition circuit in segregated America. Micheaux oversaw all aspects of production, including writing and directing, for a wide variety of seriously themed, well regarded films primarily made during the 1920s and 1930s, including *Within Our Gates, The Symbol of the Unconquered,* and *Ten Minutes to Live*.

Studio Production in Hollywood and Internationally

The Hollywood studio system typically imposed significant constraints on cinematic artists while offering substantial technical and artistic resources. *Alfred Hitchcock* was able to work within the studio system while establishing a strong identity as a director. His movies, such as *Notorious*, from 1946, and *Rear Window, Vertigo,* and *North by Northwest* from the 1950s, show us how a director could establish a unique and recognizable visual and thematic style. Hitchcock's films consistently established narratives that capitalized on the perspective and editing of cinema to engage, enthrall, and provoke the viewer. Many other directors—such as *Howard Hawks* and *John Ford*—were able to work within the studio system and create motion pictures that display distinctly unique visions and mastery of visual storytelling.

Figure 5-8 Actor Henry Fonda at left and director Alfred Hitchcock holding strap on New York subway location shooting for *The Wrong Man*. *(Courtesy Warner Bros./Photofest)*

Professional relationships between studio administrators and filmmakers working within these systems are seen in many of the countries of the world. For example, at Toho, Daiei, and Shochiku studios in Japan, directors such as Yasuhiro Ozu, Akira Kurosawa, and Kenji Mizoguchi were able to work constantly, generally producing at least one movie each year. *Yasujiro Ozu* is an example of a director who developed a highly individual approach to framing and editing in his treatment of recurring themes, such as those involving family and the passage of time. *Akira Kurosawa's* films show an astonishing array of stylistic solutions to cinematic expression and dynamic storytelling in such famous and still popular films as *Rashoman* and *The Seven Samurai,* both from 1950. *Kenji Mizoguchi* is well known for his lyrical treatment of themes linked to human spirituality and the persecution and resilience of women, yet like many filmmakers, he developed his skills directing movies in a wide array of types and styles, including crime films, comedies, war movies, working-class dramas, and motion pictures strongly influenced by German expressionism.

Other filmmakers have built international careers making movies. *Max Ophuls*, born to a Jewish family in western Germany, was able to create a body of work in which he had to cross many borders during decades of struggle to find financial and administrative support for his talents. Ophuls was a wizard of visual style and showed mastery of the diverse skills needed for a director, including working with actors, orchestrating camera angles and movements, and building distinctive rhythms in his films. After directing movies in Germany, Italy, France, and Holland, Ophuls fled Europe at the

Figure 5-9 Toshiro Mifune in Akira Kurosawa's *Yojimbo*. *(Courtesy Toho/Photofest)*

Figure 5-10 Director Max Ophuls preparing a scene with actress Joan Fontaine for *Letter from an Unknown Woman* from 1948. *(Courtesy Universal/Photofest)*

Figure 5-11 Director Billy Wilder and actress Shirley MacLaine preparing a scene in *The Apartment. (Courtesy United Artists/Photofest)*

beginning of World War II, found work in Hollywood, and then returned to Europe in the 1950s where he made such classics as *Madame de . . ., La Ronde,* and *Lola Montès.*

Among the many filmmakers who arrived in Hollywood after beginning their careers abroad, **Billy Wilder** began to write movies in his native Germany before moving to the United States, where he became a relative rarity for his time: the writer-director. Wilder wrote his scripts with a partner and directed many of the most highly appreciated films ever made, including the comedies *Some Like It Hot* (1959) and *The Apartment* (1960), *Sunset Boulevard* (1950), one of the sharpest films about Hollywood, *Ace in the Hole* (1951), a scathing critique of American media culture, and the early film noir *Double Indemnity* (1944).

Wilder, like Hitchcock, provides an example of an artist establishing strong individual identity amidst the powerful forces of the studio system. This was not typical. Many filmmakers in the studio system had to fulfill projects under the strong control of studio executives, and their names were rarely well known, like many filmmakers today. **Delmer Daves** was a writer-director working in the more typical mode of studio organization, executing projects in relation to the opportunities and needs of the corporate system. Nonetheless, his films are consistently notable for their qualities of sensitivity to diverse cultures, exploration of the tension between community needs and personal independence, and a subtle and lyrical integration of varied settings in the depiction of story.

Figure 5-12 Delmer Daves, seated on crane, directs Gary Cooper in *The Hanging Tree* (1959). (Warner Bros./Photofest)

Independent Artists and Collaboratives

The collaborative nature of motion picture art has rarely been more successfully expressed than in the movies of director **Michael Powell** and writer **Emeric Pressburger**. During a nearly two-decade run, their British production team, The Archers—including cinematographers Jack Cardiff and Christopher Challis, art director Alfred Junge, and composers Allan Gray and Brian Easdale, among others—created some of the most vibrantly original, provocative, and independently spirited movies in film history, such as *I Know Where I'm Going!, A Matter of Life and Death,* and *The Red Shoes,* made from 1945 to 1948.

With the recent growth of independent production, many filmmakers have developed their projects through partnerships with investors and distributors. One of the most prolific has been **John Sayles**, who began his work in film as a screenwriter and soon started to direct his own movies, including *Matewan* (1987) and *Eight Men Out* (1988). Sayles and many of the filmmakers of the late twentieth century and early twenty-first century originate their own projects with the support of a production team, as **Woody Allen** had begun doing in the 1970s and as **Spike Lee** had begun doing in the 1980s. Often these filmmakers work consistently with a core group, such as with **Jim Jarmusch**, an American director who writes his own scripts and retains a great deal of control of his material (in fact, not only does he maintain final cut on his movies, he secures the rights to the negative) while working with such colleagues as cinematographer Robby Müller and editor Jay Rabinowitz.

Figure 5-13 Actor Roger Livesay standing at right, facing Emeric Pressburger and Michael Powell who are seated to actress Kim Hunter's right in a production meeting for *A Matter of Life and Death*. *(Courtesy Getty Images)*

Figure 5-14 Agnès Varda, standing at left next to the camera, directs *One Sings, the Other Doesn't*. *(Courtesy Roger Viollet/Getty Images)*

This independent strategy is seen throughout the filmmaking world. French director **Agnès Varda** has maintained a long career in which she has led her own production company and has made films that have established her highly personal integration of community life and a spontaneous method and style in her films. Varda has created some of the most innovative and free-spirited short and feature films of her time shooting with an impressively wide range of approaches: feature film productions in 35mm; documentary-sized crews using 16mm cameras; videotape; and digital video.

Agnès Varda, Jim Jarmusch, and other contemporary filmmakers have created movies at the margins of current production standards and propelled

Figure 5-15 Thought-provoking use of moving images in a frame from *Plain Talk and Common Sense (Uncommon Senses)*. *(Courtesy of Jon Jost)*

by budgets in the many millions of dollars. There are also well-established traditions of filmmaking that exist almost entirely outside of the mainstream theatrical distribution chains that crisscross the United States and the globe. **Jon Jost's** filmography has been created through personal investment and the support of film foundations and public funding. During his long career, he has made innovative and provocative films like *Plain Talk and Common Sense (Uncommon Senses)* (1987) and *The Bed You Sleep In* (1993) with a minimal crew or even alone, striving to achieve the technical qualities he desires while working with equipment and processes accessible within small budgets. With the advent of digital formats, he and many filmmakers who lack corporate funding are now choosing to shoot digitally.

Choices such as those made by Jost are representative of filmmakers whose styles run counter to established norms, whether in narrative or non-narrative formats (discussed in the next section). Similar choices for independence can be seen in the implementation of highly mainstream productions as well. **Robert Rodriguez** created an in-house production studio after he built on the phenomenal success of his student film *El Mariachi* (1992). Rodriguez has taken full advantage of digital advances in filmmaking to control a wide variety of aspects of production for his films such as the *Spy Kids* series.

Diverse Forms and Content across the World

Many of the people making movies today work in a variety of media. Like many directors today, **Michel Gondry** began filmmaking during his youth, by

Figure 5-16 Robert Rodriguez (in hat) directing Antonio Banderas in *Spy Kids 2. (Courtesy Dimension Films/ Photofest)*

Figure 5-17 Michel Gondry directing *Be Kind Rewind. (Courtesy New Line/Photofest)*

crafting movies for himself, his friends, and his family. He later directed music videos and began to merit a strong reputation for his inventive, idiosyncratic approach that paid close attention to the content of the song. This served as a springboard to work in commercials, where many contemporary directors earn a great deal of their income, and for feature films such as *Be Kind Rewind* (2008) and *Eternal Sunshine of the Spotless Mind* (2004). Numerous filmmakers today work specifically in the commercial world, although some,

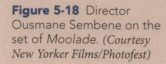

Figure 5-18 Director Ousmane Sembene on the set of *Moolade. (Courtesy New Yorker Films/Photofest)*

like Gondry, **Spike Jonze**, and **Jonathan Glazer**, produce motion pictures for a variety of media.

Naturally, these are just a few examples of the people who have helped to create the vast number of entertaining, persuasive, moving, and thought-provoking works that make up the history of moving images. We can find inspiration and learn of powerful frustrations and satisfactions when we investigate the work of a variety of filmmakers from across the world. Ranging in length from under a minute to many hours, the motion pictures of filmmakers such as **Ousmane Sembene** of Senegal, **Yasmin Ahmad** of Malaysia, **Abbas Kiarostami** of Iran, **Mira Nair** of India, **Zhang Yimou** of China, **Jane Campion** of Australia, **Patricia Rozema** of Canada, or **Alfonso Cuarón** of Mexico can help us to consider fresh perspectives and understand diverse individuals and societies.

- *Do you follow the work of any filmmakers? What is it about that person's work that interests or attracts you?*

- *Motion pictures are also made by non-professionals for a variety of reasons and in many different ways. Do you ever watch movies made by family members or friends? Why were they made? Will they be kept or used for any other reason?*

- *Have you previously made any movies? Did they follow any structure or did you edit them at all? Have you had an opportunity to show them to an audience? Where?*

- *What opportunities do you have in your area to see motion pictures on a big screen? Chain theaters? Independent cinemas or arts centers that show movies? Local public institutions, such as libraries? What types of moving images are shown in these places? Do local people have any access to show and share motion pictures at any of these locations?*

Figure 5-19 Abbas Kiarostami (in cap) filming *ABC Africa*, shot on digital video. *(Courtesy New Yorker Films/Photofest)*

Figure 5-20 Filmmaker Mira Nair directing Tabu on the set of *The Namesake*. *(Courtesy Fox Searchlight/Photofest)*

Paying for the Picture

In the century since the birth of motion pictures, the production of moving images has taken on many forms and has assumed a role of great significance for contemporary societies. Today, the creation and use of the moving image are at the core of an immense range of activities, whether for creative enrichment, entertainment, news, personal communication, or business activities and promotion. Millions of people are generating, manipulating, and utilizing motion pictures every day.

In these early years of the cinema, the struggle between creative expression and financial pressures began to develop. This was not a new story: the history of the practice of creative arts is consistently balanced between the actual creation of novels, poetry, paintings, and other works, and the need to earn a living and receive just compensation for one's work. While the studios recognized the need to create works that attracted the public through new, fresh concepts and high production values, they were also led by businesspeople who were primarily interested in attracting the largest possible audience into the theater. Thus, artistic choices were constantly weighed against perceived tastes and reactions to motion pictures, and the concept of previewing and using test audiences became a standard step in the process leading up to film distribution.

Motion Picture Economics

The tension between independent creative expression and economic pressures has been at the core of filmmaking throughout its history. As a creative medium dependent on significant technological apparatus, laboratory processes, and additional costs for distribution, filmmaking was an entrepreneurial venture from its inception. The necessity to develop proper financial outlets for motion picture distribution quickly emerged, and competition between producers was present within the first decade.

This was only exacerbated by the battles over copyrights and litigation concerning motion picture systems, particularly instigated by Thomas Edison. The Trust, a monopolistic association of film companies founded in 1908 by Edison and several competitors, hired enforcers to stop independent productions. As director Allan Dwan explained, "They found that by shooting holes through the camera, they could stop their use and that became their favorite method."

With the triumph of the studio system, two seemingly opposing forces were readily apparent: the desire to create motion pictures that demonstrate originality and authenticity versus the directive to conform to perceived popular tastes and to produce a conventional product. These two values, and the infinite nuances between the two poles, generate a great deal of the dynamic in film production. Much of the history of film production and many of its human conflicts and dramas revolve around the tension between these forces.

When you study the movies made within the studio system, you will see many examples of both tendencies. Certain filmmakers developed distinguished bodies of work and were able to flourish within the studio system. Studios benefited from the creations of artistically celebrated directors and could use this to promote their product, as with Fox studios in the 1920s with their amazing lineup of John Ford, Frank Borzage, F.W. Murnau, Raoul Walsh, and Howard Hawks. On the other hand, many writers, directors, and other creative personnel have regularly found themselves at odds with tendencies to conform excessively to what is already expected by film audiences. These propensities for conformity commonly thwart authentically creative solutions in the arts and the development of a genuine personal vision by a creative artist or a shared and mutually developed conception by artists working in collaboration.

Types of Motion Pictures

The second half of our inquiry concerns the classifications of moving images: "What types of motion pictures are there?" Having studied the sources of motion pictures and the ways in which they are controlled and brought to audiences, we will classify the forms that they have tended to assume and the ways in which we can describe their communicative varieties and structures.

There are two pairs of divergent concepts that are essential to consider. In this unit, we will examine the contrasts between narrative and **non-narrative** films. In the next unit, we will continue with the second pair of complementary concepts, **documentary** and **fiction**.

This unit's pair of contrasting concepts deals with the issue of storytelling. Here, we ask the question: Is the film telling a story?

- **Narrative** films tell a story through a succession of images and can be fiction or documentary, although they are more commonly seen in fiction films. In a narrative, both within shots and between shots, we must perceive a series of events that have a cause and effect relationship in time and space. The viewer must have ample information from the sequences of the motion picture to understand the series of events as being physically linked to create a chain that forms a story, even a brief one, such as with a commercial that recounts a very short narrative.

- **Non-narrative** motion pictures form a broad category of films that do not tell a distinct narrative but which instead offer a series of shots and sequences that convey a communicative or artistic statement without structuring their progression around events that build to a story. In order to communicate effectively with viewers, non-narrative films adapt structures so that the ideas, artistic statements, and aesthetic experiences they wish to relay are meaningful to the audience. Filmmakers can do this by juxtaposing images in a variety of ways to portray the subject matter. Certain non-narrative films, such as documentaries or promotional subjects, can take a clearly organized approach by presenting images in topical groups (**categorical** films) or the development of an argument (**rhetorical** films). **Associational** motion pictures can apply techniques that associate images more broadly or metaphorically to deliver a message about the primary theme. Finally, non-narrative movies can even portray their subject through **abstract** patterns of light, color, movement, and sound that are structured through means similar to musical composition.

Figure 5-21 Sequence of images linked by thematic and visual elements. *(Courtesy of Carl Casinghino)*

Narrative versus Non-Narrative Sequences

Earlier, we discussed film language and the Kuleshov effect, through which Soviet filmmakers investigated how we find meaning from the relationships between shots. In narrative motion pictures, we view the images that we see with some literal cause and effect with relation to time and space. In a non-narrative film, sequences do not construct a narration of linked events but instead find their meaning through the structural techniques described above. If the structures are not clear to us, we might say "How random!" However, other viewers might point out the meanings or feelings they get from watching that motion picture.

For example, imagine you are going to shoot a short motion picture involving the Agriscience program at a school. Here are two possibilities for the short project:

- We see the following images: a student checking water quality in a large fish tank; a rabbit; a hedgehog; a different student watering plants in a greenhouse; a snake; a chicken; a tulip; a student hosing down a cage; a flower arrangement.

- We see a few people enter a greenhouse and begin tending to the plants. Two students water and care for a variety of plants. Another puts flower arrangements in a refrigerator. The group moves on to a room with large fish tanks, checks the water, feeds the fish, turns off the light, and leaves. They proceed to animal areas and continue with their work, where we see them take care of a variety of warm- and cold-blooded creatures. They finish their work, turn off the lights, and leave. We see the animals in the dim light of the room after the work has been completed.

These two short motion pictures both provide a portrait of simple functions performed by students in this program, but the first uses a non-narrative approach and the second uses a narrative approach. In the first, we interpret the images through the connections we can make between them, although none of the shots indicates any sequence of cause and effect. We can guess that we are seeing a portrait of a place where there are a variety of animals and plants and a series of related activities that occur regularly. We can understand the images by association, particularly if stylistic choices such as lighting and framing are designed to indicate that these figures and actions exist in a similar setting.

With the second example, we link the events together because we see a chain of events that have a cause and effect relationship. Naturally, it is a very simple narrative. To enhance the level of interest generated by the story, the author can introduce character development and apply basic elements of drama or comedy.

Mixing of Forms

These broad categorizations can sometimes be tricky to apply clearly. There are many examples in which we can see cases of classifications being mixed. Viewers will debate the application of one category or another with certain films. Nonetheless, they can be used to establish a dialogue about the forms that motion pictures assume and to develop a more complete and clear understanding of the ways in which moving images function. What we are trying to do here is to *understand* motion pictures, and we can most appropriately do this in a manner similar to scientists by observing and noting the attributes and behaviors witnessed in a subject. We might uncover some surprises, for example distinct similarities in communicative form between certain commercials and cutting-edge, artistically challenging movies of the avant-garde.

Filmmakers can create narrative movies using a non-narrative sequence of images. In the short black-and-white film *Sea Space* from 1972, director William Farley used a recorded statement by the helmsman of a ship to serve as the basis for a motion picture about a tragic accident at sea that was kept secret by a small group of sailors. In the opening static shot of a sink, the viewer slowly perceives that the water in the basin is moving (Figure 5–22). This is because the sink is on a ship, and during the following sequence of images—an extreme close-up of a character asking a question; an unmade bed in darkness; a long, slow zoom into a porthole until the viewer sees a rough sea in close-up—the viewer observes an evocative, non-narrative sequence of images that provide a contemplative counterpoint to the confessional tale heard on the soundtrack. Many filmmakers have used the interplay between

Figure 5-22 Opening image of a sink on a ship from *Sea Space. (Courtesy http://www.farleyfilm.com)*

narrative and non-narrative elements in images and sounds to stimulate audiences' reactions to their movies.

The Development of Film Form

In the first two decades of the cinema, almost all of the developments of the communicative potential of moving images centered on narrative fiction. Within the technical limitations of this new medium, the most controllable and lucrative method of producing motion pictures was through staged fiction. Filmmakers applied long-established and widely understood traditions of storytelling—familiar through both the spoken and written word—to movies. As you have seen in this text, directors made many breakthroughs as they worked to use the perspective of the camera, expressive qualities of light, arrangement of subjects, and the possibilities of editing to devise ways of storytelling distinct to motion pictures.

It is certainly no surprise that the studios stuck to the most widely accessible and familiar structure for their moving images to be shown in given blocks of time: narrative fiction. This was also a format remarkably well suited to the most important component of the moviemaking business: the star system. Quite early in film history, audiences reacted overwhelmingly to certain actors that they saw in movies, and it became quite clear that the marketing of these personalities—and their faces and bodies—could form a lucrative aspect of motion picture production. The identification of audiences with various actors grew quickly with the emergence of fan clubs and the development of **serials** in which audiences could return to watch their favorite actors in familiar roles. Studios realized that they could craft personas for their stars and they developed advertising campaigns and roles that would satisfy the desire of audiences to see their heroes up on the big screen.

Genres

Another manner in which producers developed interest in their products and controlled marketing through a particular set of expectations and values was the establishment of film **genres**. As studios began to produce films, it was useful for them to group productions according to particular needs of setting and other logistical concerns. At the same time, many traditions have existed in literature and other art forms in which creators and the public have classified types of work according to a set of identifiable characteristics, so it was natural for the cinema to adapt many of these basic classifications, such as with tragedy or comedy. **Westerns**, **comedies**, **horror** films, **musicals**, **crime** films, and **science-fiction** could be geared to particular targeted markets and

Figure 5-23 Many serials featured episodes that ended with the star in a seemingly impossible situation, from which the term "cliffhanger" derives. In this contemporary version from Nash Edgerton's *The Pitch*, cinematographer Tom Gleeson leans over the edge filming stuntman Brett Praed while Andrew Horton assists *(photo by Louise Smith). (Courtesy Blue-Tongue Films)*

viewers could arrive with an initial understanding of what they might expect to see.

Throughout the history of the cinema, certain aspects of the industry have rewarded predictability while avoiding any motion pictures that challenged the expectations or prejudices of audiences. With similar consistency, many viewers hunger for fresh themes and more complex modes of visual storytelling in their movies. While many films closely stick to established story and style elements, others play with the conventions of genre traditions by countering the preconceptions of the viewer in subtle or extreme ways. On television, notable series have played with conventional expectations in provocative ways, from the long-running comedy series *M.A.S.H.* to the genre-bending international hit *X-Files* to the Joss Whedon creations *Buffy the Vampire Slayer* and *Firefly*.

Non-Narrative Formats

During the final decade of the silent cinema, while narratives began to develop more complexity, filmmakers started to explore the possibilities of images to create meaning and feeling outside of straight narrative sequences. A number of directors yearned to engage and challenge viewers in ways other than through sequences that built to a story. They were interested in exploring the ability of moving images to express ideas and impart artistic experiences to viewers through methods not linked to the cause and effect we see in storytelling. They found they could use editing of shots to create sequences that expressed meaning through their patterns of activity, light and shadow, shapes, and faces, or through presentation of visual information that did not follow a story.

Figure 5-24 Patterns of umbrellas in Joris Ivens's *Rain*. *(Courtesy Photofest)*

Filmmakers linked to artistic movements in Paris began producing motion pictures that built on ideas from painting, music, and poetry, such as René Clair's *Entr'acte* (1924), Fernand Léger's *Ballet Mécanique* (1924), and films by Luis Buñuel, Dimitri Kirsanoff, and Man Ray. These movies, generally grouped under the title of avant-garde, sought to explore new forms and challenge viewers' perceptions. They enthralled some viewers, perplexed others, and even enraged a few.

There were also movies that were not part of aggressive artistic manifestos. Some non-narrative films of this time offered portraits of city life through a succession of images linked by geometry, grouped activities, and patterns of movement, but without a traditional story in sight. For example, *Rain* (1929) by **Joris Ivens** depicts the interplay of weather, the city, and people using the patterns and physical effects of a rainfall to arrange the moving images. During his long career filming in Europe, Asia, Africa, North and South America, and Australia, Ivens often worked in documentary format, and throughout his life he developed methods for structuring his films using a variety of non-narrative techniques. Ivens made a number of movies that could be described as poetic essays which centered on the relationship of people to the natural world, such as with his last film, *A Tale of the Wind* (1988).

Using Non-Narrative Motion Picture Language

Filmmakers began to use non-narrative moving images to communicate in inventive and original ways and to challenge the status quo. **Jean Vigo**, a young French filmmaker, was energized by the possibilities of the camera to capture the rhythms, peculiarities, behaviors, and inequalities of modern life. He made *A Propos de Nice* in 1929 with cinematographer Boris Kaufman, a sometimes graceful, overall scathing city portrait, followed by *Taris*, a short

Figure 5-25 Dita Parlo and Jean Daste in Jean Vigo's *L'Atalante. (Courtesy Gaumont/ Photofest)*

starring a famous French swimmer which starts by demonstrating swimming technique and ends as a poetic evocation of the human body in water. Before his tragically early death, Vigo made the notable narrative films *Zéro de Conduite* (1933) and *L'Atalante* (1934), which are infused with the lyrical and groundbreaking spirit of the non-narrative cinema.

New techniques of faster editing and linking shots through a variety of patterns soon became part of Hollywood practice. In what became known as a **montage** sequence, a series of images could express an idea or feeling in a non-narrative manner but still add to the storytelling of the entire film. Early Soviet filmmakers such as Lev Kuleshov, Vsevolod Pudovkin, and Sergei Eisenstein created montage sequences that featured provocative juxtapositions of shots described as "collision" or "linkage." Montage is also used to augment narrative by condensing time and relating key information, as in *A Farewell to Arms* from 1931 (directed by Frank Borzage). When the main character engages in battle and is wounded, there is a sustained sequence of shots that depicts the disjointed violence of a terrible defeat but does not focus on events that proceed in a cause-and-effect manner from shot to shot. It is a series of images linked by the overall experience of war—a non-narrative sequence used to advance the narrative of the film.

In the 2009 movie *X-Men Origins: Wolverine,* the history of Wolverine and his brother Sabertooth is shown through a montage that spans their participation in wars over the course of a century. The uses of motion and exposure effects heighten the stylized compression of time. Montage types of editing are used consistently in commercials and Internet applications to express ideas and impressions through associative cuts and visual impact. These types of cutting, both narrative and non-narrative, often work well with musical passages in motion pictures and are seen in a wide variety of fiction films and in many music videos today.

Figure 5-26 The lyrical, distinctly personal perspective of Carlo Delle Piane's character takes form through the editing of director Ermanno Olmi's section of *Tickets. (Courtesy Fandango/Medusa Produzione/ Photofest)*

In the late twentieth century and early twenty-first century, motion pictures in theaters and on television consistently demonstrate rapid editing techniques, whether in continuity editing mode or through non-narrative techniques. There are also many variations on montage techniques, used in impressive introductory or epilogue sequences for a number of dramatic television series (such as *The Wire* or *Lost*) or in the dynamic editing seen in films by such directors as Steven Soderbergh, Richard Lester, or Ermanno Olmi. In the work of these and other filmmakers, the viewer can see many examples of sequences that are linked by memories, interior perceptions of place and time, and association or contrast of ideas and forms that bring the viewer into the perspective of a character or shape a distinct viewpoint of the setting or context of the images. Other contemporary examples are found in the disjointed arrangements and repetition of sequences in films by Quentin Tarantino, or "hip-hop" editing in *Requiem for a Dream* (directed by Darren Aronofsky, 2000).

Mastering the Techniques of Non-Narrative Moviemaking

There are also entire films that use non-narrative formats. These may be fiction films or documentaries, or they may be quite difficult to classify. Certain filmmakers have brought highly personal, often dream-like portraits to the screen, such as in **Maya Deren's** *Meshes in the Afternoon* (1943). Others have made movies known as "structural films" that focus on the process of film resources to create the content of the film itself, such as with **Michael Snow's** *Wavelength* (1967), which consists of a 45-minute zoom in towards the far wall of a room with a variety of changes in image and sound to shift perceptions and contribute meaning to the film.

Finally, some directors have combined various approaches to create quite individual responses to the resources of motion picture media, such as Britain's **Derek Jarman**. In *War Requiem* (1989) and other projects, he incorporates Super-8 and video footage made with family and friends to add texture, personal resonance, and a vibrantly brilliant use of color to his films. With long-term collaborators including actress Tilda Swinton and composer Simon Fisher Turner, his work uses collage techniques of creation and culminates in his final film *Blue* (1993), a 76-minute meditation on life, illness, death, and love that consists entirely of a screen of blue inspired by the paintings of Yves Klein.

Figure 5-27 Derek Jarman filming with his Super-8 Camera. *(Courtesy International Film Circuit/Photofest)*

Across the full range of motion picture production we can witness examples of non-narrative moving images being used to establish compelling visions and convey unique sensations, whether in highly commercial projects or in films that resolutely challenge normal viewer expectations. In animation, a number of films by the **Walt Disney** studios feature extensive non-narrative portions, including the groundbreaking and still popular *Fantasia* (1940). **Norman McLaren**, one of the most distinctive animators in motion picture history, created pixilated and hand-drawn cartoons that used many approaches to convey intricate and inventive messages and sensations through abstract and representational patterns. The history of animated film is full of examples ranging from American studios such as UPA—which often produced commercials for corporate clients while inspiring fellow animators with their pioneering style—to the intricate stop motion work of such masters as *Jan Švankmajer* and the *Brothers Quay*.

A Moving World

In many ways, the development of motion picture creative traditions, formats, and usages serves as a mirror to the world in which the moving image has evolved. The economic parameters and uses of motion pictures are inextricably linked to the progress of modern commerce and advertising. The science of the cinema reflects understanding and progress in the full range of scientific domains, from biology to chemistry to physics, as they have developed from the late nineteenth century to today. The themes and dramatic content of motion pictures typically stem quite directly from the societies and times in which they are produced. Reciprocally, the moving image also has had a powerful impact on the history of the twentieth century and fundamental modes of human communication and perception.

Many occupations use the moving image at the core of their activities. Professionals in cinema and television production rely directly on the moving image for their livelihood, and it stretches into an expansive range of domains, including journalism, industrial activities, education, sports, military, gaming, the legal system, and many applications in the arts. There is also a great deal of amateur use of motion pictures, for personal records and exchanges among families and friends and for establishing new lines of communication.

Figure 5-28 Visuals can communicate through the singularity of a unique image or in the context of sequences that provide cause and effect or related meanings. *(Courtesy of Carl Casinghino)*

VIEWFINDER

"I want to thank anyone who spends part of their day creating—I don't care if it's a book, a film, a painting, a dance, a piece of theater, a piece of music—anybody who spends part of their day sharing their experience with us. I think this world would be unlivable without art."

–Steven Soderbergh-

Director, cinematographer, and writer whose films include *Traffic* (2000), *Erin Brockovich* (2000), *Ocean's Eleven* (2001), and *The Informant!* (2009)

The ways in which motion pictures communicate to us depend greatly on their intended use, the skills of the filmmakers who are creating them, and our ability to interpret their various messages. These meaningful and expressive possibilities form the extraordinary range of informational, aesthetic, and enlightening experiences that moving images can bring to us. Whether a brief sequence intended to promote a product or an epic tale that takes place over many hours of episodes, images can be used to clarify or to distort, to offer a clear narrative or to weave a rhythm of light and color.

It's a Wrap!

In Chapter 5, you have investigated a number of essential questions about moving images: "Who makes motion pictures?" "Why are movies made?" "How do they get to us?" "What types of movies are there?" As you have seen, motion picture sequences can be broadly categorized into narrative and non-narrative formats. Many expressive traditions exist within and between each type, and filmmakers use these forms to convey a vast range of ideas and imagery. In the work to follow, you will have opportunities to develop analytical and creative skills that build on the broad communicative possibilities we have explored in this chapter.

Analysis: Non-Narrative Moving Images

Meaning through Image—*Until now, narrative film has been a central concern of our analytical work. For this Analysis exercise, you will watch a series of non-narrative and narrative short subjects, including* This Unfamiliar Place *by Eva Ilona Brzeski and* Perpetual Motion *by Kimberly Miner (see included DVD), to investigate stylistic choices and visual forms observed in motion pictures that may or may not assume as their central concern the telling of a story.*

For each sequence, indicate the following:

1. **Narrative** – First of all, discuss the content of the motion picture. Is there a narrative of connected events that form a discernable story, or is it a non-narrative motion picture? Why do you come to this conclusion?

2. **Image**

    a. What is seen in the frame?

    b. How would you describe the camerawork? Is there a particular approach to the use of the camera in relation to perspective, framing, or movement?

    c. What are the qualities of light, dark, and color?

3. **Editing**

    a. What is the pace of the editing? Is it constant or are there noticeable shifts or patterns in the editing?

    b. Is editing used to establish particular ideas in the footage? How are editing and motion control (variable frame rates to create slow or fast motion) used to establish a pace that helps to set a tone or style to the movie?

4. **Sound**

    a. What is heard during the motion picture?

    b. Is sound used to add coherence to the motion picture? Is the absence of particular sounds used to help to establish its lack of narrative? (For example, not hearing the voices of people who are clearly talking.)

    c. How is sound used to establish a style and tone to the film? Is it used in contrast to the images or only to accentuate the pace and visual qualities of the images?

5. **Context and Outcome**

    a. What is the intended context of this motion picture?

    b. What seems to be the objective of the creators of this motion picture?

    c. What seem to be the intended emotional effects of the images? Are these consistent with the context and objectives of the movie?

    d. What do these moving images communicate to you? Do you find the motion picture effective in expressing or provoking ideas or feelings to or in you?

Writing: Portraits and Landscapes

When examining non-narrative motion picture forms, there are some links that can be made with traditions of portraiture and landscapes in painting, in which narrative elements—the depiction of an action that also suggests preceding and following events—are not present or reduced to a minimum. In this writing, we will begin to develop material for considering purely descriptive elements in the visual arts.

Characterization and Setting – In this piece of writing, you will select a subject to describe in detail without recounting any actions or events. The piece of writing should contain multiple paragraphs for ample development of the portrait. Go beyond the bare details to illustrate a thorough, insightful portrait of the person or place.

1. **Person** – Write a description of yourself or someone you know. Concentrate on physical description, including manners of gesture and movement. Describe the person in a setting or settings, but without reference to a series of narrated events. You may reference both image and sound in your description.

2. **Place** – Write a description of a place with which you are quite familiar. Include wide perspectives and details that are seen from close up as well as sounds that accompany the place.

Project: A Portrait

For this exercise, you have a great deal of creative freedom to produce a short that depicts of portrait of a place or person. You are encouraged to express the essence of a place or person through a succession of images and sounds. You will determine the structure, pace, tone, and style of the movie without the need to develop a narrative.

A. **"A portrait"** – You must plan, shoot, and present a short video piece that offers a personal interpretation of the idea of "a portrait" to the class. Choose one:

   1. A self-portrait

   2. A portrait of a person with whom you are personally familiar.

   3. A portrait of a place—interior or exterior

B. **Objectives and preparations** – If requested by the instructor, submit the following:

   1. A four- to six-sentence description of your objectives for this project, including visual plan, desired tone, and structure of the short.

   2. A production list including: personnel; locations; dates of shooting and editing.

C. **Guidelines**

   1. From three to eight minutes in length, showing a structure that allows for comprehension by the viewer, such as through elements found in music.

   2. This is an individual project.

   3. You may use material generated through Writing 5, although this is not necessary.

   4. Attention to sound editing is important, whether through selective cuts, mixing, or sound design (may include voice(s), sound effects, music, and so forth).

Report

Exercise Work—*Comment on the fulfillment of objectives in creating this portrait. Please note the following:*

1. **Pre-production**–Was preparation sufficient to complete the shorts successfully?

2. **Objectives**–Were the goals of the production fulfilled through the final product? Were the elements of structure, image, sound, and editing effective in communicating the intended themes, ideas, and stylistic intentions?

3. **Motion Picture Fluency**–In what ways do you feel that you are using motion picture communication to your satisfaction? Are there particular sequences or moments that you find particularly successful in either of these projects? Are there improvements you feel that could be made in these projects or adjustments you anticipate in future work?

Glossary

Abstract – Non-narrative films and sequences that structure their images around abstract patterns, such as those found in music and abstract painting, which can consist of actions, shapes, colors, rhythms, and similar elements.

Associational – Non-narrative films or sequences in which juxtaposed shots are linked by themes and shared references in order to evoke emotions or make a statement about the topic of the motion picture.

Avant-garde – This term from the French has come to be understood as artistic creation that strives to develop new modes of expression that reject conventional forms and well-established parameters of style, content, and theme.

Categorical – Non-narrative films or sequences whose structure is based around images grouped into categories.

Comedy – In film, comedy builds on the traditions of the theater in which authors intend to create humor through the overall situations and style of the narrative; comedy includes genres such as slapstick, screwball comedy, and parody.

Crime film – Crime films are those that involve crime as the central force of the narrative, including gangster films, film noir, detective films, and thrillers.

Development – Term used to describe the initial stages in the creation of a motion picture, particularly the writing of the script in which story concepts, treatments, and drafts of the script are generated. Once financing is secured, development is completed and personnel are hired to move the film into the production process.

Documentary – A motion picture based clearly on fact dealing with real people, places, and events in a similar fashion to literary non-fiction. Documentaries typically illustrate or investigate their subjects through analytical structures, archival or primary source footage, interviews, and commentaries.

Fiction – A film that is composed of imaginary characters and events or primarily staged interpretations of events based on factual information.

Final cut – Right to have the final decision over the completed edit of a film. This authority may be accorded to a director in a production contract.

Genre – Grouping of movies into categories in which they contain similar settings, plot outlines, character types, themes, and visual styles.

Horror – Type of film fundamentally intended to cause fright, terror, or revulsion in the audience. This typically involves supernatural, gruesomely violent, or monstrous elements at the core of the story.

Montage – Editing that compresses time and space for various artistic and storytelling effects, such as montage sequences which use dissolves, jump cuts, associational cuts, and related techniques to convey information, states of mind, memories, and other non-narrative communication to the viewer.

Musical – A film genre in which songs performed by actors in the motion picture are imbedded into the sequences of the movie. Common musicals are those that evolve from stage musicals with narrative interwoven with song and dance.

Nickelodeon – Early motion picture theater, often a converted local business, in which short movies were continuously shown.

Non-narrative – Motion pictures that do not contain a narrative of events linked by cause and effect and typically include many types of documentary, promotional, avant-garde, and educational films. Four broad categories have been defined by various film theoreticians to classify patterns present in non-narrative films: categorical, rhetorical, associational, and abstract.

Pitch – A term related to "sales pitch" in business in which originators of a project seek investment through an oral presentation of the premise and attractive potential of the movie in meetings with studios representatives or funding sources.

Post-production – Phase of motion picture creation that generally consists of editing, sound design and mixing, digital effects, and printing.

Pre-production – The phase of motion picture creation in which all of the elements necessary for principal photography are prepared. Locations or studio settings are built, arranged, and dressed, costumes are prepared, rehearsals take place, and all of the other logistical aspects of the production are completed.

Production – The phase of motion picture creation during which the core images of the movie are generated, referred to by the term principal photography.

Rhetorical – Non-narrative motion pictures that present evidence to support or debate their premises, common to documentaries because of their organized presentation and analysis of a topic.

Science-fiction – Genre that consists of speculative narrative based on principles of science and current technology and is typically set in the future.

Serial – Motion pictures in which the narrative is intended to take place over a number of distinct episodes. First popularized in the 1910s with such series as *The Perils of Pauline*, serials brought spectators back to the next episode until the main action was resolved after a certain number of installments. They continued through the 1950s with detective, science fiction, and superhero serials as these techniques shifted to television through episodic series.

Studio – This term is used in filmmaking to designate two concepts: first, a company that oversees the production and distribution of motion pictures; and, second, a space designed and built for the production of motion pictures (often consisting of soundproof stages).

Western – The most distinctive film genre to many viewers, the western is understood to be a motion picture set in the western continental United States or a region resembling it during the time period of the settling of the American frontier (generally the second half of the nineteenth century). The stories and themes of westerns revolve around the conquering and settling of the Western United States by white Americans and involve conflicts among these settlers (often cowboys and outlaws) and between them and Native Americans.

David Riker, at right, directing on the set of La Ciudad. *Riker also co-scripted the award-winning screenplay of* Sleep Dealer *and is the director of* The Girl. *(Courtesy of David Riker)*

Close-Up
Behind the Scenes with Director
David Riker

Q In what ways did you first become involved in making movies?

A I began taking photographs as a young teenager and remember building my first darkroom in the boiler room of our house, and standing there, sweating, as I tried to teach myself how to wind my negative film into a Patterson developing tank. By my senior year at university I had assembled a large portfolio of images and was dreaming of one day joining the Magnum Photo Agency, home to so many of the great documentary photographers. But then I had a strange epiphany. Looking through my portfolio one day I realized that I didn't know the names of most of the people I had photographed. I realized I knew next to nothing about the subjects of my photos. The photographs had visual integrity, and some of the images were quite strong, but I couldn't help feeling that they were lacking in some fundamental way. I wanted the people in my photos to speak, and I felt that I had somehow rendered them mute. In what was one of the most painful experiences of my life, I put my camera down and stopped taking photographs. Then, after some delay, I realized that if I wanted the subjects to speak I would have to begin making films.

The first footage I ever shot was on a hand-cranked 16mm Bolex; the longest shot limited to about twenty-five seconds. But I was still using the camera as I had my still cameras – I filmed footage of Puerto Rican children breakdancing, of women trying to shut down the Wall Street Stock Exchange, demonstrators protesting the U.S. war in El Salvador. But I still didn't know the names of the people I was filming, and the Bolex was silent.

A few years later, Sony introduced the Hi-8mm Handycam and I rushed to make a documentary – for the first time with sound. Over the next few years I made a number of documentary videos, teaching myself along the way, but realized that I needed to deepen my understanding of film. I knew that great films were capable of stirring the deepest feelings, but I didn't know what the secret was to their power. I was twenty-seven when I enrolled in graduate film school.

At film school in the early 1990s, students learned their craft by shooting on 16mm cameras and editing on flatbeds. There were no digital non-linear editing systems. In the first year, everyone was expected to shoot in black and white, and the films were silent. Frustrated at first that I was still working without sound, I began to realize that the key to cinema is visual language. And slowly, deliberately, I started to learn its vocabulary and rules. It was a second epiphany for me, like uncovering some long-hidden mystery.

It was during this period of intense discovery that I began to make my first feature film, *La Ciudad*. I was inspired in part by the Italian films made right after WWII, the so-called neo-realist films – *Paisan*, *Bicycle Thieves*, *La Terra Trema*. These were films that seemed to reflect life as it was really lived, but with a lyrical voice. Unlike many contemporary 'realistic' films that were using a gritty, handheld style, the neo-realist films were eloquent, the choice of images—deliberate, striking, even poetic. I know that as I struggled to find an articulate language in my own film, the images from these masterpieces were hanging above me like golden signposts.

Q In screenwriting, do you develop how the visuals will communicate the story?

A It is tempting, when writing a screenplay, to think in images, and to some extent it's necessary to "see" the film as you're writing. But the essential task of the screenwriter is not to visualize the film but to understand and control the dynamics of the story itself. The craft of writing a screenplay is separate and distinct from the craft of directing a film.

Q What has been your experience of the collaborative nature of filmmaking?

A All filmmaking is collaborative, and this makes it one of the most complex and powerful of the arts. Many of us know that *Avatar* was made by James Cameron, but we should also know that he was assisted by a crew of more than ten thousand. I think the most important experience for young filmmakers is to learn as many aspects of the craft as possible – to understand the unique challenges of the writer, the cinematographer, the gaffer, the sound recordist, the actor, the editor. A composer must learn each of the instruments before composing for an orchestra.

Visit the textbook website to read the entire interview with David Riker.

Recording and Presenting Reality

CHAPTER IN FOCUS

In this chapter you will:

- produce a short documentary
- analyze non-fiction media traditions and standard documentary methods
- evaluate major technical and ethical considerations of documentary filmmakers

Exploring New Territory

In 1910, Robert Flaherty, a 26-year-old American mineralogist, was hired to travel to the Hudson Bay area of Canada to search for iron ore deposits. During the next six years, Flaherty experienced the local Inuit culture firsthand, writing of his encounters in diaries and developing a great respect for the traditions and skills that have allowed this group of people to survive in the harsh climates of the Arctic.

Figure 6-1 Director Robert Flaherty inspecting documentary footage in 1949 with his wife and collaborator Frances in the background. *(Courtesy Getty Images)*

By 1914, Flaherty was also filming the sites and activities of the Inuit people. From many hours of footage, he edited a completed project, *The Eskimo,* in 1916. This film was destroyed by fire in 1917. Despite this apparent setback, Flaherty felt that he had learned from the mistakes he had made in creating this motion picture (including holding a lighted cigarette near the film negative), and he wanted to return to the Arctic to create a film that would tell the story of Inuit customs and lifestyles.

After a long struggle, Flaherty was able to secure financing for the project. He traveled north for two months to reach the eastern coast of the Hudson Bay where he would work for nearly a year and a half. He proceeded to select the people that suited his plans and who would become an integral part of the making of the film. He already knew the man who would be his main character, "Nanook of the North." Allakariallak had been a traveling companion during his previous treks north and would serve as a charismatic center to his film. Flaherty cast the people who would play the members of Nanook's family, and they began to shoot footage of traditional Inuit family life.

Subjects and Participants

Flaherty wanted to depict the nearly extinct crafts and survival methods of this culture, so he set out to photograph a family engaging in a variety of pursuits over the course of a year. Having surveyed his own earlier film and other travelogues, he felt that he needed dramatic elements to engage the viewer, so he organized the shooting around a series of events and movements that would give a structure to the feature film. As the film progressed through examples of daily life, viewers would witness the struggles and joys of an Inuit family during the course of a motion picture.

Figure 6-2 Mother and child from *Nanook of the North.* *(Courtesy Pathé/Photofest)*

By this time, Flaherty had mastered the entire filmmaking process, having learned to develop and print his own films. He recognized the value of considerable shooting when dealing with a natural setting and unpredictable events and—as his own cinematographer—had honed a keen sense of visual expression and timing. These attributes would combine with his storytelling gifts and compelling subject matter to produce a film that became a landmark in the evolution of documentary film and a resounding success with the public.

Flaherty involved the Inuit extensively with his methods, screening rushes with them and discussing events and activities they could film that would tell the story of their culture. In fact, the Inuit were totally integrated in the shoot, learning to take apart and rebuild a camera, process film, and assist Flaherty with all aspects of production. The physical conditions are captured in the movie one can see today. The cold could transform the film into thin frozen glass-like strips. Flaherty cut a hole the size of a 35mm frame in the side of his completely light proof hut, attached a printing machine to the wall, and then used sunlight to expose his film. While shooting, Flaherty and his group barely survived blizzards and difficult treks across frozen stretches of land.

Dilemmas of Documenting Reality

In *Nanook of the North*, we see many of the most essential components of non-fiction filmmaking and a number of the most important sources of controversy in documentary traditions that have been debated ever since its debut. With this film, Flaherty depicts a group of people living in their natural setting. They are involved with tasks and actions that make up their daily lives. However, in wishing to depict and preserve a vision of the traditional lifestyles of this ethnic group, Flaherty made decisions to remove any traces of influence from contemporary industrialized culture, such as the rifles that the hunters would actually be using or certain clothes that they would have been wearing by then. In addition, aspects of events were staged for the camera when sufficient or acceptable footage was not forthcoming.

By taking a camera, bringing it to a natural setting, and having people perform activities that were relatively natural and true-to-life, Flaherty created a motion picture that deals with the factual reality of passed-down traditions and lived experiences of a group of people. The choices he faced in the depiction of people, events, and settings are those confronted by any documentary filmmaker when addressing their topic drawn from reality. At the time of the movie, no one had considered what a "documentary film" would be. Flaherty was proceeding as he saw fit to produce a motion picture that would engage audiences and show them the lifestyle of the Inuit in their natural environment. When Nanook and the other characters partake in most of the activities of the film—ice fishing, building an igloo, traveling in a kayak as a family—they are performing activities that had been standard aspects of daily life in their culture and that were being transformed or supplanted in the face of modern life.

VIEWFINDER

"That is the cornerstone of documentary filmmaking. You have to have respect and you have to be humble and you have to submit to the reality that you wish to capture."

–Mira Nair–

Indian director of fiction and documentary films whose projects include *Salaam Bombay!* (1988), *Mississippi Masala* (1991), and *Monsoon Wedding* (2001)

Figure 6-3 Michael Moore (in hat) framing a shot for *Roger and Me. (Courtesy Warner Bros./Photofest)*

When documentaries are produced today, choices of sequence of events, of **authenticity**, and of staging activities can be debated hotly by participants and viewers alike. When his film *Roger and Me* came out in 1989, filmmaker Michael Moore elicited unfavorable responses from some critics, because the order of certain incidents in the movie depicted the timeline of events inaccurately. Later, his films have been accompanied by extensive footnoting and meticulous research to support the essay-like approach of documentaries such as *Fahrenheit 9/11* (2004) and *Sicko* (2007).

Just Turn the Camera On

As described in Chapter 2, the first motion pictures introduced two particular forms for moving images: the documentation of real events through recorded light and the depiction of narrative through a staged filming. Essentially, documentary and narrative fiction films were born in their most elemental of forms.

Framing the Discussion

- *Have you seen a documentary or journalistic show recently? How could you tell that these were in a non-fiction format?*

- *What types of formats can you think of that present non-fiction moving images to an audience? Are there particular types that interest you the most? Are there some that you find more effective than others?*

- *What techniques do you usually see in documentary motion pictures? In what way are they crafted to express a particular point of view? Do they present the images very directly or was there considerable editing and commentary to present the moving image documents in a distinct manner?*

- *Documentary* films are the cinematic equivalent to the non-fiction traditions of writing and include a wide range of styles and formats. The material of the film concerns true events and often consists of real-life, **archival**, or journalistic footage, interviews, informative explanations, and essay-like **commentary**. In this chapter, the term non-fiction film will also be used to describe documentaries.

- *Fiction* motion pictures are those that depict people, places, and events that are either imaginary or largely invented and staged for the camera by actors or other representational means.

For most of the existence of motion pictures, the significant majority of theatrically released and widely viewed films have been fiction, but the beginning of the twenty-first century is proving to be a turning point in the history of the documentary. In the decades preceding the turn of the century, documentaries and moving image journalism were nearly always seen on television, but after a number of financially successful documentaries in the 1990s, the early twenty-first century has seen the emergence of broadly distributed documentary films in theaters and through significant sales of DVDs and similar media.

The evolution of television broadcast and Internet video journalism have followed certain traditions in print media—such as newspapers—while also developing practices and techniques that capitalize on the potential of moving images to deliver news and analysis. As television stations developed formats for journalistic offerings to viewers, they used the moviemaking institution of the soundstage studio to serve as a control center for the creation of segmented news programs. Using multiple cameras, editing would often be performed directly using a **switcher** that allowed technicians to alternate between different video or audio sources. Many techniques evolved for the creation of news segments, such as the use of the **teleprompter** so that reporters could read news reports and commentary while looking directly at the camera. Titles and transitional techniques, such as **wipes**—a transition from one shot to another in which the new image gradually occupies the frame to replace the first image as if it were being "wiped away"—were adapted from fiction filmmaking and developed their own uses in journalistic practice, from major network shows to community television.

Blurred Lines

The distinctions between documentary and fiction traditionally have been quite recognizable and clearly defined by the creators of films at the times of their development. However, the differences between the two forms can be blurred, and twenty-first century trends in moviemaking have seen an unprecedented mixing of fiction and non-fiction in terms of style, technology, methods, storytelling, and other factors. Some simple examples are when documentary films show restaged events, or when fiction films include newsreel shots and sequences to provide context, to link the story to real events, or to add authenticity. The concept of "Reality TV," whose name suggests that

Figure 6-4 A historical photograph of the racehorse Seabiscuit. *(Courtesy Photofest)*

Figure 6-5 An image from *Seabiscuit*, directed by Gary Ross, a fiction film that tells a historical story. Which photo looks more "real" to you, Figure 6–4 or Figure 6–5? *(Courtesy Universal/Dreamworks/Photofest)*

it centers on motion pictures that document reality, often presents highly prepared and staged situations in which the documentary aspect becomes thin to the point of disintegration.

There are also films that obscure the distinctions between documentary and fiction or play around with their typical styles and methods significantly. In contemporary motion pictures, sequences from one form will sometimes be seen in a film of its opposing type, such as with the voice-over sections of *Seabiscuit* (2003, directed by Gary Ross) or scenes in which archival and staged footage will be purposefully jumbled together, as with *JFK* (1991, directed by Oliver Stone). American filmmaker Erroll Morris has consistently explored issues of truth, perspective, and methodology in his documentaries, such as *The Thin Blue Line* (1988), *Standard Operating Procedure* (2008), and Academy Award-winner *The Fog of War* (2003).

Invention and Re-Invention

Other filmmakers play with stylistic devices that tend to be seen in particular formats. In the contemporary era, a number of feature films and television motion pictures have used documentary techniques to tell fictional stories. This type of fiction film, now well known as the mockumentary, first received popular recognition with *This Is Spinal Tap*, directed by Rob Reiner in 1984, and then became a vehicle for many filmmakers, most notably in the films of Christopher Guest, such as *Best in Show* (2000). For television, the format has proven to be successful in shows like *The Office,* a creation of Ricky Gervais and Stephen Merchant for the BBC that was later adapted for an American context.

Figure 6-6 Production photo from Erroll Morris's *The Thin Blue Line*. In this documentary about a man on death row for the murder of a policeman, director Erroll Morris re-staged events as part of his investigation of the crime and its full story. *(Courtesy Miramax/Photofest)*

When many people think of non-fiction motion pictures, they imagine the clear presentation and discussion of a topic through the use of interviews, printed facts, and an obviously structured arrangement of events or analysis. However, documentary films can follow approaches that are highly unorthodox and creative. In the same decade as Robert Flaherty, Soviet filmmaker Dziga Vertov directed *The Man With the Movie Camera* (1929), a non-narrative documentary that highlights the role of the cameraperson in its influential and wildly inventive portrait of the Soviet city in the late 1920s.

Vertov and his collaborators invented the term "Kino-glaz" to describe the camera as an eye, the creative instrument of the cinematic artist. Vertov explained his goal as a filmmaker to be "Kino-pravda," meaning cinema-truth, which he described as capturing "life caught unawares." In *The Man With the Movie Camera*, he and his creative team wanted to express the potential of this "eye" to communicate directly to the viewer, so their silent film did not include any written explanations. Vertov's unit filmed a wide range of images on streets and public spaces and in factories and apartments, and together they created an associational essay on the communicative power of motion pictures and their ability to depict life in the Soviet Union at that time.

Turning the Camera to the World

From its inception, one of the most important abilities of the camera has been to capture a view of the physical world of its time. It is no surprise that the most common practices of amateur filmmaking are in the realm of the documentary. A parent will turn on a camera and shoot footage of the family. People will be standing on the sidelines of school games, cameras set

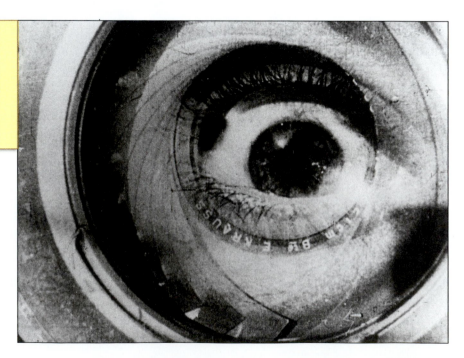

Figure 6-7 Still of an eye reflected in the lens with aperture visible from *The Man With the Movie Camera,* directed by Dziga Vertov. *(Courtesy Amkino Corporation/ Photofest)*

to record. With the integration of sound, we also talk to each other in front of the camera or speak directly to the camera.

Even with these simple examples, we can see how tricky documentary filmmaking can be. When we watch home movies, we are often aware of the ways in which people may be unnatural or may "play to the camera." It can make the actions we see or words we hear seem untruthful or affected. The integrity of documentaries revolves greatly around the ways in which films achieve an appropriate representation of whatever topic is being presented, that it makes sense within the point of view, style, and tone of the complete motion picture. Does this sound familiar to you by now? You thought about these same issues when building narrative structures and visual approaches for fiction films.

A variety of professionals are involved in the creation of non-fiction motion pictures. Some fiction directors make documentaries as well, such as Michael Apted, Bertrand Tavernier, and Mira Nair. In an interview, Tavernier explained, "Fictional characters are so invasive that I need to do documentaries to take a break, to return to reality."

Of course, there are filmmakers who specialize in documentary films, and many investigative journalists do their work primarily or exclusively through motion pictures, whether shown on television or through the Internet. All of these people document the world around us using moving images filtered through the lens of their various perspectives and expressed through cinematography, editing, and commentary on phenomena and events of the world.

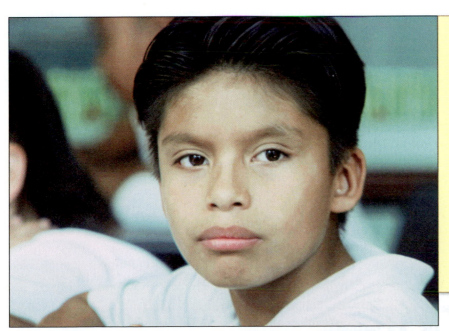

Figure 6-8 For the fiction short *Immersion*, cinematographer Frazer Bradshaw sought a documentary look with the digital RED camera through hand-held shots and a minimal amount of carefully added light. Director Richard Levien also used a documentary approach with the children in the film to facilitate a comfortable dynamic between untrained actors and the camera. *(Courtesy Richard Levien/Frazer Bradshaw)*

Figure 6-9 Director Bertrand Tavernier on the set of *Holy Lola,* one of many contemporary fiction films that use some stylistic and logistical techniques of documentaries. *(Courtesy TFM/Photofest)*

There is a great array of techniques, methods, and philosophies employed in the range of moving images that we call non-fiction. In this chapter, we will survey some of the important currents in the evolution of the broad classification of motion picture we call the documentary, and we will discuss the approaches and issues faced by filmmakers—and you—as non-fiction movies are created.

The Origins of Non-Fiction Films

You have read about how the Lumière brothers set up cameras in many natural settings around their home city of Lyon, France, and recorded a variety of everyday activities such as the arrival of a train in a station, workers leaving their factory at the end of the day, and parents involved in feeding their child. Within the next decade, many films continued with this tradition of filming unscripted events from reality, particularly travelogues that displayed sites from around the world or people involved in activities that highlighted cultural practices and behaviors.

Just as the development of projected motion pictures stemmed in part from the traditions of the lantern show, the formats of what have become known as documentary films also find their origins in this phenomenon. Lecturers would use the medium of the lantern show to accompany their discussions of scientific principles and discoveries, exotic locales and cultures, and contemporary events. The first reality-based films mirrored these conventions, and the topics of early travelogue and journalistic motion pictures echo the subject matter seen in nineteenth-century traveling lectures accompanied by projected photographs and illustrations.

Many early non-fiction films were made to be accompanied by a lecturer. This person would stand by the screen and deliver a lecture that functioned

Figure 6-10 Lantern show used for a travelogue lecture.

in relation with the moving images seen by the viewers. This practice would be adapted later for motion pictures with synchronous sound by the use of interviews or voice-over with the image on the screen.

Developing Structure

However, these early films did not sustain the interest of viewers. In the first decades of motion pictures, notable fiction movies developed framing, staging, and editing of shots to establish the dramatic interest and understandability of the story. Non-fiction films were limited to individual shots that depicted single events or a landscape, and "news" movies were often only fictional reenactments of major events. These motion pictures can be witnessed for their historical evidence, but they do not hold the attention of audiences for significant periods of time. In addition, films linked to current events were pertinent for only a limited time, so they did not make enough money for their producers.

How could filmmakers put together shots to present a topic in an organized, analytical format? How could viewers understand a topic through images that created meaningful and interesting relationships and patterns for the viewer? What was necessary was the development of methods that would give an appropriate structure to the motion picture. In that way, the viewer could begin to link the images on the screen and make sense of the ideas they expressed in a thoughtful way.

Shaping Reality

The simplest decisions shape the moving pictures that are captured by the camera. Every choice for cinematography and sound recording determines the "reality" seen on the screen. Once these images become a record of reality, they are to be transformed even further by editing and other post-production techniques. The documentary filmmaker must continually ask: How do I record an accurate representation of this scene or this person? How do I offer appropriate perspective? What are the important facts that must be provided? For his 1974 Academy Award-winning documentary *Hearts and Minds*, director Peter Davis wove his portrait of the Vietnam War from the testimonies of civilians, active soldiers, veterans, and leaders from both the United States and Asia. The film has been noted as a landmark for its "evenhandedness in counterpointing the American and the Vietnamese experience," as stated by film journalist Judith Crist.

Before you even turn on a camera, it is vital to consider core ethical issues that documentary filmmakers share with journalists, historians, artists, and scientists. When filmmakers record documentary images, what is the relationship of the images to their subjects? Will the people, creatures, or settings in the movie be harmed in any way? Will any individuals face negative effects or unwarranted attention, or are they freely accepting of their presence in this motion picture? Or does the historical, sociological, or journalistic importance of these moving images merit their existence?

Figure 6-11 Filmmaker Amanda Micheli, whose documentaries include *Double Dare* and *La Corona*, shooting in difficult conditions. *(Photo by Tecia Esposito, Courtesy Runaway Films)*

Ethical Considerations

As you consider examples in this chapter and among the movies that you watch, think about the role of the filmmaker in the events that have been recorded. From *Nanook of the North* to the contemporary documentary *Hoop Dreams* (1994), ethical concerns have confronted filmmakers regarding the ongoing experiences that they are chronicling. Sometimes filmmakers are subjected to great danger and they must consider the well-being of their crew and themselves.

For the film *Harlan County, USA* (1976), Barbara Kopple and her crew were swept up in an intense, violent standoff between labor and strikebreakers in a mining area of Kentucky, and they were shot at. Many non-fiction motion pictures made in war zones and locations of conflict or tension entail significant risk. In producing the Academy Award-nominated documentary short *La Corona* (2008), filmmakers Amanda Micheli and Isabel Vega traveled to a women's prison in Colombia to film a surprising event: a beauty pageant. A significant part of their work entailed earning the trust of the prison officials and the inmates. Once they were able to manage those difficulties, their focus was on depicting the stories of the women whose lives were at the heart of the event.

Physical conditions dictate many aspects of documentary production, chiefly because of the inherently unpredictable nature of many non-fiction motion pictures. Yet again, changes in technology are intertwined with shifts in practices and communicative styles in movies. By the early 1960s, more widespread use of lightweight 16mm cameras and faster film stocks led filmmakers to embrace new approaches in recording reality. In the 1990s, the arrival of digital technologies triggered a boom in documentary filmmaking as directors capitalized on the high image quality of digital recording and

Figure 6-12 A contestant in the beauty pageant from *La Corona*, directed by Amanda Micheli and Isabel Vega. *(Photo by Petr Stepanek, Courtesy of Runaway Films/Vega Films)*

editing in comparison to videotape. Many filmmakers have taken advantage of such opportunities throughout these decades, which in turn has helped motion picture technology to be introduced into the public sphere more quickly and aggressively than ever before.

Roles of the Documentarian

When we think of documentaries, particular impressions might come to mind: hearing an authoritative voice presenting a topic illustrated by a series of dissolving photographs; following a person around as they go about their daily life; seeing jittery images filmed in a crowd or on a battlefield or amidst dangerous natural conditions. The approach to filming and editing moving images and audio molds the perceptions and reactions of viewers. Some non-fiction motion pictures follow conventions and formats that are quite familiar, while others depict their topics in unusual or inventive ways. In order to appreciate the range of formats and styles seen in documentary film, we will investigate a variety of representative examples.

You have learned about how the first documentary films followed in the tradition of presentations accompanied by projected lantern shows for audiences. Many of the speakers delivering illustrated lectures were recounting personal exploits, adventures, and scientific discoveries. Their intimate relationship to the subject matter was one of the primary attractions of the event.

Entering the Picture

One of the first options to consider is the place of the filmmaker in the content of the motion picture. Very often in journalistic non-fiction filmmaking, a key member or members of the creative team will be a part of the movie. The viewer will see this person during interviews or walking in the settings of the movie. On some occasions, the voice of the director will be heard delivering narration and analysis to the images. Another option is for filmmakers not to use oral commentary but to include **titles** throughout the film to provide contextual information or explanations.

In television formats, the journalist often will be highly present in the material. For example, in the long-running news magazine *Sixty Minutes*, individual journalists who are heard and seen throughout the segments present the pieces. The perspective of the filmmaker and his or her involvement in the

Framing the Discussion

- *Can you think of examples in which filmmakers have played an inappropriate role in the depiction of events through moving images? Can you think of examples in which they acted appropriately in a difficult situation?*

- *If events are occurring as filmmaking is taking place, what are the responsibilities of the filmmakers to the unfolding of these events?*

generation of the motion picture is embedded in the fabric of projects such as these. Sometimes the filmmaker is not seen but heard, as in *A Stranger in Her Own City* (2005), by Khadija Al-Salami, in which the director provides commentary and cultural perspectives in her portrait of a young girl living in Yemen. This is also an example of the content of the film being a result of its production conditions: the director was operating the camera.

Voice-over, interviews, and dialogue play an important role in documentaries such as these. Therefore, scripts are written for many documentaries. Since the process of creating a documentary or news program is quite different than a fiction motion picture, there is a screenplay format that suits the needs of documentary production. The **two-column script** format is commonly used for documentaries so that picture description and matching dialogue can be lined up on the page. This is particularly well suited for voice-over, an important component of news programs and many documentaries. The reader can understand clearly the parallel of picture and sound.

Seeking Truths

The search for truthfulness in the images and statements of people in motion pictures is at the center of many debates about documentary film. One approach to filmmaking that has provoked lively discussions is known as **cinéma vérité**. In this type of documentary, whose name was inspired by Vertov's "Kino-pravda" and coined in the early 1960s by one of its instigators, Jean Rouch, the filmmakers use very small crews and try to elicit an authentic view of the life of its subjects, which includes active participation on the part of the filmmakers.

Figure 6-13 Nejmia, the thirteen-year-old subject of *A Stranger in her Own City*, talks on the street. *(Courtesy of Khadija Al-Salami)*

Figure 6-14 A frame featuring director Agnès Varda's hand in her documentary *The Gleaners and I.* As discussed in Chapter 5, Varda has made a wide range of fiction and documentary films, and for *The Gleaners and I* she used low-cost digital technology to create an award-winning feature. *(Courtesy Ciné-Tamaris)*

The intent is to create truthful, spontaneous reactions from the subjects of the movie, and the appearance of the filmmakers is embedded in the search for truth in the motion picture, as one can see in documentaries by such filmmakers as Marcel Ophuls and Nick Broomfield. Variations on the techniques of cinéma vérité movies have been used significantly by contemporary films that feature their directors, such as in the documentaries of Michael Moore and in mockumentaries that accompany the filmmaker.

Filmmakers who have made documentaries in which they are physically present in the images have employed a wide variety of methods. In the feature film *The Beaches of Agnès* (2008), director Agnès Varda uses the presence of beaches in her life as a storytelling cornerstone for this autobiographical film. She invited family members and friends to participate in this memoir that explored her over five-decade moviemaking career and other adventures, including her marriage with director Jacques Demy until his death from cancer. Discussing the use of clips from her movies for this documentary, "The selections from my films were treated as if the ensemble of my work was an information bank and I could use a fiction or documentary scene outside of its context."

For his movie *Super Size Me* (2004), filmmaker Morgan Spurlock centers the entire film around a personally-directed experiment to create an exposé on American gluttony and fast food culture. In films such as this one, since incidents are taking place just as they are filmed, the presence of the filmmaker can be the essential instigator of what we see.

Documentaries that are autobiographical or that recount a family memoir often feature the presence of their creator throughout the film, which can

Figure 6-15 Filmmaker Agnès Varda in *The Beaches of Agnès. (Courtesy Ciné-Tamaris)*

Figure 6-16 Director Eva Ilona Brzeski's father in *This Unfamiliar Place. (Courtesy Eva Ilona Brzeski)*

also be achieved through audio. In *This Unfamiliar Place*, a 1992 short film memoir about the experiences of the director's father, Eva Ilona Brzeski is not physically present in the footage shot for the movie. When filming her father for her movie, it was clear that the tragic events he experienced as a youth in Poland during World War II were difficult to discuss, and there is little traditional interview footage in the movie. She uses voiceover to tell his story from her perspective and to offer reflections on the role of catastrophic events in her life.

The Observer

On the other hand, documentarians can choose to be absent from the visual and audio content of the film. This was the choice of Robert Flaherty when he made *Nanook of the North*. During the evolution of documentary formats, many filmmakers have striven to follow an approach that reduces the tangible presence of the filmmakers and maximizes the ability of the footage to capture reality. Building on the new technical opportunities of the early 1960s just like the cinéma vérité filmmakers, a number of documentary directors adopted a similar attitude in terms of getting out into society and capturing authentic human experiences. However, the approach that they employed removed the presence of the director to focus on a direct depiction of events. They were out in the field, recording events as they transpired, and adopting strategies to present the films in close relation to the reality of the events. This approach to filmmaking has been labeled **direct cinema**.

A key aspect to the success of documentaries that attempt to show the lives of their subjects as naturally and truthfully as possible is the ability of filmmakers to work unnoticed. Movies that capture behavior and interactions honestly and accurately are often the result of successful collaborative practices and techniques in discretion on the part of the filmmakers. Filmmaker Nicolas Philibert spent many hours in 2000 and 2001 with his crew filming *To Be and To Have* in a one-classroom elementary school in a sparsely populated, mountainous region of France. In order to make this documentary, it was necessary for the film crew to earn the comfort and trust of the students and their teacher while they recorded footage of the class in action. They needed the cooperative and technical skills to be able to work so "unseen." The resulting motion picture is a remarkable view of the learning process and the unique experience of a classroom with students aged four to twelve.

Figure 6-17 Teacher Georges Lopez with students in *To Be and To Have*. (*Courtesy New Yorker/Photofest*)

Frederick Wiseman began making movies in the 1960s, and the titles of his films reflect the observational mode of his filmmaking: *Hospital, Welfare, Model, Deaf, Blind,* and *Zoo* are among his many documentaries spanning over four decades of work. In one of his first movies, *High School* (1967), Wiseman, working as sound recordist, went with cinematographer Richard Leiterman to a high school in Philadelphia and recorded many hours of everyday activities taking place at the high school. Instead of interviewing people about what they do and think about the high school, he simply filmed many different scenes, in classrooms, administrative offices, and hallways. As is typical in his films, there is no voice-over explaining what one sees, and there are no statistics or written explanations. Wiseman projects his own viewpoint into the film through the choices in shooting footage and the editing of sequences in which he develops a structure for the movie, even if it does not follow conventional narrative or character development.

In order to let the events speak for themselves, Wiseman and other directors may use long takes to allow sustained observation of people and places. For the 2003 short film *Good Morning Yokohama*, filmmaker Satoshi Ono shot footage of morning rush hour at a railway station in Japan. The documentary structures itself around the stages of the commute: putting tickets in the turnstile; waiting on the platform; being stuffed into the train. In its categorical depiction of the repetitive and spontaneous behaviors of commuters, the documentary presents a portrait of public behavior in which viewers must observe societal interactions and interpret what they see.

Stylistic Innovation

Other films use techniques of direct cinema but employ formats and styles to create motion pictures that do not look or feel like traditional documentaries or non-fiction segments on television. In the 2003 short documentary *Mojave Mirage*, filmmakers Kaarina Cleverley Roberto and Derek Roberto recorded shots of activity around an odd phenomenon: a phone booth in the middle of the Mojave Desert. The movie consists primarily of sequences of people speaking on the phone (both making and receiving calls) and talking to each other about the reputation and use of the phone booth. The filmmakers develop rhythm and meaning in the movie by editing sequences categorically, cross-cutting recurring conversations, and using digital methods of **superimposition** and **split-screen** effects.

Some contemporary documentaries have capitalized on digital techniques to employ animation and visual effects. For their 2002 documentary on movie producer Robert Evans, *The Kid Stays in the Picture,* directors Nanette Burstein and Brett Morgan used digital techniques extensively to animate still photographs into movable layers, which energized their subject matter through stylistic innovation and reinvigorated the use of archival photos in documentaries. The documentary *The Prisoner* (2006) by Petra Epperlein and Michael Tucker draws on footage shot with different cameras under a variety of circumstances along with animated sequences to tell the amazing story of Iraqi journalist Yunis Abbas. In a similar fashion, the documentary

Figure 6-18 Viewers can see a variety of digital effects in contemporary documentary films, such as this use of a split-screen along with superimposition in *Mojave Mirage. (Courtesy Kaarina Cleverley Roberto)*

Prom Night In Mississippi (2008), which was initiated as a result of Morgan Freeman's challenge to a small-town high school in Mississippi to integrate its segregated prom, includes animated sequences to portray scenes described in interviews. There have also been some documentaries that are primarily or entirely animated films. In 2008, Israeli director Ari Folman drew on his personal experiences from the Lebanon War to create the animated documentary *Waltz With Bashir*, which won many international awards.

As you have seen through our discussions in the last chapter and here, documentaries can follow narrative and non-narrative overall structures. If the documentary revolves around telling a story through linked events of cause and effect, then it is narrative in nature. If the documentary does not contain a series of events that are linked by cause and effect—as with storytelling—it is non-narrative. A recent motion picture that returns us to our concept of motion picture language and that echoes non-verbal traditions from throughout film history—such as in the work of Dziga Vertov and his collaborators—is the non-narrative film *Baraka* (1992).

In his film *Baraka*, Ron Fricke arranges footage from across the globe into a mosaic of observations of human behavior and scenes of the natural world. At the other end of the spectrum from lightweight 16mm cameras and Nagra sound recorders, Fricke used cameras of his own design in 70mm format to create images that can play on extremely large screens (such as IMAX) and employ many sequences of time-lapse photography to capture sharp detail and wide views. The images of *Baraka* are designed to paint a portrait of the interconnected nature of life on Earth, and the filmmakers juxtapose shots to develop associations that form ideas purely through visuals.

Subject Matter

When selecting subject matter, filmmakers are often drawn to topics that hold great personal interest. They might wish to expose an issue to the public. They could film a memoir or topic concerning a family member or friend. They might want to craft an artistic or intellectual statement using real-life footage as their source. Much of the creation of documentary films has been undertaken far from the realm of major studio production and the large budgets of fiction features, so the history of non-fiction filmmaking is filled with stories of projects that are developed and nurtured by an individual or small group of collaborators.

Having just discussed the technical complexity of *Baraka*, let us return to the simplest films of all: the first non-fiction movies of the Lumières. There are lessons that can be learned from these single shot films. These first films serve as documents of their time and place, and most of their interest to us today stems from the choice that is typically the first in the creation of a non-fiction film: subject matter. It was the decision faced by Louis Lumière when he proceeded to use his new cinematograph: What is the camera going to record?

Among the most compelling of these early films are the ones in which we see interesting human activity and behavior. Films such as *Demolition of a Wall, Feeding Baby, Snowball Fight in Lyon, Woodcutters in Paris,* and *An Arab Knife Grinder at Work* are particularly appealing because of their depiction of human interaction or the achievement of a task. By contrast, many of the films featuring famous figures such as royalty or religious figures are far less engaging because of their static nature. They are seen standing,

Figure 6-20 Filmmaker Adam Keker documenting the dangerous work of gem miners in Cambodia: There are many unexploded shells in the area. *(Courtesy Invisible City Films)*

waving, or walking in a setting and manner that tend to be particularly dull.

Today, one of the first shots we think of when we imagine a documentary is the close-up for an interview. However, it is important to remember the lessons of the first non-fiction moving images from cinematic history: we like to see events and actions take place before us. Many young people creating a documentary choose a topic and then seek out appropriate people to interview about that subject. While interviews can be appropriate and interesting, the value of witnessing the successful progress of movement and action—whether by people, living creatures, or the natural world—is quite significant.

Time Factors

Since non-fiction films deal with the reality of the world, one of the most important factors affecting the subject matter of the film is *time*. If the events of the motion picture are unfolding during production, this can affect the work of the filmmakers profoundly. Sometimes it can compel a need to produce images aggressively and rapidly, or it can mean following the subjects of the motion picture for a substantial period of time. These factors all involve a concept that is dealt with by both documentary and fiction filmmakers: coverage.

Coverage is the collection of individual shots recorded during production of a film. The term "coverage" is used to indicate that the scene has been properly *covered* by the various shots. Consequently, there will be enough different angles and compositions to properly edit the footage into a satisfying sequence. In fiction films, this is helped by shot lists and "lining the script," as you will explore in Chapter 8. In documentaries, this is achieved by the expertise of the filmmakers who must shoot enough footage to edit the scene successfully.

During a real-life event, particularly one with lots of action and unpredictable events, getting coverage can be quite challenging. For example, this can mean filming important shots of a key event and sufficient cutaway footage to allow for choices in editing. On the other hand, if the filmmakers are pursuing a historical subject, or at least a topic that is not developing at the time of filming, the forces concerning time are different. In these cases, there are other pressures to consider, such as research and the time-consuming process of gathering and selecting archival footage.

For documentaries that are produced independently, the commitment to a project can be considerable. Dayna Goldfine and Dan Geller, award-winning documentary filmmakers, began the making of *Ballets Russes* in 2000 after a suggestion to film a major reunion event of legendary dancers of the Russian ballet in New Orleans that year. It was after initial interviews that they were convinced of the potential of the subject matter. They proceeded to record dozens of hours of interviews, events from the reunion, and visits to dancers in Los Angeles, Dallas, Cincinnati, New York, and London. The archival research for the film led them to seek out sources in Chicago, Australia, New York, and the homes of former ballet dancers from across the world. Finally, their editing process was so extensive it took them over two years to finish it, and the final release of the film was in 2005.

Economic Considerations

Many independent filmmakers have pursued topics of personal interest. At first, they may seek funding, such as when Robert Flaherty secured financing from the French fur company Réveillon Frères for *Nanook of the North*. With the development of marketing and advertising early in the twentieth century, it became clear to certain companies that it could be in their interest to initiate a project. Thus, subject matter can also be propelled by a corporate entity or production source. This is seen in the career of Flaherty, who in 1948 made the film *Louisiana Story* fully through the funding of Standard Oil (although not truly a documentary, it does contain non-fiction elements common to Flaherty's films).

Figure 6-21 Archival image researched and used for *Ballets Russes* directed by Dayna Goldfine and Dan Geller. *(Courtesy Geller/Goldfine Productions)*

In all of these different circumstances, part of the work of the filmmaker is to develop **outlines** and proposals to pitch projects to investors, studios, and broadcast networks. Many professionals spend a considerable amount of their time seeking **grants** from arts and humanities councils, government-run

Figure 6-22 An example of contemporary digital production techniques: filmmaker Eugene Corr, a veteran of major Hollywood productions, shooting the documentary *From Ghost Town to Havana* with an HDV camera and a minimal crew. *(Courtesy of Tamsin Orion)*

endowments, and **foundations**. In addition to public support, one of the most common sources of documentary funding is through television.

Broadcast media projects are developed as a result of expressed interest by investors, a group of producers, or wide cross-sections of society. In some cases, public television networks run thematic series that follow a formatted design employing a specific creative team. Conversely, other programs can feature projects that are pitched by independent filmmakers and produced for inclusion as a segment of a show. Cable networks, particularly HBO, have proven to be major sources of investment in documentaries.

Across the World and Back Home for Stories

One of the most enticing attractions of the early cinema was to bring far away places to one's local theater. In fact, the word "documentary" comes from the French word *documentaire,* which was used for the earliest travelogue shorts. Later, when non-fiction films began to be made in lengths over five or ten minutes, movies that served as voyages to foreign lands continued to be the norm. Audiences were interested in seeing exotic locales and cultures. Merian Cooper and Ernest Shoedsack, who later made *King Kong*, filmed an enormous migration of people and animals through the Zardeh Kuh mountain area in *Grass* (1925) and shot *Chang* (1927) about a family living in the jungles of Siam. Many of the films in this genre reflect intensely stereotyped views of foreign cultures. Often they were made by filmmakers who represented colonizing nations and who wished to reinforce attitudes of ethnic and cultural superiority towards various peoples of non-European ancestry.

As documentary filmmaking traditions evolved, certain filmmakers saw the value in depicting topics closer to home. In Great Britain, John Grierson headed a documentary film unit which produced many films in the 1930s that were funded by various British corporations and marketing boards. During travels and studies in the United States, Grierson had been inspired to use films to teach and inform societies about important issues and facets of contemporary life, and he organized a team of filmmakers who pursued topics that met commercial demands but that also were guided by significant personal interest. With films of this period such as *Drifters, Song of Ceylon, Night Mail*, and *Housing Problems*, the personnel under Grierson's supervision crafted a series of films that strove to employ striking images, inventive sound work, and the recording of footage that depicted their subjects in a vibrant but honest manner. Grierson said he wanted to "bring the citizen's eye in from the ends of the earth to the story, his own story, of what was happening under his nose . . . [to] the drama of the doorstep."

Contemporary Examples

In contemporary documentaries, subject matter continues to be fueled by personal interest, topical relevance, and commercial potential. When Steve James, Peter Gilbert, and Frederick Marx set out to produce a documentary about inner-city teenagers trying to succeed as professional basketball players, they planned on making a thirty-minute motion picture for public television. Once the filmmakers began shooting, they were compelled by the subject matter to continue their work. They filmed hundreds of hours of footage as they depicted the high school years of two adolescents from Chicago who are recruited by a private school to play basketball. The feature film they completed in 1994, *Hoop Dreams*, became one of the most acclaimed motion pictures of its time. This narrative documentary is driven by the personal drama of families struggling to get by in the face of great adversity and the social significance of race, class, and athletic competition in America.

The subject matter of *Hoop Dreams* centers on a highly intimate portrait of two families from inner-city Chicago. Many films pursue subject matter focused around characters that the viewer can accompany through the course of the motion picture. Such movies often tell a story. As we have seen before, they can also follow alternative approaches. In *Rivers and Tides* (2001), a portrait of multimedia artist Andy Goldsworthy directed by Thomas Riedelsheimer, the structure of the film stems from the individual projects pursued by Goldsworthy as he endeavors to create works of art that fulfill his inspirations. It does not follow an ongoing narrative or overall story arc, but it does provide an intimate glimpse of the artist's working process and driving passions.

Figure 6-23 Arthur Agee goes for a layup in the documentary *Hoop Dreams*. *(Courtesy Fine Line Features/Photofest)*

Other films center on an idea or abstract theme for their subject matter. In the movie *The Corporation* (2003), filmmakers Mark Achbar, Jennifer Abbott, and Joel Bakan present an exposé on the phenomenon of the corporation through interviews, wide-ranging visual records, and voiceover that offers historical perspective and analysis similar to that of a non-fiction writer. The distinct style of the film derives in large part from an original use of music and sound editing, graphic organizers, and juxtaposition of opposing viewpoints. For student or amateur filmmakers, this type of topic can pose great difficulties because of inaccessibility of archival footage and lack of focus or structure. Typically, directors must contend with substantial reliance on interviews in such projects.

In his highly acclaimed documentaries such as *The Civil War* (1990), *Baseball* (1994), *Jazz* (2001), and *The National Parks: America's Best Idea* (2009), filmmaker Ken Burns has employed significant historical research, striking archival images, interviews with experts in the field, and strong narration to build his motion pictures. In order to compose a well-rounded investigation of a topic and earn the respect of reviewers, filmmakers must typically weigh their sources and avenues of inquiry in the same manner as an academic researcher or non-fiction author.

Inspired by Reality

There are as many ways to depict the world as there are to experience it. The sources of inspiration to document reality are as extensive as the potential for human observation and imagination. Award-winning documentarian Erroll Morris explains:

> Truth is not relative. It's not subjective. It may be elusive or hidden. People may wish to disregard it. But there is such a thing as truth and the pursuit of truth. We must proceed as though, in principle, we can find things out—even if we can't. The alternative is unacceptable.

Often filmmakers are prodded by the events of the world surrounding them to create new works of vision and substance. They might be inspired by the wonders of the natural world or ecological concerns, as seen in Academy Award winners *The March of the Penguins* (2005) and *An Inconvenient Truth* (2006). They may be compelled by conflicts to depict the human stories at the heart of widespread strife. When making the 2007 Academy Award-winning documentary *Taxi to the Dark Side*, filmmaker Alex Gibney was inspired by the experiences of his father, a World War II veteran, to give perspective on events over a half-century later. As a child, filmmaker and journalist Pierre Sauvage was sheltered along with his family and thousands of Jewish refugees by courageous villagers in the town of Le Chambon in France. He returned to

Figure 6-24 Lyrical imagery helps to define the setting of Laos in *The Betrayal*, photographed by director Ellen Kuras. *(Courtesy of The Cinema Guild)*

Figure 6-25 Archival image that helps to document Thavisouk Phrasavath's extraordinary journey in *The Betrayal. (Courtesy The Cinema Guild)*

this setting to film *Weapons of the Spirit* (1987), which captures this moving story and its full context of treachery contrasted with selfless sacrifice.

In 2008, acclaimed cinematographer Ellen Kuras completed her directorial debut, *The Betrayal,* a chronicle of a Laotian immigrant family in the United States. She had been shooting the movie for twenty-three years. It all began when she sought lessons in Laotian and met Thavisouk Phrasavath. As she started to record footage of the family's experiences, she "wanted to be able to use imagery to speak as loudly as words . . . I wanted the audience to vicariously experience what was happening; I wanted the film to feel as if we were entering into Thavi's memory." Phrasavath, who ended up sharing a co-directing credit with Kuras, comments, "I've been able to become a filmmaker, the first Laotian filmmaker. Now I'm a role model for the youth and that's because Ellen, as a good American, felt obligated to do something because people would never know the truth."

Filmmakers work to create visual and sonic experiences that build from source material to construct a personal vision. Approaches to non-fiction subjects are most successful when the creative presentation of the material reflects or stems from the meanings and themes of the actual topic. At the heart of the production of documentary motion pictures is the knowledge of and respect for the subjects of the film and a similar regard for the audience.

It's a Wrap!

In Chapter 6, you have continued to explore motion picture forms by investigating the wide range of approaches seen in non-fiction movies. You have studied similarities and contrasts between documentary and fiction techniques, and now you will have opportunities to develop skills in evaluating and using these methods. Moreover, you will be introduced to the distinct challenge of depicting a non-fiction subject as you produce a documentary.

Analysis: Short Documentaries

For a series of short documentary films including Looking Back *by Emile Bokaer (see included DVD), you will discuss the following questions. Select two of the films for an analysis of contrasting approaches to documentary filmmaking. For the choices, consider the following methods present in the films:*

- Voice-over in first person
- Filmmaker present in the images
- Journalistic mode: third person voice-over (reporter) or written titles (informational)
- Methods of direct cinema (generally observational camera)
- Methods of abstract or non-verbal non-narrative cinema

A. **Content**

1. In one sentence, describe the central subject of the motion picture.

2. What provides information to the viewer about the topic of movie? List the types of footage and visual and sonic elements of the documentary.

3. Pick three moments from the film that stand out to you. Why are they important?

B. **Structure**

1. If you were to break the film down into three to five sections, what would be the parts? Describe them briefly (one sentence or less each).

2. Looking back at how you divided the motion picture, what happened at the transition points between each section?

3. Is the motion picture narrative or non-narrative? Or do you see it somewhere in between? Why?

4. In either case, how does the motion picture structure the images so that they are understandable?

C. **Cinematic Style**

1. Describe the cinematography of the motion picture, including use of movement, framing and depth, and qualities of light, dark, and color.

2. What is the pace of the editing? Are many shots held for more than 10 seconds? Note if those shots are interviews.

3. Do sequences move forward in terms of a straightforward narrative or presentation of clearly progressing images, or is there an alternative pattern to the arrangement of shots?

D. Documentarian Stance

1. From your answer to the question about "what provides information" (A2), what are the perspectives offered about the topic during the film? Is there any way to determine the goals of the filmmaker from the presentation of information? Explain.

2. From the following descriptive terms (from Erik Barnouw's book *Documentary)*, what one would you select for the person (or people) responsible for this documentary: reporter; prosecutor; promoter; observer; poet. Explain your choice with examples from the movie. If you think that two terms are necessary or if you want to use a similar noun not on this list, do so, but explain your choice.

3. From our discussion of the ethical issues often faced in documentary filmmaking, do you see evidence of proper or improper methods or approaches in the filmmaking?

Writing: Documentary Writing

Documentaries do not use an invented script to shoot their footage—when they do, they are fiction! However, documentaries can involve a great deal of writing. One of the most prevalent examples is in the composition of voice-over as the footage is shaped through editing and the rhetorical structures of the film are solidified. In your writing for this unit, you will draft preparatory pieces to be used in developing your projects. The first two parts of this exercise will consist of notes and preliminary work for the completed writing project.

A. **Brainstorming** – You have watched a number of non-fiction sequences and complete documentary motion pictures. What topics interest you? What subjects could you investigate properly in a non-fiction project? Use the following steps to generate subject matter for the production of a non-fiction motion picture. Remember that you should use brainstorming activities to generate possibilities. Even if initial responses do not seem particularly feasible or possible, note them. They may lead to other more practical choices. For each of the following categories, generate one or two examples from the questions:

1. Person – Is there someone whose personality, activities, achievements, or other characteristics you find interesting or inspiring?

2. Place – Is there a natural or man-made setting that holds particular meaning to you or that has sparked your interest for further exploration?

3. Activity – Is there an endeavor that you are regularly involved with or that interests you?

4. Behavior – Is there a behavior that you witness regularly among peers or other groups of people that strikes you as interesting or worthy of investigation?

5. Business – Is there a local economic activity with which you are familiar?

6. Event – Is there a current event you are aware of that could provide subject matter?

7. Academic or thematic concept – Is there an issue you have examined in any of your courses at school that you wish to investigate further?

8. Moving images – Do you already have personal footage linked to a person, event, or definable topic?

B. **Feasibility** – Now that you have generated a list of potential candidates for your project, it is useful to think about the chances you may have to create a motion picture from any of these subjects. For each of the preceding subjects you listed, consider whether or not there is any chance to pursue the possibility of making a non-fiction motion picture based on that subject matter.

1. Appropriate – Is the topic acceptable in relation to school or sponsor guidelines?

2. Accessible – Is treatment of the subject possible in relation to guidelines or agreements that may be dictated from outside sources, whether they be school-based, corporate driven, or subject approved? If you are unsure of this, you will incorporate a timeline for approval and initiation of the project.

3. Size – Is your topic *too small?* Mark down the ways in which you can examine the topic and make sure that the subject matter is significant enough to hold the viewer's interest. Essentially, it depends on the proper treatment of the topic and how you can imagine its study; the "smallness" of a topic depends greatly on our own conception of it.

4. Scope – Is your topic *too big?* This presents far more of a challenge than a topic that is "too small." If you can't imagine a way of treating the topic satisfactorily, then there is a good chance it might be a bad idea to select it as a central subject of a motion picture. Ask yourself: Is there any way to tackle *one aspect* of the topic? In addition, a topic that centers on an *idea*—and not an observable activity, event, or narrative involving people—can be quite difficult to treat effectively. It is very useful to determine in advance your approach with an *idea*-based topic. (Examples: teen gambling; senioritis; dating; etc.)

C. **Development** – From the preparatory work you have done so far, select one of the topics. You will now draft a piece of writing to initiate the development of this project.

1. For this piece of writing, you will choose the most appropriate and useful type of material for the topic and your needs. Pick from the following choices:

    a. Pitch – Draft a letter to a prospective investor.

    b. Subject – Compose a letter to a subject of or involved participant in the project.

    c. Crew – Write a mission statement that will be shared with the production team.

    d. Blueprint – Write a "script" for the movie that includes research for voice-over or written information for the screen.

2. Regardless of the format you select for your writing, include the following information:

   a. Subject – A statement of the primary topic of the documentary, including people who will be filmed or discussed during the motion picture.

   b. Objectives – Why do you want to make this motion picture? Include at least three reasons.

   c. Personnel – Who will be involved in the creation of this movie?

   d. Setting – Where will the documentary be made?

   e. Timeline – What are the stages of production and post-production for this project?

Project: Documentary

From the drafted preparations of your Writing exercise in this chapter, you will produce a documentary motion picture. If your initial work does not lead to a feasible project, you may shift strategies or embark on a project that is different from what was outlined in your preparatory writing. If you start a new topic at this time for this exercise, make sure that you are sufficiently prepared to complete the motion picture by any deadlines set for the project.

A. **Guidelines** – Compile the following information to initiate your project.

1. Class members will share topics during collaboration sessions supervised by the instructor. Different class members can discussion cooperative work or interest generated by various proposals.

2. Students are advised to work in groups of two or three, although some projects are well suited to be completed by a filmmaker working alone. If working in a pair or small team, tasks must be specifically delineated prior to production. Here are sample tasks for a documentary that will be designated during shoot preparations:

   a. Writing / Research

   b. Cinematographer

   c. Sound recordist / designer

   d. Director / Interviewer

   e. Editor

3. This film is to be a minimum of eight minutes in length, and a maximum of twenty minutes. If a different length is desired or necessary for your topic, you must secure approval from your instructor.

B. **Regulations** – At the outset of this class, there were basic guidelines established for your exercises. For documentary work, here are additional guidelines that will be discussed with your instructor:

1. You must obtain permission to record images of the people appearing in your video, in addition to shooting in any public or privately owned space. For a ticketed event, make sure that information is printed on the ticket that indicates consent to the use of their image, or post a sign at the entrance to the venue in consultation with the responsible parties.

2. Students will afford each other and their subjects with the same respect that they are expected to do while interacting appropriately in person. The produced video will not be used to misrepresent or malign the reputation of any of the involved individuals.

C. **Pre-production** – Compile the following information to initiate your project.

   1. Equipment list and technical logistics, including editing
   2. Locations for recording of real-life footage and events to be filmed
   3. Interview subjects, including place of interview
   4. Personnel necessary for production with breakdown of tasks
   5. Schedule for the shoot, including contact list of personnel and subjects
   6. Projected schedule for post-production, including personnel list

D. **Evaluation** – Please note that your evaluation will be based on the intended depiction of your subject through the recording of footage that appropriately portrays that topic and the construction of an editing structure that fulfills the objectives agreed upon by the filmmakers and the instructor.

Report

Write a minimum of four paragraphs analyzing your work on this project. Comment on the fulfillment of objectives in creating this documentary. Please note the following:

1. **Collaborative Work** – Describe the primary roles of each contributor to the film and specify your tasks.

2. **Pre-production and production** – What steps did you go through to make this film?

   a. Who was contacted?
   b. Who was interviewed?
   c. What research was conducted?
   d. What footage of non-fiction events and activities was filmed?

3. **Post-production** – Describe the course of editing the film, including key steps in the process and decisions in developing structural elements for the motion picture. For example, how did you move from a rough cut to fine cut to final cut? Were any major changes made during the editing process? Was there any reshooting?

4. **Product** – Were the *objectives* of the production fulfilled through the final product? Were the elements of image, sound, and editing effective in communicating the intended themes and ideas and presenting the subjects seen in the motion picture?

Glossary

Archival – Motion pictures that have been stored and are used for study, research, and placement in other motion pictures. An archive is a place where moving images are preserved for public or private use.

Authenticity – In filmmaking, the genuineness or truth of footage in relation to the actual events or experiences being shown or depicted.

Cinéma vérité – Term from the French meaning "Cinema Truth" originally applied to documentaries that sought truth about events through active participation and eliciting of testimony by filmmakers, although it is often used to describe methods involving direct recording of events with minimal intrusion by the filmmaker.

Commentary – Remarks delivered by a person, usually an off-screen voice, concerning the topic of the motion picture, often given as an authority perspective.

Coverage – Group of shots filmed for a scene regarding their appropriateness for editing. Full coverage implies a range of different framings, angles, and movements of individual shots in relation to the content and continuity of the scene. [Note: There is also a second distinct meaning for coverage in filmmaking: a report by a script reader evaluating a screenplay for its merits and deficiencies.]

Direct cinema – Documentary traditions that seek to record events and activities as they occur with minimal evidence of the presence of filmmakers, including interviews.

Foundation – An institution that holds an endowment dedicated to funding projects, including documentaries and other non-mainstream motion picture production.

Grant – An amount of money distributed by a governmental organization or foundation for the purpose of completing a project, such as a motion picture. In virtually all cases, specific procedures and terms are in place to apply for the grant.

Outline – In documentary film, an outline typically consists of a two- to three-page summary of the project and is used to apply for grants or studio subsidies.

Split-screen – Visual effect in which the screen is divided into two or more frames, with separate or repeated images occupying each individual field of the screen.

Switcher – A board consisting of control levers and buttons that allows a technician to select and mix video and audio signals directly in a studio to produce completed segments for broadcast media and related formats. Full term is production switcher.

Teleprompter – Video device that displays a script directly in front of the camera, allowing reporters, commentators, or actors to read aloud as they look into the camera lens.

Titles – Words applied to the image on the screen that convey information to the viewer, including opening and closing credits, superimposed writing, or subtitles that translate the dialogue into another language.

Two-column script – This type of script, also known as split page, is common to the documentary format or multi-camera productions, using two columns with description of visuals in the left-hand column and the corresponding voice-over and dialogue in the right hand column.

Wipe – Transition from one shot to another in which the new image gradually occupies the frame to replace the first image as if it were being "wiped away." As opposed to a dissolve in which the images are transparently combined during the transition, with a wipe the new image enters the screen using a horizontal or vertical line, circle, or other geometric shape that delineates the new image as it crosses the frame or enlarges to take over the screen.

Close-Up

Behind the Scenes with Editor and Director

Deborah Hoffmann

Q Did you have any early inspirations to use moving images to communicate?

A In college, I got very involved in still photography, and the one connecting thing – other than liking working with images – was that I got very involved with putting on exhibits, and I really liked thinking through the order of the images, so that viewers can have a specific type of experience going to the event. It took a while for me to get from there to being involved in making documentaries, but that was where it began.

Q What were your initial steps professionally?

A I began by volunteering as an assistant editor on a documentary. They got funding very quickly after I began, and there I was, I had a job. I went from assistant editor to sound editor, and I was very determined and very devoted, and I was able to start making deals, "I'll be assistant editor if you let me edit a scene." That happened on one project, then on the next project I edited enough scenes to be associate editor, and then I was off and running and editing film.

Q What lessons did you learn from your early efforts?

A I remember very early on, when I was an assistant working with an editor, he said to me, "You know, the relationship between the editor and the director is more difficult than a marriage." And I've always remembered that, and there's a lot of truth, not that it needs to be difficult, but it is a very complicated relationship, and of course when I became a director, now I've seen it from both sides. Directors are handing over their baby, and that's their point of view. And the editor feels like, "I can really see what's working and what's not, and the director is too close to the material." So there's that tension, and I think that this tension can be really helpful in film. And when I teach, and students are editing their own films, I always tell them, "You are doing the most difficult thing possible." You go out, you round up the subjects, stand in the snow and rain to film them and go through all that, you become convinced you've got a masterpiece and every frame is wonderful. And the person who didn't do any of that and they're just seeing what ended up in the footage—and not what the entire surrounding experience was—they can see more clearly. So when you're editing your own material, you have a unique challenge compared to when you're editing someone else's material.

Q What challenges do you face as an editor of non-fiction motion pictures?

A A documentary editor has a thrilling job because you really make the story in the editing room. You do wonderful things as a fiction editor too, but you're not sort of *writing* the story, and I feel that you really *are* doing that as a documentary editor. It's a wonderful thing, and you really can discover unexpected things in the editing room.

Q Was your previous work as an editor helpful to your role as a director?

A If I ruled the world, or at least the world of documentary film, I would make every director be an editor first, because I do think that you learn so much about what makes a scene and what tells a story by actually having to do it in the editing room. So I felt it was really, really helpful that I had been editing before I was directing. The first thing I directed was a personal film I made about my mother and Alzheimer's, and that was almost not a decision, it was just an overriding need that I had to make that film. And then I thought, this is kind of fun, you get to make all the final decisions.

Right now, documentarians can be a one-man-band. A lot of my students go all over the world, take one crew person with them, do everything incredibly cheaply, and then they edit it at home with Final Cut Pro. The expenses have come down in a lot of ways, but it's still tough in a lot of ways and the constant search for money can really beat you down. It's grueling work, but it's thrilling work, so until you get burned out, your problem will not be that you're unhappy at your work. It is a way to go places and meet people that you would otherwise have no way of experiencing. You have the excuse of making this film, and you meet the most fantastic people in the world.

Visit the textbook website to read the entire interview with Deborah Hoffmann.

From Page to Screen

CHAPTER IN FOCUS

In this chapter you will:

- create an original short narrative screenplay in standard format
- investigate traditions and methods of storytelling through motion pictures
- evaluate narrative structure and character development in a variety of movies

Storyteller

Where do our stories come from? Do you tell someone about your actions and experiences? Do you make things up? Do you type out stories to store on a laptop? Do you write in a journal? Do you only read or hear or see stories but never think of recounting a narrative yourself? Do you ever think of a story in which the first ideas that come to your head are a sequence of images? Or do you pick up a camera and start shooting movies, making up a story as you go?

Many filmmakers in Hollywood like to describe themselves as "storytellers" who happen to work in the visual and aural medium of motion pictures. As discussed earlier, these storytellers nearly always work from a plan. In this chapter, you will complete essential steps in the development of screenplays and other forms of preparation for motion picture production, and you will hone skills in the analysis of screenplays and movie narratives.

Screenwriters work in a variety of ways and use countless sources of motivation for the development of ideas, characters, and thematic material. The essential difficulties of the task of the screenwriter have been shared by storytellers and artists throughout the history of human creative expression. Here is a description of the working process of Billy Wilder, a writer-director-producer who was presented in Chapter 5. He is talking about collaborating with his writing partner I. A. L. Diamond:

> *We meet at, say, 9:30 in the morning and open shop, like bank tellers, and we sit there in one room. We read* Hollywood Reporter *and* Variety, *exchange the trades, and then we just stare at each other. Sometimes nothing happens. Sometimes it goes on until 12:30 . . . and we go to lunch. Or sometimes we come full of ideas. This is not the muse coming through the windows and kissing our brows. It's very hard work, and having done both, I tell you that directing is a pleasure and writing is a drag. Directing can become difficult, but it is a pleasure because you have something to work with. You can put the camera here or there; you can interpret the scene this way or that way; the readings can be such and such. But writing is just an empty page. You start with nothing, absolutely nothing, and I think writers are vastly underrated . . .*

Figure 7-1 Writer/director Billy Wilder, in hat, working with Charles Brackett on the screenplay to the 1942 film *The Major and the Minor. (Courtesy Paramount Pictures/ Photofest)*

Devising Plans

In this brief description of his work as a writer, Billy Wilder brings up why screenplays exist at all. The preparatory stages for filmmaking have started with words for the overwhelming majority of fiction motion pictures viewed by audiences across the world. Essentially, this is because it is more manageable, time saving, and cost effective for a writer to create a plan for the movie than to have a crew and actors standing around trying to devise solutions for a story idea created or selected by the directors or producers of the motion picture. It is also easier for producers to retain control of the project, and most uses of **improvisation** as the basis of the filmmaking process have been through independent ventures or by creators who have distinctively earned the trust of producers.

In the earlier chapters, we established the most basic elements of motion picture storytelling, and you have worked on a variety of original scripts by now. In this chapter you will be studying the screenwriting process in more depth to examine additional concepts and practices familiar to screenwriting. Consider the questions in "Framing the Discussion" below to pursue this investigation.

Among the motion pictures you have seen for your work with this book, you have observed some examples of stories that closely follow familiar storytelling formulas and others that pursue storylines and ways of revealing narratives that are quite different from what is considered comfortable and "normal" to the general public. There are also a wide variety of creative approaches in the development of narrative blueprints for motion pictures. Some filmmakers have used improvisational techniques with actors in features and television shows. In Chapter 1, you read about the storyboarding conferences initiated by the Disney studios in the 1930s. Storyboards have been used as integral tools in the story development process by such directors as Alfred

Framing the Discussion

- *At the outset of a writing project, what is important for a screenwriter to consider?*

- *What are key issues to contemplate in the development of a story?*

- *What are standard formats and strategies of motion picture storytelling?*

- *What are some alternatives to standard screenplay format in pre-production material for a motion picture project?*

Hitchcock, who strove to create precisely illustrated plans for his films. In this chapter, we will investigate a variety of creative and collaborative techniques such as these.

Narrative Traditions Applied to a New Medium

As you have seen throughout this text, motion picture narratives reflect dramatic principles learned from and shared with oral storytelling traditions, short fiction and novels, and plays. In the first decade of the twentieth century, film production outfits churned out short movies rapidly to zip them off to their growing audiences.

Since the movies were short and the filmmakers needed to shoot quickly, there was little compulsion to spend time preparing for the movies by writing. Literature was a common source of early cinematic plots, such as the novels of Jules Verne or classical drama, which functioned well during production since the creators would be familiar with their key dramatic moments.

Moreover, with filmmakers needing to work quickly and to craft simple sequences that required little or no writing, they constantly stole ideas from each other. In fact, this phenomenon was so extreme that one unit would often directly duplicate a film soon after it was made by another studio. A member of their group would see the movie and then return to begin shooting their own version of that movie. Since movies were only a few minutes long, it was not very difficult to reproduce the story shot by shot.

Figure 7-2 Director Alfred Hitchcock, seated, gestures to collaborators at a storyboarding conference for the 1940 film *Foreign Correspondent*. (*Courtesy Wanger/UA/Photofest*)

There are two main problems with this. First, it was inevitable that copyright laws would be established for the moviemaking world so that filmmakers could not simply duplicate the work of another producer. Second, audiences want to experience something new. Have you ever started to watch or read a story and rolled your eyes, grumbling to yourself (or the person sitting next to you): "Oh, that's so unoriginal, I've seen exactly this thing before."

New Material for Motion Pictures

One director who understood the importance of original narrative was Alice Guy Blaché. She describes the genesis of her 1906 French film *The Alcoholic Mattress* in this passage from her memoirs:

> *Searching for a setting for a film . . . I [saw] a mattress-maker had installed her frame for stretching the canvas. She finished filling it with wool which she had just carded . . . and went away for a few minutes. Almost at once a drunk arrived, climbed the mound and rested in contemplation before the half-finished mattress.*

From this experience, Guy Blaché created a motion picture in which the mattress maker starts to refill an old mattress, then leaves to go to a café. A drunken man walks by, sees the cozy stuffing, and climbs into it. The woman returns, sews the mattress shut to finish her work, and then is astonished to see the mattress begin to move, followed by a series of comic turns and dramatic resolution.

At this time, scripts either existed in the head of the filmmaker or consisted of a few sketched notes, which reflected the length, visual simplicity, and lack of sync sound in motion pictures. Since motion pictures did not involve dialogue and were typically shot with a minimal crew, there was little need to create detailed continuity for production. However, it was also at this time that filmmakers began to recognize that they needed to develop interesting stories to attract audiences and generate notoriety for their production firms.

There are two basic ways to generate story concepts for a motion picture: an **adaptation** of an existing work of fiction or an **original screenplay**. That is why there are two screenwriting categories for the Academy Awards and at similar international ceremonies and festivals. Although the tasks and challenges of each type of script exhibit differences, the basic elements of screenwriting remain quite similar whether the author is adapting an existing story or creating an original narrative.

The Business of Writing

By the early 1910s, movies began to lengthen and increase in complexity, and it was clear to directors and production chiefs throughout the world that the most engaging and publicity-generating movies were those that grabbed viewers by showing exciting and funny stories. As a result, moviemaking studios began to hire writers specifically for the development of movie material.

In 1910, director Alice Guy Blaché was living in America where she oversaw the creation of Solax production studio in New Jersey, and she arranged a system of project development using a team of writers. Out west, Hollywood began to establish itself as a hub of filmmaking activity. The New York Motion Picture Corporation sent director Thomas Ince to California in 1912 to become west coast production head, and he acquired many acres of land to take advantage of local landscapes for more authentic westerns and war films. Like Guy Blaché, Ince recognized the importance of generating plenty of story material for new projects.

Studio Organization

Ince organized the entire production process along highly industrialized lines and endeavored to reduce the personal investment of writers in a particular narrative project. He focused on organizing the writing process into a collaborative endeavor overseen by the production unit, but this cooperative venture was credited to one person: Ince was notorious for taking credit for all the work in his name. Throughout the history of motion pictures, many executives have striven to reduce the personal commitment of screenwriters

Figure 7-3 Maurice Tourneur directing silent film actress Mary Pickford in *The Poor Little Rich Girl* (1917) from a script by Frances Marion and Ralph Spence with Lucien Andriot at the camera. By this time, movies used scripts like this one in which the writers tailored the story to suit its star. *(Courtesy Fort Lee Library)*

Figure 7-4 In a script conference, such as this one with author Anita Loos in hat, writers and the production team may review a screenplay for a variety of objectives, whether they are dramatic, creative, or commercial. *(Courtesy Photofest)*

to individual projects by methods of studio supervision and production management decisions.

A chief tactic of controlling the ownership and decision-making power in film production was to keep the various contributors to a project separate and to reduce their ability to communicate, and in no area was this more effective than with screenwriters. Certain Hollywood practices developed that continue to be industry norms to this day, such as having numerous writers rework scripts in a significant quantity of drafts, sometimes at the same time, and keeping the writers separate from directors during the various phases of the production process.

Struggles over legal rights to written material have recurred throughout the history of screenwriting. The studios held all rights to original stories written by screenwriters under contract until writers banded together in unions during the 1940s and were able to secure rights to material they authored and to establish procedures for applying proper screen credit on projects (although that has remained a contentious issue since that time). In the early twenty-first century, the Writers Guild of America engaged in a long strike over compensation for motion pictures appearing on the Internet and in other media, which halted many television productions for months.

Developing Narratives for the Screen

In the early 1900s, movie studios also actively solicited stories from the general public. One of the most celebrated and talented screenwriters of the early cinema got her break this way. Anita Loos was in her early twenties when she sent in her story "The New York Hat" to Biograph studios in 1912. They bought it to make a movie directed by D. W. Griffith with star Mary Pickford. Biograph proceeded to invite her to visit because they were buying many stories from her. Loos later said that upon her arrival they thought that her mother was the writer. Soon, her charisma, sense of style, and wit charmed moviemaking society. Her talents for crafting original narratives uniquely suited for moving images led her to become one of the authors who would help to establish the norms of writing for the screen. At the beginning, Loos provided brief story outlines typically consisting of a page or two. By the 1920s, she was writing scripts that were about fifty pages long.

When American film studios had sought material to make early short motion pictures, they were looking for stories written in the style of short fiction for magazines. As motion picture storytelling traditions grew, effective approaches to writing for the screen evolved as well. It had taken a number of years to recognize the need for scripts in the preparation for a motion picture, and then to develop an approach to writing for film. However, once this occurred, the norms that were established proved to be remarkably resilient. The basic principles that are reflected in the motion picture scenarios of the late 1910s and the 1920s are still quite evident today.

This can be seen in the screenwriting manuals that were published during the time, such as Anita Loos's own *How to Write a Photoplay* (credited to Loos and her husband John Emerson). Many of the approaches described in the pages of this book are echoed in screenwriting books from over a half-century later, including employing one sympathetic **protagonist** to drive the story, basing the plot on a clear conflict with a central **antagonist**, structuring the

Figure 7-5 Anita Loos with seated actress Jean Harlow in a publicity still for *Red-Headed Woman*. *(Courtesy MGM/Photofest)*

story around a three-part conception (beginning-middle-end), and keeping all the developments of the story to a central plot. While there have been different cycles and trends in mainstream Hollywood storytelling during the decades since then, many American screenwriters have regularly returned to these values.

The Motors of Story

In order for characters to drive the narrative forward, they must make choices that affect what will happen next. For a choice to be truly dramatic in nature, its alternatives must be compelling. For example, an actor who is simply running from one life-threatening tight spot to the next is probably showing us activity but not making dramatic choices. When thinking about the actions of characters in a movie, it is useful to ask the following questions:

- Is this action helping to define the character?
- Is it an independent choice or only a reaction?
- Is it affecting the outcome of the story?
- Is there anything at stake in this decision?
- Will a different choice lead to a completely different situation for the character?

In other words, choosing what to have for dinner is probably not an important dramatic decision. That is, unless the two options represent a major turning point in the existence of the character, which is doubtful. Running away from bullets is not a *dramatically* meaningful decision either—it is normally just a reaction without any significant alternatives.

Conflict and Antagonists

In classical drama, the primary obstacle to a protagonist achieving his or her goals is the antagonist. The antagonist is generally a person who stands in the way of the main character's ability to reach an objective. However, in short films the antagonist is often a non-human obstacle or situation.

When developing or examining a story, think about these questions: what is the goal of the character? What is the central conflict of the story? If there is a character who can be seen as an antagonist—such as a bully—are that character's actions affecting the central conflict? If not, the narrative of the story is probably not being driven by the protagonist. Events tend to seem to be taking place around such protagonists who are simply reacting to the events. These characters are **passive**.

Again using theatrical traditions as a guide, some screenwriters look at their scripts as a succession of scenes where each one must move the story forward. Writer and director David Mamet offers a set of what he calls "The Three Magic Questions" that must be asked about each scene: "1) Who wants what from whom? 2) What happens if they don't get it? 3) Why now?"

Unconventional Approaches to Narrative

As you have observed in a variety of movies, there are many different ways that filmmakers approach storytelling. You have probably witnessed this in life as well, through how people describe their experiences and tell stories.

Figure 7-6 What does the main character want? What conflicts with that objective? What will the character do to achieve the goal? Writers can be inspired by an image to create narratives for characters. *(Photograph from a series on Palestinian children, Courtesy S. Smith Patrick)*

Cultural backgrounds, artistic objectives, and educations can all lead to vast differences in writing practices. David Lynch, who has written for television and feature films, says "I sit and dictate what comes to me . . . [My assistant] sits at the computer and I sit in a chair, and I try to catch ideas and say them . . . the idea tells you how—as you read a book you picture it, you hear it, and it makes an impression. So you stay true to that impression as you translate it to film."

Numerous filmmakers have used approaches that do not follow the "how to" dictates of cinematic narrative developed by different generations of Hollywood experts and executives. Acclaimed American filmmakers such as Quentin Tarantino, Spike Lee, Robert Altman, Woody Allen, and Steven Soderbergh have made movies that break from conventional storytelling in different ways. For example, the story may feature a large number of important characters or may not move forwards in a straight time line. As a movie viewer, you have probably watched feature films that do not follow standard methods of Hollywood screenwriting. Reflect on the following questions:

- *Within the first ten minutes of the movie, are you sure who the one or two main characters are? This is not true if there is a group of characters who are equally important to the plot of the story.*

- *Has it been made clear to you "here is the good guy and here is the bad guy" during the first twenty or so minutes of the movie?*

- *As the movie moves past an hour or so, have the main characters of the movie clearly indicated their feelings to other important characters, including anyone with whom they are in conflict?*

Figure 7-7 Writer and director Spike Lee (with G on forehead) with actor Giancarlo Esposito in *School Daze* from 1988, one of Lee's films that contains strong autobiographical elements like his 1994 film *Crooklyn*. *(Courtesy Columbia Pictures/ Photofest)*

- *Does the main character have a clearly defined obstacle to overcome? During the last five minutes of the movie, is that conflict resolved, or is there a clear statement of finality to the central dramatic situation of the movie?*

If you answered "no" to any of the questions above, the script is taking an approach that differs from the most conventional styles dictated by American screenwriting formulas. Sometimes motion picture narratives can diverge from the standard methodology in small ways, and at other times they can tell stories in unfamiliar and innovative fashions. Take the example of *Napoleon Dynamite* (2004), written by Jared and Jerusha Hess. It does not propose a clear central conflict for the main character to overcome. However, its rejection of many of the standard practices of character development and plot construction is a reflection of its main character's persona. In fact, the primary purposeful actions of characters in the movie are achieved by characters around Napoleon, particularly his friend Pedro who runs for class president. This leads to one of Napoleon's strongest and most successful actions, his dance. Clearly, a great deal of the movie's success with viewers results from its originality and its ability to capture an insightful, if skewed, view of life for an American adolescent. As Napoleon tells us, he's going to do "whatever I feel like I wanna do. Gosh!"

In the United States, many of the most celebrated screenwriters have been those who craft clear-cut stories that weave the tale of a resolved journey or challenge for a main character. Genres set up particular expectations of viewers, but whatever the type of film, certain basic foundations tend to remain the same. Successful screenplays are typically those that achieve a balance between a well-structured plot and memorable dialogue that are both used to move the story forward in an emotionally engaging way. Most of all,

Figure 7-8 Writer and director Woody Allen discussing a scene with cinematographer Carlo DiPalma for the film *Hannah and Her Sisters,* which features multiple storylines and central characters. *(Courtesy Orion Pictures/ Photofest)*

Figure 7-9 Efren Ramirez and Jon Heder in *Napoleon Dynamite*, directed by Jared Hess. *(Fox Searchlight/Photofest)*

the audience must believe in the story and the dilemmas and desires of the characters. When this does not occur, viewers and critics often complain of a lack of credibility in the characters or their world. As you have seen many times, that world is created through the use of the language of cinema and the depiction of a reality that sticks together on the screen in terms of style, tone, and meaning. Our experiences of seeing and hearing that world need to make some logical and instinctual sense to us, thematically and artistically. Often, the screenwriter is the person who sets the first foundations for that world.

Constructing the Story

Writers of many of the most celebrated motion picture scripts talk in terms of building a structure for a motion picture. Charles Bennett, the writer of numerous classics from 1929 to the 1960s, including Hitchcock's *The Thirty-Nine Steps* and *The Man Who Knew Too Much*, described his primary talent as a *constructionist*. He refers to the *architecture* of the story as how elements work together to build a chain of events that makes sense to us as a story. This architecture was defined in Chapter 3 as the *structure* of the story. However, it is hard to develop a structure before we know what we are building or what we are using to build it!

Premise is the central concept or dramatic situation of the film. Often, a writer can successfully describe in one sentence the premise of a story. Here are some examples:

> *Upon hearing the news that he is terminally ill, a therapist who is leading an empty life disconnected from all the people surrounding him is motivated to interact with them in a genuine way.*
> (Our Time is Up, *written and directed by Rob Pearlstein*)

> *A woman riding on a tramway in Germany is disturbed by the presence of a black man sitting next to her and shares her racist views with the people in the car, prompting an inventive, non-violent revenge from the silent target of her verbal attacks.*
> (The Black Rider, *written and directed by Pepe Danquart*)

It is possible for the premise of a story to be the starting place of a writer. It can be the "aha!" moment of imagining a particular action or turning point in a conflict between two people. The previous two examples are for short films, but similar exercises can be done for longer formats, such as television programs or feature films. When a viewer is introduced to a motion picture such as a television program or feature film, the premise is typically used in the selling of the movie, whether a thirty-second advertisement, a movie trailer, or on occasion a poster.

The Importance of Time

Time is often an initial consideration of any storyteller. Two angles must be contemplated: the length of the motion picture and the story length. When a writer creates a screenplay, there may be outside forces that dictate the length of the intended motion picture. Perhaps running times have been set by a teacher, a festival board, or an employer. Is it a short motion picture of one, five, ten, or twenty minutes? Other standard lengths are those for the half-hour or one-hour television show. Finally, there are the durations of feature films which generally range from ninety minutes to two-and-a-half hours. Naturally, the length of the script can simply be the choice of its creator: the story that the writer wanted to tell was suited to a film of that length, so that is why it ended up at that page count.

The length of the motion picture affects many of the choices by the screenwriter. From our consideration of the running time of the motion picture, the other angle in relation to time is *story* duration. With short films, it is quite typical to center the narrative on a single event and a small number of clearly delineated characters. Many of the most successful short films center on one scene in which a conflict between two or more characters finds dramatic expression. The 2002 four-minute short *I'll Wait for the Next One* centers its entire narrative on the metro ride of a lonely woman. Although she does not speak a line of dialogue, the depiction of her character is remarkably expressive, and the movie's poignancy helped to earn it an Academy Award nomination.

It can be quite challenging to depict an extended period of time in a short film in a satisfying way. However, the use of flashbacks, reference points, and other film language devices can be appropriate to express the story. In the 2003 animated short film *Das Rad*, the filmmakers convey a narrative that covers eons of time from the perspective of stones. In Tom Tykwer's short starring Natalie Portman from *Paris, I Love You* (2006), the filmmaker shows the extended romantic story arc of a young couple in Paris using rapid editing, musically-arranged voice-over, and only one dramatic scene between the two main characters. From the same film, the *Place des Fêtes* segment by Oliver Schmitz depicts the tragic story of an African immigrant in Paris from the lyrical perspective of the main character. Interestingly, the core events of each of these segments are quite short, but through the illustration of personal perspectives, longer periods of time are successfully shown to the viewer.

In short films, the story often hinges around a single strong dramatic moment, a solid core. In many fiction shorts, the drama of the motion picture is built around the setup to that moment and the resolution of the conflict. In shows and feature films that unfold over an extended series of scenes, this development is more complex. A term commonly used when discussing screenplay structure is the **act**, from the theatrical term used to designate major breaks in a play. A standard broad conception used when discussing movies is the three-act structure, consisting of a setup, confrontation, and

Figure 7-12 Natalie Portman screaming in the Paris metro in Tom Tykwer's segment of *Paris, je t'aime. (Courtesy La Fabrique de films/ Photofest)*

resolution. As indicated earlier, this concept dates back to the first decades of the cinema. However, let us consider terms indicated by Kristin Thompson in her book *Storytelling in the New Hollywood*, in which she freshly examined story constructions of feature films to see how they were built.

Turning Points in Narrative

Motion picture narratives are propelled forward by key turning points in their major actions, when they seem to "shift gears." As researched and demonstrated by Thompson, these tend to fall rather evenly throughout the story, resulting frequently in four sections (and occasionally three or five). Thus, a two-hour movie nearly always falls into four major parts of about a half hour each, although these lengths can vary and still work quite effectively. The most frequently observed and logically divisible portions of feature films have been labeled and described by Thompson as follows:

- Setup – *During the first section of the story, the initial situation of the narrative is introduced, including relationships between characters.*

- Complicating Action – *The main character or characters have to react to a conflict that changes the initial situation of the film and the ability of characters to fulfill goals or function normally.*

- Development – *At this point, the characters have been pursuing their goals and confronting obstacles in a variety of ways, and they must fully confront their struggle in this section.*

- Climax and Epilogue – *This part begins with a final major turning point and all of the core obstacles to the characters' goals have been established. Typically, this is a section of distinctly rising dramatic action to result in a final confrontation or resolution of conflicts in the film.*

A screenplay that received many awards and accolades by the press during the first decade of the twenty-first century was *Juno* by Diablo Cody.

To understand how story structure can work in a feature film, consider this interesting Academy-Award winning example:

The script quickly establishes the central dilemma of its main character, the sharp-tongued adolescent Juno: She is facing an unplanned pregnancy. In the Setup section, she deals with the initial news and arranges to terminate the pregnancy. At 20 minutes into the film, she leaves the clinic, creating the first major turning point of the film: she will go through with the pregnancy. In the Complicating Action section, which lasts 22 minutes, she deals with the pregnancy by selecting a couple for adoption and telling her parents. This section ends near the midpoint of the film when she decides to go to the couple's house alone. This action builds on the initial connection she made with Mark, the adoptive father of her baby: she is "crossing boundaries," as her step-mother will soon tell her. The Development section lasts 24 minutes, during which the drama of her relationship with the biological father of her baby, Paulie, builds to a conflict, and she establishes a bond with Vanessa, the adoptive mother. Juno initiates the final major turning point when she makes a conscious choice to ratchet up her relationship with Mark: She calls him and puts on lipstick before driving to their house to exchange mix CDs when he is alone. During the 26 minute Climax and Epilogue section (the three-minute epilogue is primarily a song performed with Paulie), Juno works to resolve the conflicts in her life and achieve her objectives. There are other devices used to set up sections and establish rhythms in the film, such as the labeling of seasons and musical passages, but the major dramatic turning points divide the film quite neatly into four sections with an important, but seemingly subtle, choice falling right at the mid-point of the film.

Figure 7-13 Jennifer Garner, Jason Bateman, and Ellen Page in *Juno*, directed by Jason Reitman and written by Diablo Cody. *(Courtesy Fox Searchlight/Photofest)*

Figure 7-14 A story can start in the writer's mind as a single dramatic image in which an action provokes a series of events. *(Courtesy Adam Keker)*

Breaking it Down

It is always possible for writers to break the story down into smaller parts, right down to individual scene cards. Thus, motion pictures narrative can be divided even further for story **beats** and patterns of smaller actions and conflicts. Remember that characters have to *make choices* to create the turning points which generate the structure. Consequently, a key source of inspiration for many writers is that the characters drive the story. Quentin Tarantino commented: "When I start writing, I let the characters take over… I have to write from beginning to end because the characters are kind of telling the story."

You learned earlier that narrative is defined by connected cause and effect, and storytelling traditions depend on actions that initiate change. When characters face obstacles to the fulfillment of their objectives, conflict is created. However, there are many factors that impact these very simple conditions. Who are our characters—what type of people are they, what sort of things do they do, what are their roles in society? How do we perceive them and react to their choices? What is the world in which they live? The answers to all of these questions are quite dependent on the cultural values, ethnic customs, and societal role of the person who is responding.

These perspectives have great impact on the objectives and methods of storytellers. As a result, when you watch movies from a variety of cultures or by filmmakers with contrasting beliefs or goals, you often witness very different approaches and styles that tend to reflect the community, nation, or production context of the author. These factors can affect the depiction of individual characters, groups of people, and settings; the development of storytelling structure (whether separating the story into two, three, four, or nine parts); and viewpoints and attitudes concerning societies and individual behavior.

Words and Pictures: Fitting It Together

At the opening of this chapter, you were asked questions about your own initiatives to make up tales or tell stories from personal experiences. The inspirations for storytelling can spring from many sources. Consider this series of story beginnings:

- Sarah looked at Jackie and Mykki through coursing tears and said, "That's it." She let herself fall against her locker, tilting her head back a bit so that it banged on the metal. Jackie reached out too late and Mykki just stood with her arms crossed and eyes and lips scrunched in plotting. "Let's get him," Mykki said to her two friends. Sarah, eyes closed, tapping the back of her head on the locker, said "No." She opened her eyes, "No, let's just get right out there. Let's get *them*." "Who?" asked Jackie. Sarah replied, "You know, whoever we want. Let's make a list and that's how we start. Here's the name: B.W.P. Boyfriends Without Pain—I'm not getting hurt anymore."

- There was something strange going on around the corner from the Junior High. Hector stood at the kitchen table shoving cereal in his mouth while his mother talked on the phone with a neighbor as she got breakfast ready for the little ones. His mother and the neighbor were gossiping back and forth about all the wild kids being sent to juvie, but Hector knew something was up. Jerome, the latest middle grade kid to disappear was friends with Hector's little brother, and he knew Jerome would never have done anything to end up in court. Not even close. He was going to get his little brother to take him over to Jerome's place that afternoon.

- Jimmy glanced down towards his hand to see the text just before the bell rang. "Not in class today. Call now." Jimmy quickly asked, "Mr. G, can I go to the bathroom before the bell rings?" The teacher just grunted and waved his hand toward the door. Jimmy was out of the classroom in a flash. Back at her house, Carrie was waiting for Jimmy's call. She couldn't even go in to start the day in Auto Shop, she was too freaked out. Yesterday, she had removed the tarps and pulled in to the unused bay to surprise Jimmy with some extra work on his Camaro, and everything blinked. Time shifted. Was she losing her mind, or was there some sort of door, a concrete road to another time. Was this a sign? The school was trying to pull the plug on Auto Shop so that they could fit in more Advanced Placement classes. Was this some weird result of that? Carrie's ringtone made her jump up: it was Jimmy calling from the bathroom.

- Serena sat in her chair, staring down at the faded, chipped tile between her feet. She didn't want to be in this session, but she had to be. The only words she had been able to say to her parents since her brother found her were: "Okay, I'll go." She listened to the breathy, "I'm so sensitive" voice of the counselor and then followed the voices around the circle spitting out their labels: anorexia, suicide, gambling, drugs. She closed her eyes and heard her song, saw herself walking around this circle, belting out her words to wake them up, to tell the therapist where to go, to be heard for real.

- Conor grabbed his father's bowl-shaped mug because he didn't see a clean one on the rack in the kitchen. He poured coffee to the brim and ran out the door to the sound of Dan's honking car. His friend didn't like to be late to school. As they pulled out of the driveway, Conor hated this huge mug, and he gritted his teeth at himself for filling it up so much. He brought it up to his mouth, burned his lips, tried to blow on it for a moment, then winced as Dan took a sharp turn. Conor imagined himself as a free-floating gyro moving in sync with the mug as he revolved around the liquid floating in space.

Seeking Inspiration, Finding Tales

What do you think motivated the authors of these story openings?

The circumstances of all of these brief selections are situations that have been generated from real contexts of young people in settings that are familiar and detailed to them. A girl standing with friends at their lockers, feeling angry about how she was treated by a boy. Urban violence pulled from headlines—whether the result of a tragic flurry of shootings or of corrupt judges sending away innocents—explored in the form of a mystery or horror tale. Cell phones, texting, and the removal of automotive technology class from a high school serve as a trigger for a fantastical tale. A group session used as a set piece for a musical about the emotional trials of rejection and depression for an adolescent. Seniors driving to school, rushing to not be late.

Creative writing is stimulated by many catalysts. Stories we have heard, read, and seen can provide powerful encouragement to explore a theme or situation, although familiar formats and plots can lead filmmakers to pursue paths that lack originality and integrity. Everyday actions and events can initiate compelling storytelling. Often, the most familiar people and common objects can provide rich possibilities for telling stories because we know them well and we can visualize them in a variety of situations.

A key word here is "visualize." When we read a screenplay, the script must compel us to imagine *seeing* the story taking place in front of us. The text that is on the page of a screenplay must be able to be *seen* or *heard*. When reading a short story or a novel, our experience of the story often includes the author's voice, exploration of the characters' thoughts, and commentary on the context and setting of the story. For motion pictures, viewers will understand the story through what they see and hear while watching, so the script needs to propose what is visible on the screen and heard through dialogue, sounds, and off-screen voices.

In the five previous storytelling examples, there are sentences that easily translate to script form, and others that do not. In reviewing the five selections, which parts need the most work to make them screen ready? What passages seem to you to be *cinematic* or easily put into a screenplay format?

As the writing exists right now for these pieces, the first selection featuring Sarah and friends translates easily to script format. The physical setting, description of actions, and dialogue are all made clearly visible to the reader.

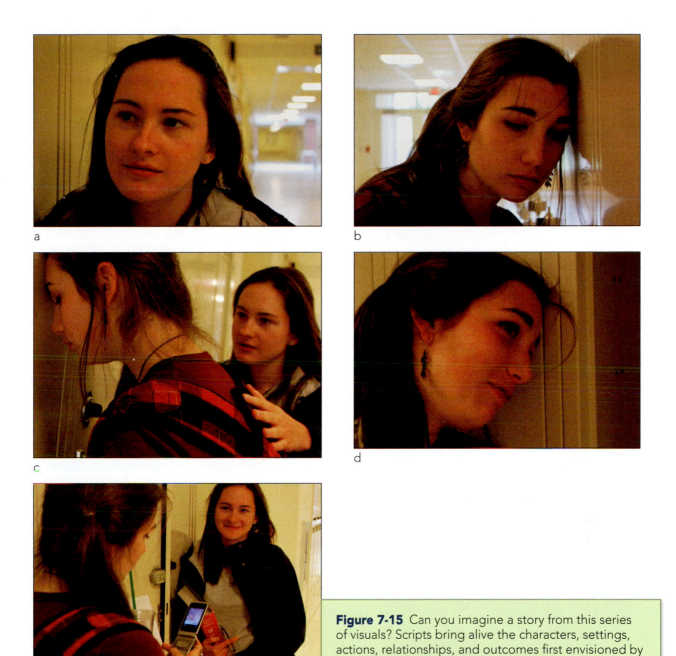

Figure 7-15 Can you imagine a story from this series of visuals? Scripts bring alive the characters, settings, actions, relationships, and outcomes first envisioned by the writer. *(Courtesy Kendelyn Ouellette)*

This selection represents the foundation of what Anita Loos describes as "a story suitable to motion picture production." The first step commonly used by early screenwriters was to write a story from the form of a synopsis, which is a clear summary of the plot in about a page (which would be a paragraph or two for a short film). The transferring of the story to a "photoplay" format was known as putting it into "continuity." Today, there are a number of approaches of screenwriters in the generation of material, including the writing of a **treatment** or a step outline, or the direct composition of a screenplay.

How to Draft the Story: Formats for the Screenwriter

When a writer puts words on a page to develop a story for a motion picture, there are a number of forms to consider. A treatment is a prose version of the story that can run from about one to forty pages, although they have been as long as entire screenplays (over 100 pages!). The primary difference from a script is the general lack of dialogue that makes up a great deal of the screenplay. In other words, treatments look quite a bit like short stories, but written in a very direct plot-oriented style. Essentially, a treatment is a longer version of a synopsis.

Another possibility for writers is to map out the unfolding of the story scene by scene, in which case they can create **scene cards** for the motion picture. These are descriptions written on index cards (or sticky notes), one per scene. If writers want to type the information onto full pages, they create a **step outline**. This is a scene-by-scene description of the story that includes a brief summary of each scene.

Figure 7-16 A straightforward logline on the poster for *Ray*, written by James L. White and directed by Taylor Hackford. *(Courtesy Universal/Photofest)*

JAMIE FOXX

Ray

THE EXTRAORDINARY LIFE STORY OF RAY CHARLES,
A MAN WHO FOUGHT HARDER AND WENT FARTHER THAN ANYONE THOUGHT POSSIBLE.

Summarizing the Narrative

The shortest summary possible is a **logline**. When making a short film, this might be the last step in writing: a one-sentence description for Internet postings or festival listings. For a feature film, it is a single line to be placed in an advertisement, or for a television show, it might be the selling line for the series. For example: "A former CIA hit-man with no memory of his identity tries to seek answers about his past while preventing his own assassination." (*The Bourne Identity, 2002,* directed by Doug Liman)

For some writers, a logline might be similar to the essence of the pitch for a project. When writers generate original projects, they will often team with a director or producer and attempt to pitch their idea to a studio or film financing source to secure funds for the project. They might pen an outline or perhaps write the entire script, but they generally need to be able to deliver their concept in a convincing oral presentation, as you read in Chapter 5.

Standard Formats

For creators of fiction motion pictures, the screenplay is the format that is the most prevalent guide during production. Scripts for individually produced motion pictures, whether short or feature length, use a standard format that was introduced in Chapter 3. **Teleplay** formats, used for some television productions, tend to follow different guidelines that can depend on the type of show and specific parameters set up by the creators. Primetime dramas typically follow standards similar to feature film formats because they are shot in a similar manner. However, situation comedies (such as *Friends* or *Seinfeld*) and daytime serials (or soap operas) often follow formats with a variety of differences. For example, dialogue is more widely spaced, action is in capitals and is less prevalent, and the script is separated into scenes and acts. This setup is designed for efficiency in the production conditions, pace, and style of shows shot with multiple cameras or recorded in front of an audience.

As you have seen in your writing so far, the standard screenplay format furnishes dialogue for a movie and descriptions of the actions and visual information on the screen. In addition to scene headings, action, and dialogue, which you have already reviewed and used, here are other writing tools at the disposal of a screenwriter:

- In addition to the **parenthetical directions** that were discussed in Chapter 3, there can be indications by the writer that a **beat** or pause is necessary to properly play the scene. These can also be indicated by ellipses in the dialogue: . . .

- Camera indications can be a part of a script, although it is consistently advised to use them sparingly: essentially, only if they are necessary to the understanding of the narrative or the scene. For example, if information is being revealed in a way that only the camera can do, a *push in* or *pull back* to reveal details or wider perspectives can be necessary to a writer. In addition, some writers may indicate a *point of view* shot for a character that provides vital perspective for the reader. However, the task of creating a shot-by-shot visualization of the movie is the job of the director through the creation of a shot list or storyboards.

- Transitions are indicated in a script when necessary for clarity or the proper visualization of the story, such as with a series of images that are used to advance the plot but are not played as full scene. The most typical indications are *Cut To—; Dissolve—; Fade to Black* (or other fade indications). Again, the important issue to consider is if the indication is *necessary* for the proper conception of how the script will become a motion picture.

As you have seen repeatedly, the most instructive way to learn about movies is by watching them closely. The same is true of screenplays. Seek out scripts to motion pictures that you value and investigate the ways in which their authors brought their stories to the page. You will witness practices that occur regularly and teach you about common routines, and you will undoubtedly see examples of highly personal choices or touches that particular writers bring to their material.

Alternative Blueprints

As you read in Chapter 1, one of the most appropriate tools available to filmmakers is the storyboard, which has a long history of use in moving image media. During the silent era, European filmmakers such as Fritz Lang and

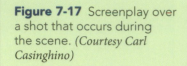

Figure 7-17 Screenplay over a shot that occurs during the scene. *(Courtesy Carl Casinghino)*

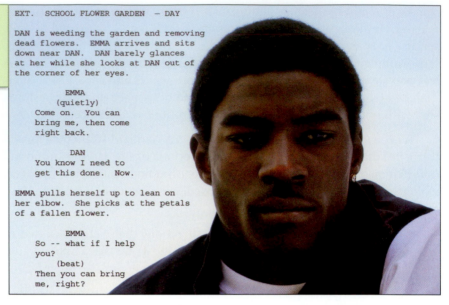

```
EXT.  SCHOOL FLOWER GARDEN - DAY

DAN is weeding the garden and removing
dead flowers.  EMMA arrives and sits
down near DAN.  DAN barely glances
at her while she looks at DAN out of
the corner of her eyes.

        EMMA
        (quietly)
    Come on.  You can
    bring me, then come
    right back.

        DAN
    You know I need to
    get this done.  Now.

EMMA pulls herself up to lean on
her elbow.  She picks at the petals
of a fallen flower.

        EMMA
    So -- what if I help
    you?
        (beat)
    Then you can bring
    me, right?
```

F. W. Murnau created complex visualizations of their movies, and storyboards evolved as a widely-used step in the pre-production process. As employed by the Fleischer and Disney animation studios, storyboards constituted what was a visual equivalent to an early draft of the script, which could later be written in screenplay format, primarily for the integration of dialogue. For some filmmakers, storyboards are very simple sketches used to create a loose game plan, while for others they are employed as an integral tool in story development and in planning discussions between the members of the production team.

Figure 7-18 Storyboard sequence for *A Frog and a Princess* (2006) by Kimberly Miner, director of the Student Academy-Award winning animated short *Perpetual Motion (Courtesy Kimberly A. Miner)*

For short form visual media, the storyboard can be the primary preparatory document. For a commercial, it can serve as the exact template for the narrative of the piece. This will often depend on the amount or importance of dialogue in the motion picture. If there is significant dialogue or voice-over in a project, written format is typically necessary.

Using Improvisation

Another approach is the use of improvisation in the filmmaking process. This can be done in moderation, where the actors are allowed or encouraged to ad-lib from the established script. It can also function as an integral part of the filmmaking process, because the actors spontaneously generate the spoken elements of the story. American filmmaker John Cassavetes used improvisation to drive the creation of his first film *Shadows* (1959), which strove to create the lives of its characters through a highly collaborative environment between director and actors. Sometimes, improvisation can be on camera, while it also can be used to create a script. British filmmaker Mike Leigh commonly works with his actors to develop characters and the content of scripts.

Improvisation has been an effective method for filmmakers who have created dramatic situations that are designed for improvisation or carefully selected collaborators well prepared for the task. Writer-director Blake Edwards and actor Peter Sellers collaborated to improvise a great deal of the Hollywood satire *The Party* (1968). Finnish director Aki Kaurismaki has prepared for some of his films using written formats that resemble treatments. Kaurismaki's familiarity with his crew and recurring actors helps him to maximize their contributions while putting onto the screen his unique vision.

Figure 7-19 Actor Jean-Pierre Léaud and director Aki Kaurismaki on the set of *I Hired a Contract Killer*. Collaboration between actors and directors is a vital aspect of the storytelling process for many filmmakers. *(Courtesy Photofest)*

On American television, writer Larry David, who was a co-creator of the show *Seinfeld*, uses story outlines for the episodes of his show *Curb Your Enthusiasm*, from which the actors improvise their dialogue and behavior from the indicated dramatic context and narrative structure.

There are many factors to consider in developing stories and bringing them to the screen. The materials you create are meant to make the production and post-production processes as fruitful as possible. From the initial inspirations and visions that provoke us to want to create motion pictures, it is a tremendously challenging process to transform them into a series of shots that make up sequences and well-developed stories.

Words and Pictures: Finding a Flow

Returning to our five story examples featuring Sarah, Hector, Jimmy, and the others, consider "putting into continuity" the second passage. The scene with Hector would require substantial re-imagining. We can see Hector eating cereal and his mother talking on the phone, but a significant amount of the information in the narration is inside Hector's head or delivered through commentary by the author. How can the screenwriter set up this story? Remember the lessons we have learned about cinematic storytelling: visual solutions are often the most effective. The screenwriter might see fit to have Hector tell another character what he is thinking or address the audience through voice-over, but how can this be done interestingly? In what ways can it be done visually?

Setting up the Story

In a movie, when a character explains the background for a scene or a situation, this is an example of a device called **exposition**. Exposition is a component of storytelling used so that audiences can understand the context of a narrative and key information that they would not otherwise be aware of through the images they see on the screen, such as character backgrounds, historical conditions, or an upcoming event linked to the past. It is often delivered by an on-screen conversation or voice-over, although it can also be conveyed through news reports, visual indications (such as signs), or written cues.

When we set up a story—and particularly a short one—a primary challenge for the writer is to bring the audience right into the narrative. Exposition—such as lengthy explanations—can make the movie drag or seem artificial. The challenge to the writer is to inform the audience of key information in a way that helps to move the story forward and adds to the depiction of the narrative. Many short films place the spectator right in front of a scene or series of sequences in which we experience the story directly through the events that we see. They may offer no **backstory** at all: What we see happening in front of us is what we get. We understand the characters only through the scenes taking place without flashbacks and explanations of past events or relationships.

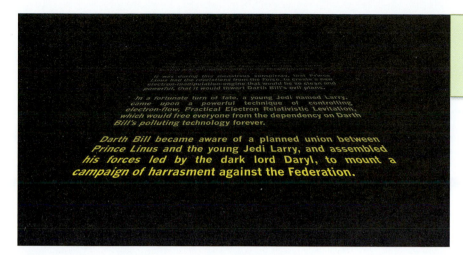

What to Show? Where to Start?

With the passage with Jimmy and Carrie, it is necessary to ask questions just as we did with Hector's scene, particularly when Carrie is introduced waiting for Jimmy's call in response to her text message. Should there be a flashback? Would we be able to understand a flashback right as the character is introduced? Are we going to hear her voice? Again, ask the important question: How can I tell this story visually? What do I want to show to the audience?

For a script featuring Serena from the fourth passage, the author would ask: is this my starting point? There is clearly a very important and dramatic series of events relevant to why Serena is sitting in the circle. Will the viewer see the events taking place from that moment on? Will we ever find out about Serena's past, and if we do how will that happen? Or will the screenwriter decide to move the beginning of the narrative of events back in time from the moment that is described?

Motivations for the Storyteller

In Chapter 3, you explored basic components of short narrative storytelling, focusing on character, setting, and structure. To move from initial sparks of inspiration to a short narrative motion picture, it is useful to explore the motivations to tell a particular story and then to seek out the most appropriate way to depict the world it entails. In general, the core elements for a story must be firmly established by the writer to build the strength of the narrative.

For example, the final narrative passage above is an idea based on a simple circumstance: trying to stop coffee from spilling. It is the job of the storyteller to bring alive the details of the situation and to make the discomfort of the main character familiar to us. This brief description could be a start to a complete narrative: where can it bring us? In this case, we must start with the important question: Who are our characters? Next: What will happen between Conor and Dan? What if Conor says, "Look, just slow down!" and Dan replies, "Just

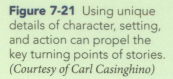

Figure 7-21 Using unique details of character, setting, and action can propel the key turning points of stories. *(Courtesy of Carl Casinghino)*

throw it out the window or gulp some of it down!"? The writer was inspired by an experience of trying to deal with a full mug of coffee, and the key is to find out why that event can be a catalyst for viewers to discover something about Conor and his world, or at least for a good laugh.

For our narrative samples in this chapter on screenwriting, you read stories on a page, so this may seem like a lesson in short story writing. As you have discovered, many of the first narrative motion pictures stemmed from short stories, novels, and plays. The lessons from various literary forms continue to serve the development of material for motion pictures. In fact, you may be compelled to write your stories in the form of short fiction, or perhaps plays or poetry. From that basis, you may feel motivated to bring the story to the motion picture screen. Or you may be inspired from the outset to go directly to the form of moving images, in which case it is extremely beneficial to create a written blueprint for you to crystallize your ideas and share them with actors, crew members, and any people involved with or responsible for the production of this work.

There are many approaches to the development of story. Deeds, movements, thoughts, words, emotions all bring substance to the world of a story; they make it happen. If the characters of a story—like those of the selections we have considered—are coursing with life in the mind of the author, their uniqueness must be brought to the page. Ultimately, the backgrounds, motivations, and actions of characters will give them life to an audience.

It's a Wrap!

In this chapter, you have deepened your familiarity with the traditions and challenges of screenwriting. Now, you will develop your analytical and creative skills by evaluating movie stories and writing your own. The actions, perspectives, complications, and reactions that propel a story are what generate the hunger of the author to want to know what will occur next in the experiences of these characters. What they do. What they say. How they seek to accomplish goals. How they get there. It is a writer's greatest challenge to make the audience share that desire to know what happens next.

The advice of Anita Loos is as apt for us today as it was nearly a century ago:

> Above all things the scenario writer should keep alive. Just keep yourself with lively, laughing, thinking people, think about new things yourself, and cultivate a respect for new ideas of any kind. Take care of these small ideas and the big plots will take care of themselves.

Analysis: Story and Screenplay

In your analytical work with this text, you have studied motion pictures from a variety of angles: motion picture language, sound, editing, cinematography, and other factors. With this unit, we will focus exclusively on the development of a story from a writer's perspective through the viewing of short films, including Immersion *by Richard Levien (see included DVD). If possible, you may read the scripts for these films, and it is also acceptable to answer the following questions after having only read scripts.*

A. Character

    1. List the identifiable characters of the movie, separating them into main and secondary characters.

    2. For the main characters of the motion picture, what are their objectives at the outset or during the course of the movie?

    3. What persons or other forces come into conflict with each objective?

    4. From these conflicts, who or what are the antagonists in the film?

B. Setting

    1. What are the settings for this movie? Are there changes of location or is the movie set primarily in one place?

    2. In what ways are the settings important to the story? Do they help to establish the characters? Do they have any impact on the actions of the narrative?

C. Structure

    1. Make a list of the scenes of the movie, writing each scene using the scene heading format. Indicate the central action of each scene in one sentence.

    2. What is the opening sequence of the movie? Does this provide the setup for the story? If not, when are the characters and central conflicts established in the motion picture?

    3. Is there exposition during the film? Does the film contain explanations of backstory or any other clues to important information needed to understand the narrative?

D. Premise and Theme

    1. What is the premise of this movie?

    2. What is the central theme of this movie? If there is not a clear theme, what are the messages delivered by the story?

    3. If there is a key dramatic moment in the movie, what is it? How does it reflect the premise? Does it solve the conflict or leave it unresolved?

Writing: Crafting a Story for the Screen

Using the tools and formats we have studied in this chapter, you will develop a story and write a script for a short film. This script should be five to fifteen pages in length in its final form. As you arrive at the final chapters of this text, you will have the opportunity to produce the most complex projects that you will have undertaken. The script you write here can be used for the projects included in Chapter 7 and Chapter 8. If your script involves a core of one to three characters and only one or two locations, it will be used for the project for this chapter. On the other hand, if your screenplay involves more than three actors who will be speaking in the film or three or more locations, you will be producing this script for the project for Chapter 8.

A. **Brainstorming** – *Use the following brainstorming activities to generate material for a screen story. If you already have a story idea, use these prompts as necessary.*

　1. **Characters** – *Let's generate some characters! They might fuel your story.*

　　a. Write character sketches of these people. Include age, physical description, personality, profession or occupation, interests, goals, family or friends.

　　　i. A person who makes you laugh

　　　ii. A person who makes you frustrated

　　　iii. A person whom you respect

　　　iv. Yourself through another's eyes

　　b. From any of these descriptions, are there traits or objectives that suggest possible conflicts with other people or outside forces? Jot down any story ideas that are suggested by these characters.

　2. **Places and Things** – *Consider physical settings or objects for inspiration.*

　　a. Brainstorm a list of the following locations or objects.

　　　i. Interior spaces where you witness activities being done

　　　ii. Exterior spaces where you see people interacting

　　　iii. Objects that you use on a daily or regular basis

　　　iv. Objects sitting in your house or at school that never seem to get used

　　b. Among any of these places or things, are there actions you can imagine that are suggested by them? Are there any particular images that come to mind?

3. **Premise** – *Do you have a central situation or thematic context that is already in your head?* Write it out as a single sentence.

   a. Write a list of possible settings for this premise.

   b. Can you see any of your characters involved with this premise?

   c. From the premise, imagine a key dramatic turning point with the situation.

4. **Resolution** - From sections 1 to 3, choose a story idea to develop.

B. **Step Outline** – As a result of the preceding brainstorming activities, write a step outline of the story that you are starting to imagine. This should consist of scene headings and brief descriptions of action.

C. **Screenplay** – For this exercise, you need to produce a screenplay of five to fifteen pages. Remember that one page of script is roughly equivalent to one minute of screen time, but if there is little dialogue on the page, this tends to stretch out the screen time. Thus, a script with significant action will most likely produce a film longer than the actual number of pages.

D. **Revising** – It is essential to rewrite your script to refine your writing and to fully develop the potential of the blueprint for your film. Working in a collaborative group, share the script or read it aloud if possible. With the group, review the following questions:

1. Is script format appropriate? Does the script follow an easily visualized flow?

2. Does the beginning make you want to continue to find out what happens?

3. Are the characters clearly defined to you? If not, is the mystery surrounding any characters appropriate to the plot, conflict, or resolution of the story?

4. Do you feel that the action is either too detailed or too thin or vague? Why?

5. Does dialogue dominate the script? If so, is it appropriate to the intentions of the writer (in relation to the premise, subject matter, or theme)?

6. Are you surprised by any of the events of the script? If not, why?

7. Are you satisfied with the ending? If not, does it provoke your mind so that you continue to ponder the events in a contemplative way? If not, why?

E. **Final Draft** – Make sure to revise to reach your final draft. Make sure to save copies of each draft separately and note the number of the draft on the title page. Since this will be a shooting script, it is useful to number the scene headings. As explained in Exercise 7, you will line the script and create pre-production materials such as shot lists, storyboards, floor plans, and schedules.

Project: The Visual Storyteller

Now it is time to take your screenplay and tell its story using moving images. You will work in collaborative groups to produce this project. For the projects of Chapter 7 and Chapter 8, you should work with collaborators to produce the scripts you have written.

If you wrote a script that only has one to three speaking roles and contains one or two locations, you will produce it now for "The Visual Storyteller." Those who wrote screenplays that involve more than three speaking actors and three or more locations will work as crew or actors for the directors of this current project. Later, those who are directing for the current project will function as part of the creative teams that will be assembled for the Chapter 8 project. For that final exercise, you will create and use production schedules, art direction, and cinematography plans.

A. **Pre-production** – One useful pre-production technique of a director is to *line the script*. This task is done to prepare coverage of the script shot by shot. From the shot list for the motion picture, lines are drawn along the length of the script to see the section of the script that each shot will cover. This is done because shots overlap in shooting, and part of the job for the director is to make sure that there is appropriate footage to enter the editing stage. This is called "having enough coverage of the scene."

1. **Shot List** – Prepare a shot list for the movie, imagining how the scenes in the script will be photographed.

2. **Line the Script** – On a copy of the script, you write the designation of the shot (1A, 1B, and so forth) at the point where the camera begins to shoot. Draw a line downwards from that point and extend it down the page for as long as that shot should be held. At the end of the shot, mark its close by a small horizontal line. If another shot is filming the same dialogue or action, begin it to the right of the first line, using the width of the page to be able to include multiple shots that are covering the same dialogue or action. Do this for each shot from your shot list to see how the script will be covered by your shots.

3. **Casting** – Select the actors for your project and arrange a production schedule. Make sure that actors are available at the times during which it will be necessary to shoot. You need to finish before any deadlines!

4. **Scheduling and Logistics** – Establish a set of deadlines for your project:

   a. Casting and rehearsal

   b. Secure locations

   c. Schedule exact dates and times of shoot – confirm with collaborators

      d. Editing sessions – gauge time from editing experience

      e. Set deadlines for assembly, rough cut, fine cut, and final cut

B. Production – Remember to keep in mind length of the final project when shooting. You have taken time to develop characters that are the force behind the story you want to tell. Have they been well chosen and are they properly prepared to interpret the script? Communication between the director and actors of a motion picture is one of the primary tasks of the director and is one of the most important elements of the success of a project. Your skills at cooperative work are vital to the effectiveness of the production.

C. Post-Production Guidelines – Completed short is between five to twelve minutes.

Report

Project Work – Describe your work on this project. Use the following questions to guide your analysis of your own work.

1. Was your pre-production effective? Were the actors properly prepared to interpret the script?

2. In what ways did the production progress effectively? What elements of the projects were possible through successful collaborative work? Give at least two examples.

3. Were the structural elements of your story effective once they reached the screen?

4. Once the edit was complete, was the style and pace of the completed motion picture a reflection of the feel of the original script? If not, describe the differences. Were improvements made during shooting or post-production? Explain key decisions in the movement from script to production to edit.

5. Comment on the overall effectiveness of the motion picture. Take into account visual elements, sound design, editing, and overall creation of a world on the screen.

Glossary

Act – In dramatic writing and performance, an act is the main division of the overall work. Plays are generally structured in one to five acts, and scenes are used to divide acts. In film, three-act structure is used to describe story conception that divides narratives into first (setup), second (conflict), and third (resolution) acts.

Adaptation – A screenplay based on a pre-existing work, such as a novel, play, or previous motion picture.

Antagonist – The figure of a story that opposes the protagonist and is the primary source of conflict with the main character. The antagonist, who may be clearly a villain or simply in opposition to other figures in the narrative, often drives action and instigates turning points in the plot.

Backstory – Events in the lives of the characters of the story that occurred previous to the on-screen narrative.

Beat – (1) In theater, a beat is a moment of pause for the actor, and this is the source of the use of the word within screenplays, in which it is a synonym for pause. (2) A beat in screenplay analysis describes a structural unit of the story signaled by a significant change in the narrative, although beats can also be broken up into smaller units, such as distinct dramatic moments within a scene.

Exposition – A storytelling device through which the audience is provided with information pertinent to the narrative of events occurring in the story.

Improvisation – The spontaneous creation of lines of dialogue or unscripted actions during the production of a motion picture.

Logline – A one- or two-line statement of the plot of the film.

Original screenplay – A script written directly for motion pictures, not adapted or based on a previously created work, such as a novel, play, or another movie.

Parenthetical direction – In screenwriting, a short indication placed in parenthesis on a separate line preceding dialogue that provides information about the dialogue delivery or state of the character.

Passive – A passive character does not make independent decisions and lets outside influences drive the situations and events of his or her life.

Premise – The dramatic situation that is the source of the actions and conflict of the narrative in a story.

Protagonist – The main character in a motion picture (or play or other literary work).

Scene card – Written breakdown of a scene on an index card or similar size surface. Scene heading and a brief (approximately one sentence) description are noted.

Step outline – Summary of the story that breaks it down into short descriptions for each intended sequence, including scene headings and brief action summary.

Teleplay – Script for a fiction television program with formats varying depending on the type of show. Some use formats similar or virtually identical to feature films, while different approaches are used with multiple camera series such as *Seinfeld*

Treatment – Prose version of a story intended to be made into a motion picture, typically drafted as a stage between the outline and screenplay. They tend to range from twenty to fifty pages for a feature film and are written in present tense using simple descriptive language with minimal dialogue.

Close-Up

Behind the Scenes with Writer
Pamela Gray

Q What are some lessons from your early efforts screenwriting?

A I was surprised to discover that screenwriting structure was so difficult. I had a love and a talent for writing dialogue and creating fully-developed characters, but I didn't realize how difficult it was to keep a story moving forward, to keep track of what my story was about, and to learn to stay on course and not wander off from the spine of the screenplay. I also hadn't realized how important it was to think visually, and I had to train myself to see pictures and not just hear what my characters were saying. I was also surprised and pleased to discover that my skills as a poet could be helpful, because my years of trying to find images helped me develop that visual sense.

Q What is important for beginning screenwriters to consider?

A Beginning writers often don't know what their story is about, *who* it's about, who their characters are, what their characters want, and what actions those characters will take to reach their goals. Beginning writers often start scripting before they've taken the time to clarify the story and to fully develop their characters. This has a detrimental affect on the story structure as a whole. The script meanders, and individual scenes don't move the story forward; they're often too long, too wordy, and lacking in conflict. Beginning writers often rely upon dialogue instead of action and visuals to tell the story and move it forward—and the dialogue itself doesn't sound like it's spoken by specific, individual characters. There's often "on-the-nose" dialogue, lacking in nuance and sub-text, or dialogue that just states exposition, rather than organically incorporating exposition in interesting, subtle ways.

Whether the screenplay is full-length or for a short film, writers need to take the time to do the preparation outlined above. Rushing through a script will ultimately get in the way of the *writer's* goal to create a great screenplay.

Q How does the screenwriter fit into the filmmaking process?

A The ideal way for the screenwriter to fit is to have a good collaboration with the director from the start. In the best-case scenario, the screenwriter's opinions are included through pre-production—the director would welcome their thoughts about casting and include the writer in all rehearsals. The writer would also be welcome to share thoughts on art design, props, wardrobe, hair and makeup. Most importantly, the writer would be on the set throughout the production. At that stage of the game, the story is now in the hands of the director, but in an ideal world, the screenwriter would be there to rewrite scenes that aren't working, to hear actors' suggestions and requests for changes, and to make adjustments to scenes if the need arises during the course of production.

The screenwriter and the director should have an ongoing dialogue throughout the filmmaking process—albeit one in which the writer respects the director's vision and understands that it is now the director who has creative control over the script. The director can benefit from the writer's ideas, especially because the writer continues to hold a vision of the work as a whole, while the director is faced with so many immediate demands that it's sometimes not possible to focus beyond the scene being shot at that moment.

Q What have been some of your greatest challenges?

A As a professional screenwriter, I am constantly challenged by my inability to retain control of my screenplays. It's devastating to pour my heart, soul, and sometimes years of work into a screenplay that doesn't get produced. It's also heartbreaking to be "fired" off a project and to watch my baby be handed over to someone else to rewrite.

Q What have been among your most fulfilling experiences?

A While it's definitely thrilling to see the name of my film on a marquee, and to watch people walk into a theater with tickets to the movie I wrote, I find production to be the most exhilarating part of the process. You find yourself standing on sets that were just one-dimensional images in your mind; you're hearing actors say words that you alone spoke out loud in front of your computer. Those movie moments you've lived with in your head are suddenly ALIVE. Despite the heartache and struggles that this career can bring, I keep writing screenplays because of my desire to see my work produced, and to have my vision inform the finished film. What keeps me going is my love of the craft of screenwriting; patience and persistence; the ability to handle despair; my belief in my own skill and talent; and my passion to tell stories.

Visit the textbook website to read the entire interview with Pamela Gray.

The Production Process

8

CHAPTER IN FOCUS

In this chapter you will:

- create a short motion picture that features multiple production departments
- investigate personnel roles in pre-production, production, and post-production
- evaluate the work of key crew positions in the creation of motion pictures

The Collaborative Process

Through every chapter of this book, you have been studying and using the production process. The flow of ideas, communication, and physical work that generates the creation of motion pictures has been at the heart of all of the exercises in this text. Now you will expand the range of your perspective.

In this chapter, you will review the key steps of the production process as they exist in contemporary moving image media. As a result, you will investigate the primary jobs that are part of live-action motion picture production, centering on film and television occupations. The types of positions necessary to a project depend on many factors, particularly the budget. For animated or computer-generated moving images, the division of labor stems from the needs of those formats (such as character modelers or background artists). However, the organization of creative departments follows similar patterns to standard film production processes. Even in the making of interactive games, the staff will break down the duties in relation to production needs, many of which mirror those of feature films. In their case, the solutions are those of the virtual reality world.

Managing Cooperative Endeavors

Motion picture productions function in ways that reflect countless other fields of human endeavor, from construction projects to scientific research to the creation of a high school or university course. Typically, there are various stages: setting goals and planning the mission; creating, gathering, and selecting the physical elements and evidence; and assembling and evaluating the product to try to achieve the desired result.

You have been developing cooperative skills and measuring the success of collaborative ventures throughout the work of this text. As you have probably seen numerous times, the effectiveness of an undertaking depends greatly on the proper coordination of tasks and contributions of each team member. At this point, your response to that statement may be "Easier said than done." As you have observed, the parts to a creative puzzle tend to be very difficult to piece together.

In addition, there are many pressures on the completion of a project. The contributors to the final product have their own perspectives and goals, and these can be very hard to combine. Outside forces, such as costs or weather, can bring production to a halt. Work can break down because of personality conflict, illness, or poor planning. Perhaps you have dealt with all of these problems in your exercises!

Figure 8-1 Collaboration can be a difficult process: conflicts and breakdowns can occur over creative, financial, technical, and logistical clashes. They can also stem from personality differences, power struggles, or the basic inability to collaborate harmoniously. *(Courtesy Kendelyn Ouellette)*

(continues)

(continued)

Organizational Challenges

Stanley Kubrick, the director of such classic groundbreaking films as *Paths of Glory, Dr. Strangelove, 2001: A Space Odyssey*, and many others, also served as producer for the majority of his films. He observed:

> *I am deeply involved in the administration, because it is in this area that many creative and artistic battles are lost. You've got to have what you want, where you want it, and at the right time, and you have got to use your resources (money and people) in the most effective way possible because they are limited, and when they are seriously stretched it always shows on the screen . . . and the conclusion that I have come to is that the making of a film is one of the most difficult organizational and administrative problems to exist outside of a military operation.*

You have also witnessed that moviemaking conditions can involve anything from a single creator to personnel that number in the hundreds or thousands (and it can seem limitless when watching the credits of some movies). At the outset of projects, filmmakers organize the tasks that need to be done to make the movie. How can the work be organized? How many people are needed? Who is responsible for each decision or confirming that an assignment is completed?

The necessary steps to complete a project will guide your investigation of motion picture production from conception to completion. At the outset of a production, filmmakers must fully analyze their project to determine what is needed to make the motion picture. These needs dictate the organization of the production process.

Figure 8-2 Stanley Kubrick, in foreground, on the set of *Dr. Strangelove. (Courtesy Getty Images)*

Figure 8-3 Crew preparing an interior shot for *The Pitch*, directed by Nash Edgerton. Personnel in this photo by John Myles are (left to right): Saskia Donkers (hair and make-up), Tom Gleeson (cinematographer), Billy Mitchell (armourer assistant), Nash Edgerton (director), Kieran Darcy-Smith (actor), Sotiri Sotiropolis (safety officer), Andrew Horton (camera assistant), Dan Oliver (special FX), Arthur Spink Jr. (sp. FX supervisor), Catherine Hart (sp. FX), and Narayan Moore (sp. FX). *(Courtesy Blue-Tongue Films)*

According to the requirements of a particular motion picture, many departments and jobs may be called into play. You will review the steps to the moviemaking process for a variety of types of motion pictures, in which contrasting needs can result in different roles and personnel. You will learn about the workers seen on standard feature, television, or commercial productions. Naturally, keep in mind that size relates to budget: a feature production that could employ fifty people in the most important roles from pre-production to post-production (and many dozens or even hundreds more in smaller positions, particularly if there are significant **visual effects**) would see similar tasks completed by perhaps a dozen key people or even less on a small independent production.

It is critical to note that professional practices can vary widely in different countries. Differences in legal systems, accounting practices, and working traditions can greatly influence how people produce motion pictures. In addition, funding can come from contrasting sources, including government grants, public television systems, and international partnerships. Because these differences can become quite complicated, the production practices and occupations you will be studying are specifically from the American example, which presents a highly developed, competitive system.

To Produce a Motion Picture

The four broad stages of creating a motion picture have been defined as *development*, *pre-production*, *production* (or *principal photography)*, and *post-production*. In the last chapter, you dealt with one of the main aspects of development and pre-production: writing. The genesis of concept, characters, and setting, then the writing of a screenplay or other story blueprints constitute the essential building blocks upon which the work in pre-production is assembled.

When a motion picture is simply an idea or an inspiration or a product pitch, who is involved with its creation? There are many possibilities. It may be a screenwriter who is trying to get a **producer** interested in the project. Perhaps it is a commercial writer who is preparing a proposal for a client. Or it may be a production team delivering a concept to a television studio. Whatever the situation, the person or group of people who initiate the furnishing of materials and a budget and who provide the organization and logistical support for the motion picture to be made are considered the producers of that project.

Framing the Discussion

- *From your experiences making motion pictures, what have you found to be the most important tasks to complete during pre-production?*

- *What have been the most important factors for you during production?*

- *What are the primary challenges during post-production?*

- *What factors have contributed to decision-making during the filmmaking process?*

- *To you, what are the most enjoyable aspects of production? Are there parts that have been difficult or less interesting to you? Why?*

Figure 8-4 Actor Roy Scheider, producer Richard Zanuck, and director Steven Spielberg on the set of *Jaws*. Zanuck and fellow producer Richard Brown bought the rights to Peter Benchley's novel *Jaws* in 1973, and they hired director Steven Spielberg to direct the movie after firing Dick Richards, their original choice as director. *(Courtesy Universal/Photofest)*

The Roles of the Producer

As their title tells us, motion picture producers are responsible for making sure that the movie gets made—that it is *produced*. They are present from the beginning of the project to the end. What do producers do? When you created schedules for your shoots, managed money (such as paying for supplies or food), and made administrative decisions about a motion picture, you did the work that is done or supervised by a producer. You functioned as a producer! While the director is the person responsible for overseeing the artistic decisions in making a movie, the producer is responsible for the financial and administrative oversight of a project from start to finish. When you do both of these things, you are producer *and* director (and you were most likely the writer as well).

Essentially, producers must ensure that the production moves from the very first step of creation through each successive stage until the motion picture is actually being shown to an audience. Producers are the resource managers of a motion picture, and they assume professional responsibility for the completion of the project with the film studio or financing group for the project. After having overseen the financing arrangements for the project, they must supervise hiring of personnel, coordinate all phases of production, and secure distribution deals. Sometimes they are closely involved with the decisions of the creative team of a movie, while at other times they occupy themselves primarily with the logistics of budget and personnel. This can depend quite a bit on the national traditions of a film industry and corporate practices. In some situations, producers may exercise little creative control during the production process.

On a professionally produced movie, if a writer or director is personally responsible for the actual conception of a project, he or she will earn one of the producer credits. Sometimes you will see filmmakers who take on multiple roles, such as writer, director, and producer. When directors strive to generate their own projects, they take on significant roles as producers, like Spike Lee, Robert Rodriguez, The Coen Brothers, and M. Night Shyamalan. In television, J. J. Abrams, the creator of *Alias* and *Lost*, has worked extensively as a producer while also building a career as a writer and director of feature films.

There are many professionals in the film industry who work specifically as producers. Scott Rudin, Kathleen Kennedy, Brian Grazer, Stacey Sher, and Ross Katz all work as producers for feature films or television series. Sometimes a producer is the originator of the central concept for a project, while at other times writers and directors will work to convince producers

Figure 8-5 J. J. Abrams directing *Star Trek* on the main bridge of the Enterprise. Some contemporary directors also function as producers and writers, and they vary their roles in a variety of domains, including television, feature films, music videos, and commercials. *(Courtesy Paramount Pictures/Photofest)*

to develop their projects. Whatever the situation, producers can apply a great deal of control over all processes of production, including creative decisions. In most contractual arrangements, the producer is in charge of the staff on the film, and that includes the director. If a producer is unhappy with the work being done by the director, it is possible for the producer to fire the director as well as any other person working on the film. This was an essential condition of production as it was set up by the Hollywood studios in the first half of the twentieth century. Directors who wanted more control over their own work would often produce their own material, although studio heads still retained a great deal of power in final decisions about projects.

The Production Team

There are many titles for the roles that have to do with overseeing production. Besides the basic role of the producer, here are some key positions in the production staff:

- **Executive Producer** – In major motion picture production, this is typically a CEO, executive with a studio, or chief investor, while in independent production, the writer or director may fill this position. The executive producer supervises the overall financial and administrative decision making for the movie. Other producer titles are *co-producer* (which may only indicate financial involvement or initial contributions during development), *associate producer*, and *assistant producer*. A **line producer** is seen on some projects when the administrative office wants a producer regularly on set to supervise the logistics of the shoot and the budget of the production, and whose role is similar to that of the unit production manager.

- **Unit Production Manager (UPM)** – Unit production managers are responsible for the supervision of personnel and budgetary aspects of principal photography. UPMs oversee the negotiation of contracts and purchases for the production, and they must make sure that the shooting schedule and budget are maintained. On a large project, there may also be production supervisors or secondary unit managers who oversee particular aspects of production or second unit work.

- **Assistant Director (AD)** – The **first assistant director**, or first AD, is vital to scheduling during pre-production and running principal photography effectively. First ADs assist both the director and unit production manager in assuring smooth management of the set. They devise a production board to set an overall schedule using a standard color-coded format. From that point, first ADs must work to ensure that the film is completed on schedule, which includes watching the clock during shooting. They are in charge of making sure that crew and actors are where they need to go when they need to be there. They also coordinate extras and may direct background action. Helping to maintain a focused collaborative environment is the **second assistant director**, or second AD, who assists the first AD, takes direct charge of getting actors to and from their shots, and creates **call sheets** to inform the crew and actors about the locations and schedule on a day-to-day basis.

The system is designed so that budgetary decisions are overseen by the producers, directed by the unit production manager from offices and through various communication devices, and administered daily on the set by the first assistant director. First ADs take these responsibilities right to the point of shooting, for they are the ones who "call out roll" on the set. They announce final checks to begin shooting and are the ones to declare "quiet on the set" or "picture is up" or "lock it down" right before shooting. Finally, first ADs are the ones to initiate the sound and camera when they call out "roll sound" and "roll camera."

Starting the Process

Before a project can move from the early stages of development to pre-production, administrators must **greenlight** it for financing. During development, certain creative and administrative decisions that will drive the making of the motion picture are researched, debated, and formulated by writers and by the team gathered at that time. In order to assure the support of studio executives or financiers, it is general practice to confirm lead performers and key creative personnel, such as the director and cinematographer. The matter of casting is an interesting issue in motion picture production, since financing of a project can depend significantly on the presence of particular actors. During development, the **casting director** may work with the director and producer of the project to select the actors who will play the principal roles of the feature film or show.

Figure 8-6 Director Mike Chase (in red) and actors prepare a scene for the digital feature *The Roper*. When casting a movie, the production team must look for the strengths that individual actors can bring to their roles as well as the potential group chemistry of the performers. *(Courtesy Mike Chase)*

Once the screenplay gets the go-ahead for production, then formal pre-production is initiated. Pre-production generally lasts at least a month, and the usual period is between two to four months, although major projects can necessitate a year of preparations.

The Casting Process

During the pre-production phase, the casting director will typically work with the director of the project to complete the cast of actors who will play the speaking roles of a movie. Readings with the actors can be recorded or casting can be done in live auditions (usually for smaller roles). Director George Cukor—famous for his track record as the first director to cast such actors as Katherine Hepburn, Shelley Winters, and Jack Lemmon—commented, ". . . there is no theory; there's just an instinct and a hunch . . . Maybe this seems rather touch-and-go but not really, because I think there's a deep instinct for it."

A common observation made by filmmakers is that the most important decisions by a director are made during casting, as when Ron Howard recalled Bette Davis's quip that "Once you've done [casting], stay . . . out of the way and . . . get the movie shot." Director Robert Altman said, "Actors are, without a doubt, the most important element, because they're the ones who are performing. And if it really came down to it, where we didn't have a set, we didn't have any lights, and we were sitting on a beach with a camera and four actors, we still could do something."

One of the most revealing ways to reflect on the impact of selection of actors is to look at historical examples of casting changes during development

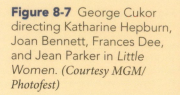

Figure 8-7 George Cukor directing Katharine Hepburn, Joan Bennett, Frances Dee, and Jean Parker in *Little Women. (Courtesy MGM/ Photofest)*

Figure 8-8 Robin Williams in *Dead Poets Society,* directed by Peter Weir. *(Courtesy Buena Vista/Photofest)*

or pre-production. One famous daring casting choice was the selection of Dustin Hoffman for his groundbreaking role in *The Graduate*. Later, Hoffman came very close to playing teacher Charles Keating in *Dead Poets Society* (1989), but for most people who have seen the movie, it would be nearly impossible to imagine anyone but Robin Williams in that role.

Location Scouting and Sets

Another important consideration to determine early on in the process is locations and sets. In order for further planning to move forward, it is important to determine any locations or **sound stages** where the movie will be shot. The filmmakers must weigh budgetary concerns, artistic advantages and disadvantages, and logistical feasibility of shooting on location or in studios. Once this information has been determined, it is imperative for the first assistant director to begin creating a schedule from the indications of the director, unit production manager, and producers.

First assistant directors must work with the unit production managers and directors to draft production schedules that arrange the order in which scenes will be shot. They take into account locations, availability of personnel, natural conditions, and any other pertinent factors. They work to minimize moves and maximize ease of shooting. This is why movies are nearly always shot out of order. The first sequence that is shot might be one of the last scenes of the actual story. The next day of shooting might be for a scene in the middle of the script. If there is a location that reappears a number of times in a movie, the filmmakers will often shoot its scenes in succession.

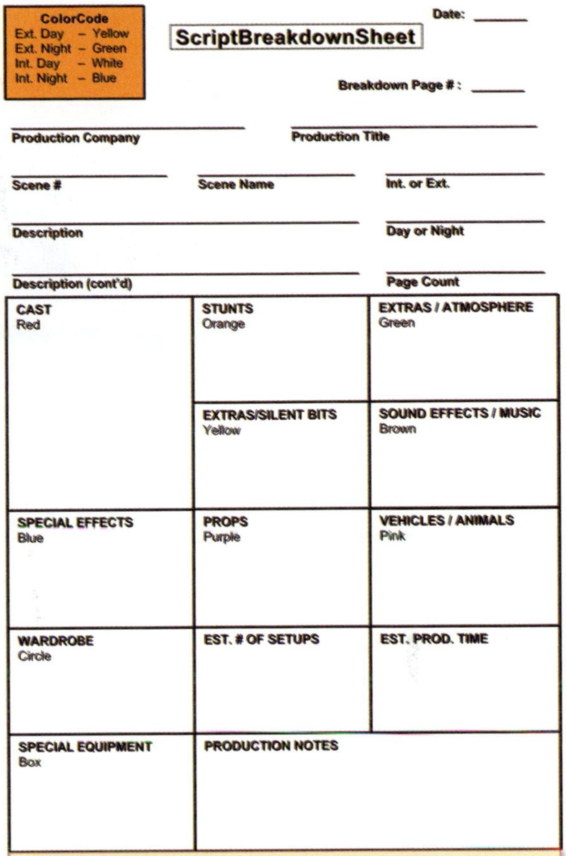

For fiction films and commercial work, script **breakdowns** are important documents that fully kick off the work of the creative team responsible for pre-production. To break down a script is to create lists of responsibilities for each department of the production. When breaking down a script into individual sheets, the camera, sound, production design, costume, and other departments all note necessary personnel, equipment, props, and vehicles for every scene of the movie.

Figure 8-9 Script Breakdown Sheet.

The Departments

What is needed to make a movie? Of course, there are also the two elements necessary for virtually every motion picture: camera and sound. In previous chapters, we reviewed essential components of each of these departments. When you learned about sound, you investigated the work done by the members of a production sound team and post-production personnel. Now, you will be introduced to the members of the camera and lighting crews as well.

Before a motion picture camera is turned on to record images, the creative personnel must decide what work must be done to create the scenes that will be filmed. What will the actors wear? Do any of the actors have to be made up or their appearance altered in a special way? What objects or vehicles are used in the movie? What will the locations look like? Do sets need to be constructed? Are there any stunts or special effects that occur during the

Figure 8-10 *The Curious Case of Benjamin Button,* starring Brad Pitt and directed by David Fincher, features extensive use of visual effects to tell its story of a man aging in reverse. *(Courtesy Paramount Pictures/ Photofest)*

action? The departments that create the physical world to be captured in the movie provide the answers to all these questions.

Finally, there is a department that has been an important factor in motion picture production throughout the history of the moving image: visual effects. **Matte** painters and **model** makers have been creating illusions that have amazed or tricked audiences since the early years of the cinema, and digital effects have become a standard tool in motion pictures of the twenty-first century. Computer-generated images have become one of the most predominant sources of moving images, particularly in the realm of interactive games, which can feature highly developed plot lines that are animated by extensive teams in digital studios.

Creating Production Value

From our first introduction to the concept of film language, we have returned to the discussion of realities that make sense to us on the screen. Filmmakers work to present to us a vision whose parts fit together, whether through performances, visual style, sound design, and overall feel. In addition, settings, decoration, costumes, objects, vehicles, and other production elements can add to the interest and can attract audiences to the world on the screen. All of these factors can serve a story to make its world believable and compellingly detailed.

Figure 8-11 Models have been used in a wide variety of contexts throughout motion picture history, as in this example from *The Sacrifice*, with director Andrei Tarkovsky. *(Courtesy Lars-Olof Löthwall)*

Production value is a term often used by filmmakers to describe the overall quality of the production as it is seen on the screen. It is often a reflection of the budget of a film, although a high compliment for creative teams on motion pictures—and particularly for production designers—is when they work on a movie with a small budget and the production value is high. A major consideration of filmmakers is the degree to which high production values serve the story. In some films, high production values are not important to the story. While style can be an important

Figure 8-12 Actor Bill Murray in front of the unique set for *The Life Aquatic with Steve Zissou*, directed by Wes Anderson. In Wes Anderson's films, production values are integral to the storytelling and the development of a finely detailed world for the characters. *(Courtesy Touchstone/Photofest)*

part of storytelling, sometimes extravagant or complex production values can overwhelm weak characters and story. Basically, a motion picture with two characters in a sparsely decorated room has low production value; a James Bond film with locations across the world, intricate stunts, many extras, and an array of original gadgets seeks to show very high production values for a great deal of its appeal.

The Camera and Lighting Units

As you know from your own productions, it is useful to devise a visual approach before shooting a motion picture. The creation of shot lists and storyboards and scouting of locations for visual preparations can be vital to the success of a motion picture. The person who is in charge of ensuring that the camera will be used effectively to bring all of this to the screen is the cinematographer or **director of photography (DP)**. Cinematographers are among the first people to join a production and have a tremendous amount of responsibility during all its stages. Their work is balanced between the artistic concerns of crafting light, movement, and framing, and the technical concerns of photography. They must also oversee a sizeable portion of the crew because everything that has to do with photography is under their supervision.

As you learned in Chapter 4, a cinematographer must supervise the use and creation of all the light that is on the scene and that enters the camera. They must select and properly use cameras, film stocks or digital media, lenses, filters, and a wide array of tools. The work can be done under difficult conditions, whether in snow, under water, on sand, or on top of a mountain. As Academy Award-winning DP Haskell Wexler explains, "My job is to help the director translate in an artful way the drama as expressed in the script and by the actors. This involves helping with framing, staging, lighting, and utilizing all the mechanical devices necessary to make the images tell the story."

Figure 8-13 Actor Heath Ledger on camel, cinematographer Robert Richardson on crane, and director Shekhar Kapur making *The Four Feathers*. Camera crews must be able to adjust to difficult conditions, as with director of photography Richardson working a Panavision rig set up for the desert location. *(Courtesy Paramount/Photofest)*

The Camera Team

Working under the supervision of the cinematographer are the camera team and the lighting crew. Often DPs do not actually operate the camera during shots so that they can work fluidly with all their assistants and concentrate on overseeing lighting. They need to be able to look at the big picture. In this case, there is a separate **camera operator** who works under the supervision of a DP. The camera operator works the camera, eye to the viewfinder, hands manipulating the controls for movement and framing.

The core members of a camera crew are the **first assistant camera** (first AC) and **second assistant camera** (second AC). First assistant cameras are the primary people in charge of maintaining the camera and lenses, cleaning

Figure 8-14 Director Tony Gerber behind camera along with camera and production crew on *Side Streets*. *(Photo by Seth Rubin, Courtesy Market Road Films)*

all of the precision equipment, and setting f-stop, shutter speed, and other adjustments to the camera from the instructions of the DP. They are responsible for measuring, establishing, and shifting focus during shots, which is why they are sometimes called *focus pullers*. If a shot is out of focus, it is typically ruined, so there is a great deal of pressure on the first assistant camera. If the camera and actors move around, this can become quite challenging. When shooting film negative, the first AC must also "check the gate" periodically to make sure it is totally clean because a single hair or speck on the edge of the gate can ruin the image of the exposed film.

The second AC works as the assistant to the first AC and is in charge of labeling and clapping the slate for each take. Second assistant cameras must note what has been shot in camera records, including all technical information. When shooting with film negative, the second AC also works as a *loader* who places film into the camera **magazines** and removes the negative to place into film cans. This work may be done by a separate loader on the crew who also makes sure that the takes are properly labeled for processing and marked on the camera reports. All work with the negative must be done in a dark room or with a **changing bag** so that the film stock is not exposed to any light. Thus, one of the skills of loaders is to be able to insert and thread film negative into magazines without being able to (or having to) look at what they are doing. Their hands are stuck inside a completely lightproof bag, and they hold the movie itself in their fingers, quite literally. .

With digital cinematography, a great deal of the work of the camera team has shifted to the verification, oversight, downloading, and uploading of the digitized footage. There have been many methods of storage of the digital footage used during the late twentieth and early twenty-first centuries, and the

Figure 8-15 On small-scale productions, many positions are filled by individual crew members, and digital filmmaking has allowed for significantly reduced camera crews. *(Courtesy Mike Chase)*

variations and ongoing changes in practices on sets from low budget projects to major Hollywood productions are staggering. The workflow for the camera crew on the twenty-first century set can include a wide variety of strategies. To give one example, the job of a camera assistant can include collecting shots on a digital card, removing the card from the camera, downloading the information onto a laptop, verifying the labeling and organization of the takes, and passing on this work so that the shot can be immediately inserted into a temporary rough cut to see how the footage works.

Lighting and Electric

To direct the lighting of the movie, the cinematographer's head assistant is the **gaffer**, or chief lighting technician. The gaffer and the lighting crew, including **best boy electric** and second electric, are in charge of maintaining, selecting, setting, and adjusting the lighting setups of the movie. Cinematographer Michael Margulies explains,

> I will discuss with the gaffer what I want, where I want the light coming from, what I want the light to hit, and usually let him decide on the units he uses. Nine out of ten times he will make the decision on the unit . . . I want the set looking in a certain way and I want so many foot-candles and that is what he gives me.

This quote from 1986 reflects a traditional approach to film lighting, and there is now more predominant use of natural illumination and minimal lighting setups in film and television. However, the dynamic between directors of photography and lighting crews, headed by the gaffer, still revolves around their ability to converse fluently about light and to use the tools at their disposal effectively.

Figure 8-16 Gaffer Eric Blum, on ladder, and crew rig lights for *Of Men and Angels*. *(Photo by Gregg Mancuso, Courtesy farleyfilm.com)*

The lighting crew must know about all the types of light units, which ones work well in particular situations, how to set them, and how to shape and manipulate the light they project. Gaffers will instruct their teams to rig lights using a variety of standing and hanging supports and to set stands that hold various **flags**, **nets**, **gels**, **reflectors**, and types of **diffusion**. The electrical demands of lighting setups in feature films can be extensive, and the person in charge of electricity is the best boy electric. Best boy electric is the first assistant to the gaffer and is in charge of power hookups and supervision of electrical materials. Along with working out electrical concerns, the electricians directly rig lights along with their **barn doors** and **scrims**. Helping in the setting up and preparation of stands for lights are **grips**.

The overall movement of materials on a film set, including elements of the camera and lighting departments, is generally the work of grips. The **key grip** joins the project during pre-production to help with the preparatory work for the shoot. Key grips oversee the implementation of all the instructions of the gaffer and supervise the variety of tasks in the grip department, which can include construction of devices to help with any needs of the camera or lighting departments. The **best boy grip** is the assistant to the key grip, serving as a set foreman and overseeing the use of materials that come off of and return to the grip truck. The **dolly grip** is the member of the grip department who is in charge of all camera moves, including tracks, wheeled dollies, and cranes. The choreography of camera moves can require a great deal of artistry, so the dolly grip must develop a strong sense of rhythm and flow in the displacement of the camera.

Figure 8-17 Director of Photography Kathleen Breeler and Director William Farley near the camera on the set of *Of Men and Angels*. In this shot, you can see metal barn doors affixed to the lights and diffusion held in place in front of the units. *(Photo by Gregg Mancuso, Courtesy http://www.farleyfilm.com)*

When audiences consider safety on a film set, the most common issue they generally think about is stunt work. However, safety is a constant concern with a wide range of activities on a film set. The amount of electricity needed for lights and the difficult location conditions of some shoots can combine to form electrical situations that demand serious professional oversight. Many light units and stands with lighting materials are placed around a set, and it is imperative that the grips set up equipment safely and sturdily. Sandbags are one of the most familiar objects on a film set.

Constructing Worlds for the Camera

Just as the cinematographer supervises everything that has to do with using the camera and lighting the set, the **production designer** oversees the creation or decoration of the settings of the movie, including all the visual details that make up that world. Moreover, design has been part of the production process for nearly as long as cinematography, starting with the groundbreaking work of Georges Méliès. Not only was Méliès instrumental in pioneering techniques such as fades, superimpositions, and jump cuts, but he also created detailed sets using illusionist techniques that he adjusted for motion pictures.

Méliès paid attention to depth, composition, and a variety of elements that are integral to film sets. He troubleshot issues with black and white photography, as he explained, "Color sets look terrible on film . . . So it is necessary to paint sets as if they were photography studio backgrounds." Méliès summed up his approach as "I was born an artist in my soul, very dexterous with my hands, skillful in most things, inventive, and an actor by nature. I worked with both brain and hands." Many designers use similar terms to describe their work.

The lessons of Méliès were not lost on future filmmakers who continued to create inventive backdrops and sets that capitalized on the illusions of perspective and camera placement. This could be the case for adventure movies set in far off lands and outer space or for realistic dramas that use design to craft a convincing impression of authentic locations. Certain trends in film style are most recognizable through their production design, whether the German expressionism in such films as *The Cabinet of Dr. Caligari* and *Nosferatu* or fanciful MGM musicals such as *The Wizard of Oz* and *The Pirate*. In working to balance the artistic desires of the creative team and the restraints of the budget, legendary designer Alexandre Trauner commented, "I cannot betray either the director or the producer." He adds, "The visual

Figure 8-18 Two cameras set up for tracking shots for *The Sacrifice* with director Andrei Tarkovsky on left and cinematographer Sven Nykvist gesturing towards the scene at the right. *(Courtesy Lars-Olof Löthwall)*

Figure 8-19 Here the tracking setup becomes a movie: Sven Nykvist shooting the dramatic finale to *The Sacrifice*. *(Courtesy Lars-Olof Löthwall)*

imagination of the spectator completes our work . . . What is reality? On the screen it is the one that the spectator accepts."

From the beginning of pre-production, the production designer will begin to create the look of the film, from any building that will be constructed to color schemes to fabric and furniture choices to landscaping and everything design oriented that will be created for the motion picture. Production designers must take into account many factors, starting with reading the script and then analyzing the full context of the motion picture including budget, genre, and tone. For example, designers working on films set in the

Figure 8-21 Méliès (on raised platform) and crew working on a set in the director's glass studio. *(Courtesy Photofest)*

Figure 8-22 Extensive use of production design by Bo Welch for Tim Burton's *Edward Scissorhands* starring Johnny Depp. *(Courtesy Twentieth Century Fox/Photofest)*

past will conduct meticulous research to depict accurately and convincingly the context of that time, while those working on science fiction films use technical information, design standards, and the tone of the film to direct their inventions. During location scouting around Japan for the James Bond film *You Only Live Twice*, production designer Ken Adam flew over an area of volcanoes with producer Cubby Broccoli. Ken Adam asked, "Wouldn't it be great if the villain could have his headquarters in one of these extinct craters?" and made a quick sketch. It became one of the most recognizable, grandiose sets in film history.

Figure 8-23 Ken Adam's set for *You Only Live Twice*. *(Courtesy United Artists/Photofest)*

Figure 8-24 Nathan Crowley's production design in action for *The Dark Knight*. *(Courtesy Warner Bros./Photofest)*

For *The Dark Knight*, designer Nathan Crowley explains that he "worked on the entire film, starting with the Batmobile, because we needed lots of time to build the thing." In explanations of his work for this movie, Crowley describes how Batman's cape, bat design motifs and logos, and a hyper-realistic approach were key considerations in the creation of a distinctive look for the project. On top of that, they wanted to build a Batmobile that could actually be driven.

Figure 8-25 Edison studio set from 1916. Note the moveable walls and hanging lights. *(Courtesy Photofest)*

After the production designer synthesizes the various design elements of the film in sketches, paintings, computer schematics, and research notes that have been discussed with the director and cinematographer, they will be passed to the **art directors**, who work to have them translated into drafting schematics and itemized reports. Art directors oversee the implementation and budgeting of these plans with the **set designer** and **construction manager**. Set constructors, decorators, and dressers are the primary personnel responsible for taking the plans created by production designers, art directors, and set designers and turning them into viable settings. Sets are constructed for films so that they allow for maximum ease of shooting through the use of **wild walls**, open ceilings for lighting rigs, and smooth floors.

Illusions of Space and Movement

Some aspects of the creation of these worlds can also involve the fabrication of complete illusion, whether through the use of mattes, models, trick photography, CGI, and other visual manipulations of perspective and layering. The collaboration involved in creating the convincing and expressive illusions of the world on the screen can be quite extensive, and the methods used to create them have a complex history. Early filmmakers discovered they could enhance their capacity to tell stories by using inventive methods to trick the eye. They could mask part of the film and run the same piece of film back through the camera, such as with a shot in *The Great Train Robbery* in which the train is seen moving through the window of the station. **Optical effects** could be produced by the camera crew, and other procedures were rapidly developed to create a variety of effects during the post-production stages of film processing. Many of these printing techniques, such as fades, dissolves, wipes, and composites now can be done digitally, and you may have performed some of them using the tools on a computer editing program.

The intersection of camera perspective and visual design has prompted ingenious solutions from generations of filmmakers. Two of the earliest concepts that still see applications today—and whose lessons have been applied to the digital world—are in the use of matte painting and scale models. From the first decade of the twentieth century, artist Norman Dawn began creating illusions by placing painted glass plates in front of the camera,

Figure 8-26 Futuristic cityscape from Ridley Scott's *Bladerunner*. *(Courtesy The Blade Runner Partnership/ Photofest)*

Figure 8-27 The future as seen from 1927 in *Metropolis,* directed by Fritz Lang, which features a dazzling array of visual effects, including both stop-motion miniatures and the Schüfftan process which combines models and moving people. *(Courtesy UFA/ Photofest)*

with the painted area melding into the scene seen through the transparent glass. By the 1930s, matte painting became an indispensable tool for some productions, allowing filmmakers to create scenes that would be impossible to build because of engineering or budget constraints. From *Gone with the Wind, The Wizard of Oz, Citizen Kane,* and *Black Narcissus* to *The Empire Strikes Back, Raiders of the Lost Ark,* and *Bram Stoker's Dracula,* painters trained in mastering illusionist effects have completed the work started by production design teams.

The use of models has also been one of the visual design team's most effective tools, seen in an early method named after its inventor, cinematographer Eugen Schüfftan. The **Schüfftan process** combines live action with miniature sets and paintings that are photographed with the ingenious use of a silver mirror. Scale models seen through the mirror could be combined with actors on a set behind the transparent glass part of the mirror, or the opposite arrangement in which the actors are seen in the mirror while the miniature or a painted scene is behind the glass. Like other techniques of cinematic illusion, the process required appropriate lighting and attention to scale and movement. The application of the Schüfftan process and other scale model techniques including stop-motion animation have been effective tools of storytelling from movies such as *Metropolis, The 39 Steps,* and *King Kong* to the films of Ray Harryhausen and *The Lord of the Rings: The Return of the King.*

Compositing

The techniques that involve the combination of parts of separate images to produce a single image can be understood under the term of **compositing**. Many techniques continue to develop the effectiveness and artistry of optical illusions, from a wide variety of matte shots, front and **rear projection**, and chroma key (**bluescreen** and **greenscreen**) technology. A common technique that has been augmented by digital technology is the use of color screens—particularly green or blue (used mainly because of their absence in skin tones)—to combine two images seamlessly. With this method, actors stand in front of the screen of green or blue, which is the color, or "chroma key," that will be removed. The green or blue in the image is made transparent so the actors appear to be standing in front of whatever image is inserted as background.

Amazingly, this technique was developed for *The Thief of Baghdad*, which was in production in London at the beginning of World War II! Producer Alexander Korda staked a substantial investment on his trust in American visual effects director Larry Butler, who boldly believed his new technique would work, despite absolute rejection by officials from the Technicolor Company. Their daring gamble paid off, and it serves as one of the finest examples of the mix of entrepreneurship, artistry, technical innovation, and collaboration that embodies the story of filmmaking. Chroma key techniques are used in many types of motion pictures, from complex feature film productions to television weather reports. Use of such technology can involve many aspects of the production process, and the collaborative nature of filmmaking is vividly seen in such aspects of production.

More recently, the use of greenscreens has become standard because digital image sensors have a higher sensitivity to green. Interestingly, for the 2002 film *Spider-Man*, visual effects supervisor John Dykstra had to oversee the use of both bluescreen and greenscreen. This was because Spiderman, whose costume has lots of blue, needed a greenscreen, while the Green Goblin had to be photographed in front of a bluescreen or the process would not have worked effectively.

Figure 8-28 Chroma key work in the studio on *Spider-Man 2*, with director Sam Raimi instructing James Franco (on ground) and Alfred Molina perched for action. *(Courtesy Columbia Pictures/Photofest)*

Visual effects are all of the alterations to the moving images made during post-production, but they typically involve preparation and oversight during all stages of the production process. The **visual effects supervisor** oversees the implementation of all artificially created images and additions and subtractions to live-action footage, most often through the use of digital processes. Visual effects are used in a vast array of contemporary moving images, from commercials to television programs to feature films. Uses range from small additions and subtractions of visual elements in primarily live-action shooting, such as adding color or leaves to plants in *Juno* or the removal of stunt wires from many action movies (or logos or a bald spot on an actor's head), to completely computer-generated backgrounds and characters. In some projects, the production revolves around the work of the visual effects supervisor, such as in *Van Helsing, Sky Captain and the World of Tomorrow*, and many films of Robert Zemeckis.

Acrobatics of Light and Bodies

The worlds created by production design teams along with visual effects collaborators are meant to be inhabited by characters. Thus, they must be designed so that what needs to occur inside of them can be done through action or through believable fakery. This is the domain of special effects and stunt personnel. Again, the traditions in this area reach back to the early years of the cinema, whether in the westerns that featured gunfights, cavalry raids, and daring rescues, the adventures of such stars as Douglas Fairbanks, or the stunt-filled comedies of Buster Keaton and Harold Lloyd. Keaton worked with his crew to devise sets that allowed for acrobatic feats of precise choreography, such as in his films *Steamboat Bill, Jr., Our Hospitality*, and *The General*.

Figure 8-29 Zhang Ziyi and Michelle Yeoh in *Crouching Tiger, Hidden Dragon* directed by Ang Lee. Some actors specialize in stunt work or they may train for many years to develop skills necessary for action sequences. Alongside natural techniques of actors and stunt doubles, stunt coordinators rig harnesses and other devices to enhance the acrobatics seen in fight and chase choreography. *(Courtesy Sony Pictures Classics/Photofest)*

Figure 8-30
Cinematographer Greig Fraser and Camera Operator Sebastian Dickens (holding camera) line up a shot on director, actor, and stunt coordinator Nash Edgerton atop a runaway car for the short film *Lucky*. *(Photo by Spencer Susser, Courtesy Blue-Tongue Films)*

In contemporary production, the **stunt coordinator** is in charge of safely preparing and executing any stunts. The work of stunt personnel can involve collaboration with many departments of a production, including the visual effects team, and they often work in tandem with the **special effects** department.

Since the integration of digital methods in motion picture production, *special effects credits* are defined as those that involve physical effects created by mechanical, pyrotechnic, or artificial means. The **special effects coordinator** supervises the creation of fire, snow, explosions, and all other effects necessary during production. Although computer-generated images have greatly influenced the creation of special effects in the production process, filmmakers continue to craft live effects for their projects. As special effects coordinator Chris Corbould has observed, "At one stage, we thought CGI would take over our roles and leave us obsolete. . . [yet] on *Die Another Day* we were running at about 120 technicians, partly due to Bond [production] policy of trying to retain as much reality as possible."

Actors Becoming Characters

The settings of the film have all been prepared and the complex arrangements of personnel are in place to bring the story to the screen. The actors have been cast in their roles and now they have to appear in the motion picture. What will they look like? How does the director imagine them? What will they wear? These questions will be answered by the makeup artists, hairdressers, **costume designers**, and **wardrobe supervisors** on the production team.

Figure 8-31 Lara Jade applies make-up to Nash Edgerton for *Lucky*. *(Photo by Spencer Susser, Courtesy Blue-Tongue Films)*

The makeup and wardrobe departments are organized in a similar fashion to the other aspects of production. The costume designer will meet early on with the director, cinematographer, production designer, and other department heads to devise plans for the movie. As with the preparations within those other departments, many considerations must be taken into account as conceptions are devised for the project. For the costume department, a great deal of the work is completed during pre-production, where the costume designer and wardrobe supervisor work from a script breakdown to plan all of the clothing changes of the actors through each scene of the movie. Costume designers are in charge of creating patterns for all original clothing in the production, of supervising the fabrication of those garments, and of selecting clothes that will be purchased or rented. They consult with the director and production designer to devise appropriate costuming for characters in keeping with overall production design. Wardrobe supervisors work under the costume designer to manage the costume department, so they work on the set to oversee dressing of the actors, schedules, maintenance of clothing, budget issues, and costuming personnel.

The key makeup artist and key hairdresser meet with the director and other department heads when production planning warrants their attention, and their primary work during pre-production generally involves test shooting with actors. Some personnel in these departments work closely with specific actors, and they may be attached to projects as a result of contractual demands. Naturally, the primary work of makeup and hairdressing occurs during principal photography. In the case of special effects makeup, experts may be hired to alter physical appearance enormously, as with aging effects or faces made up to resemble monsters or aliens.

VIEWFINDER

"Some actors have really tapped into the energy of dressing up."

–Tim Burton–

Director whose motion pictures include *Edward Scissorhands* (1990), *Ed Wood* (1994), *Sweeney Todd* (2007), and *Alice in Wonderland* (2010)

Figure 8-32 Peter Jackson directing Sean Astin as Sam Gamgee in *The Lord of the Rings: The Return of the King*. (*Courtesy New Line Cinema/Photofest*)

Now that the actors are ready to inhabit these worlds that have been prepared for them, the production schedule will be used to put into place the work of all the departments. Has the budget been properly prepared? Will shooting remain on schedule? Will the food on set be good? Will the different elements that make up the world on the screen be properly balanced to tell the story well? One of the most all-encompassing examples of the ways in which the wide variety of motion picture production tasks and techniques can come together is on the award-winning *Lord of the Rings* trilogy of films.

For this series of films, director Peter Jackson supervised the operation of a production in which a vast array of tasks had to be coordinated: production design and construction; costumes and makeup; optical effects, including scale model work; special effects and stunts; and the supervision of principal photography that occurred over an enormous range of natural settings with a cast of many actors and extras. In order to be able to accomplish the enormous challenges of undertaking such a production, initial shooting for *all three* movies was completed in an extended block of principal photography. Later, Jackson worked with a different editor on each of the movies to complete post-production manageably. However, despite the meticulous preparation involved in producing these features, extensive re-shoots had to be completed for these films because a great deal of the work of editing involves discovering new storytelling solutions and capitalizing on accidents and unplanned breakthroughs during production and post-production.

Putting It All Back Together

Early on during pre-production, each department drafts a breakdown of the script in order to itemize and organize the tasks that they need to accomplish. During the entire production process, the elements necessary to produce the completed motion picture—whether a thirty-second commercial, a television episode, or a two-hour feature film—are built up and put together, then broken apart and built up again. The final steps in this entire process are the ones familiar to you as post-production. In fact, building blocks of this aspect of filmmaking have been presented to you from the first unit of this text, and you have been using the editing process throughout your exercises. Moreover, during your studies of the sound department in Chapter 3, you investigated the work of post-production personnel such as sound designers and editors, foley artists, and composers. To complete our investigation of the production process, you will examine how the work you are familiar with compares with standard division of labor and techniques observed on professional motion picture production.

Head editors generally begin to work on a film just before the start of principal photography, at which point they may offer recommendations on certain editing choices from the information in the script. However, the major contributions of editors typically commence from the first day of shooting when they assemble the takes that have been selected by the director. On professional productions, they will work with a team of assistants to sift through the material and give initial structure to the footage. Editors work to solve problems of performance between takes and in separate shots, establish appropriate pace in sequences, oversee the development of rhythm across scenes, and offer suggestions to the director to find new storytelling solutions that were not previously apparent through script readings or during shooting. In addition, editors must develop an effective synergy with the sound editing team and visual effects department.

Contemporary Editing

In the early twenty-first century, most editing of moving images is being performed digitally, even if the initial cinematography is completed on film negative. This has not necessarily reduced the personnel for editing teams, in particular because the increase in digital shooting has been accompanied

Figure 8-33 Filmmaker Ross Martin at the editing table in a twenty-first century digital home-studio setup with dual monitors for tracking source images, sound, and edited picture on full screen. *(Courtesy Ross Martin)*

by a tendency to shoot more footage and a rise in the number of cuts in movies. Even if editors are no longer using splicers and trim bins to handle their footage, there are new tasks to manage the sequences made during the editing process. A key time-saving tool with such products as Avid software is the edit decision list (EDL), which archives editing choices to recover previous work.

From the early years of editing, many of the essential tasks of assistant editors have revolved around logging and recordkeeping of the footage from principal photography, and this is still true today. Codes must be attached to the shots in the motion picture right down to individual frames, and it is the job of the assistants to identify and keep track of this information. This must correspond between formats, particularly between film negative and digital transfers that are used in editing. Assistant editors must ensure that the editing process runs smoothly, and this involves a great deal of management of the footage as it comes in and is subsequently cut.

Discussing her work as an editor, Thelma Schoonmaker explains,

> You take one shot and connect it to another shot, and if you don't feel that little jolt of electricity that happens when you cut two shots together you know it's not working. So you reject that shot and try another one . . . The job is to get the best out of the actors and what the director has laid down, and get a rhythm going between them. In the way you overlap lines, or how long you pause after someone says a line. It's all just a matter of very careful, very detailed work that you have to keep reviewing, refreshing, and refining day after day. Then you go away from it for a couple of days and cut another scene. In some ways it's just nuts and bolts, but in other ways there is a lot of subtlety and emphasis that you can give with editing.

The Big Picture

In editing, you can see this process of breaking apart pictures and building them back together again in interesting, surprising, and satisfying ways. This can be on the scale of a thirty-second commercial whose production personnel is focused on a short span of images, or it can be observed in the sprawling range of missions on a blockbuster movie.

Whatever the scale of production, it returns to the vision that springs from human experience and imagination. Sometimes the creation is in the form of a highly personal narrative brought to screens by a single creator or small core of collaborators. In other cases, a team of professionals may be fulfilling a contractual demand from a client in which they need to devise a strong visual interpretation of a product. Whatever the source, motion pictures can be powerful expressions of the realities, dreams, and physical creations of humankind.

It's a Wrap!

In this concluding chapter of *Moving Images: Making Movies, Understanding Media,* you have conducted a final investigation of the collaboration, creative problem solving, and critical thinking that are at heart of its title. In the activities of this unit, you will have the opportunity to employ the skills you have honed through your journey with this text.

You will be accomplice, observer, and creator of the events of your time. The more you understand and effectively utilize methods of connection with families, friends, and communities across the globe, the more enriched your life will become. The images and sounds of motion pictures are among the most powerful vehicles of expression available to you. May you use them well.

Analysis: Taking Apart the Puzzle

For your final analytical work in this text, you will consider movies such as The Pitch by Nash Edgerton (see included DVD) from the production angle. In order to do this, you need the most complete available list of credits for the production.

For this series of shorts or feature films, answer the follow questions:

A. **Pre-production**

    1. From all the evidence you have, what were the most important considerations for the following tasks:

        a. Assistant director

        b. Cinematographer

        c. Sound recordist

        d. Production designer (or director, depending on type of production)

    2. What were the five most important pre-production decisions in the creation of this motion picture? Why do you choose these five decisions?

B. **Production**

    1. In what ways does production value enhance the story and the visual expressiveness of the moving images?

    2. Comment on the integrity of the performances in the film. Do they seem to reflect a coherent interpretation of the story? Does the direction of this film seem consistent to you?

C. **Post-production**

    1. What is the pace of the editing of the movie? How does the editing style serve the story?

    2. In what ways is sound used in the film? How do sound editing and design serve the story?

D. **The Big Picture** – Evaluate the overall impact of the movie, including its theme and integrity.

Writing: Pieces of the Puzzle

For this unit, you do not need to produce a new screenplay. As you saw in Chapter 7, certain scripts produced for that unit are to be produced in this chapter. If you had a script that fulfilled the guidelines for this chapter's project, you will have the opportunity to make a motion picture from that screenplay at this time.

Thus, the writing material you will complete depends on the role you plan to fulfill in the following project. Once you determine your job on this chapter project, you can complete your writing for this chapter for **one** of the following roles: director; assistant director; cinematographer; art direction; sound. Please note that some of the work is not actual writing, such as the organization of the assistant director or cinematographer.

A. **Director** – *You have written your script while working on Chapter 7, now complete the following work to prepare for the shoot:*

   1. Shot List

   2. Production Statement – *Write a brief description of your objectives in creating this motion picture, including your conception of its theme, intended tone, and style.*

B. **Assistant Director** – *Your role on this production is a cross between producer and assistant director.*

   1. Schedule, including precise shooting times and personnel

   2. Production Portfolio – *Compile the work produced by the production team in a folder and prepare a list of permissions and elements necessary to the shoot.*

C. **Cinematographer**

   1. Visual Preparations – *Prepare a storyboard or detailed floor plans from the director's shot list.*

   2. Designing the Photography – *Write one paragraph indicating intentions on camera movement, focus, and expected lighting tools and situations.*

D. **Production Designer**

   1. Screenplay analysis – *Written as a list or notes directly on a copy of the script, comments on locations, costumes, and other production design.*

   2. Design plan – *Create a blueprint or model of a location for the project.*

E. **Sound mixer/Sound designer**

   1. Schedule – *List of shoot days with locations and equipment and personnel needs.*

   2. Audio Mix – *Write one paragraph indicating intentions on audio recording and sound design for the motion picture.*

Project: Putting the Production Puzzle Together

If for the writing exercise for Chapter 7, you wrote a screenplay that involves more than three speaking actors and three or more locations, you are now ready to turn that script into a motion picture. You will work with a producer/assistant director to create and use production schedules. You will collaborate with a crew to pre-produce and shoot your film using art direction, sound design, and more advanced cinematography.

All member of the collaborative team should have begun their work for this production with this chapter's writing exercise. Now is the time to put those plans into action, whether for organizational purposes or for the visual and audio qualities of the motion picture.

A. **Pre-production** – For this shoot, you should have completed your pre-production as a result of the work from this chapter's writing exercise. The assistant director/producer compiles this work and uses it to coordinate the work of the shoot and to make sure the lines of communication are effective. The following elements are recommended for the shoot:

1. **Production Design** – If appropriate for this project, props, costumes, and other location work have been initiated by the director and prepared by an art director, as per Writing 8.

2. **Cinematography** – A visual plan for the movie has been created by the cinematographer according to this chapter's writing exercise. It is recommended to use at least three of the following elements: a form of dolly or steadycam-type device; manipulation of light with reflective surfaces, diffusers, or shading; manual focus, including focus pull if appropriate; handling of interior lighting to achieve proper exposure and avoid high levels of video noise.

3. **Sound** – It is recommended to record production audio with a boom microphone or high-quality audio source outside of the camera.

4. **Scheduling and Logistics** – Assistant director/producer will establish a set of deadlines for the project:

   a. Casting and rehearsal

   b. Secure locations

   c. Schedule exact dates and times of shoot—confirm with collaborators

   d. Set deadlines for assembly, rough cut, fine cut, and final cut

B. **Production** – As you have seen throughout this book and in this chapter, the quality of final product depends greatly on the effectiveness of the collaborative work. Each crew member has a distinct role to fulfill for this project. Establishing these roles clearly, setting deadlines, and communicating properly are all necessary for a smooth and successful completion of the work. If these steps are taken correctly, each member of the team is responsible for the work assigned directly to him or her and each task will contribute to the completion of the movie.

C. **Post-Production Guidelines** – The completed short should be between five to twelve minutes. The director will serve as editor for the project, although collaborative editing teams can be proposed.

Report

Exercise Work – Write a minimum of three paragraphs describing your work on this project. Use the following questions to guide your analysis of your own work.

1. Was your pre-production effective? In what ways were you unprepared for the logistics or challenging situations of the shoot?

2. In what ways were the different contributions of crew members effective in adding to the production value and artistic qualities of the final product?

3. Was the story brought to the screen appropriately from its script form? Did the structure of the actions in the narrative translate well to the overall depiction of the story?

4. Once the edit was complete, was the style and pace of the completed motion picture a reflection of the feel of the original script? If not, describe the differences. Were improvements made during shooting or post-production? Explain key decisions in the movement from script to production to edit.

5. Evaluate the overall effectiveness of the motion picture. Take into account art direction, cinematography, sound recording and design, editing, and overall creation of a world on the screen.

Glossary

Art director – Art directors execute the sets and other design elements conceived by production designers and may oversee the art department for a motion picture.

Barn door – Two- or four-paneled metal device attached to the front of a studio lamp to control light spill.

Best boy electric – First assistant to the gaffer and is in charge of implementing power hookups, electrical materials, and lighting setups.

Best boy grip – The assistant to the key grip, serving as a set foreman and overseeing the work of grip crew.

Bluescreen – Compositing technique originally known as "travelling matte" in which actors stand in front of a blue screen during filming, then all of the blue is removed leaving the images of the actors so that they can be inserted into a background. Uses of computers in filmmaking and printing have improved the procedure, and digital technology has widened its applications.

Breakdown – Analysis of elements necessary to produce a script done for cost estimates and preparations by location for each department working on the movie.

Call sheets – Daily schedule for crew and cast, including arrival and shooting times.

Camera operator – Crew member who operates the camera during shots, viewing the scene and adjusting framing. It may be the cinematographer or a camera technician under supervision of the director of photography.

Casting director – Individual responsible for overseeing the selection of lead and supporting actors for a feature film or television show (although not necessarily the stars with top billing) done in collaboration with the director and producers.

Changing bag – Lightproof bag with two zippered linings used for changing film rolls in magazines while on location when no dark room is available. Common option is changing tent with supports to suspend linings above loader's hands.

Construction manager – Person responsible for building of sets.

Costume designer – Head of the costume department who works with the director and production designer to dress characters appropriately and to establish a consistent and suitable style for the movie.

Diffusion – Material used to soften or break up direct light.

Director of photography –Commonly called the DP, this person is the head of camera crew and directs lighting. Also known as cinematographer, although the term director of photography is sometimes specifically employed when there is a separate camera operator photographing shots.

Dolly grip – Member of the camera crew responsible for movement of the dolly.

Executive producer – Individual who oversees the work of producers on a motion picture and overall financing of a production, often a studio chief or investor.

First assistant camera – Primary crew member in charge of maintaining camera and adjusting lens settings during principal photography.

First assistant director – First assistant director, or first AD, assists the production manager and director by creating a production schedule, managing personnel on set, and assuring the adherence to the timetable.

Flag – A cloth or other opaque surface used to cut light or shade the lens.

Gaffer – Chief electrician during principal photography, in charge of placing and operating lighting setups.

Gel – A transparent sheet used to add color to light.

Greenlight – In feature film and television projects involving financing from an outside source or client, this is the word used to indicate that the studio or financier will provide the backing to advance the project from development into production.

Greenscreen – Following from the example of the bluescreen, this is a chroma key technique in which actors stand in front of a completely green, evenly lit screen that will be removed from the image and replaced with a different background. Greenscreen use was developed because digital image sensors are more sensitive to green than to blue and a greenscreen requires less light.

Grip – Stagehand in charge of movement and placement of apparatus on a set.

Key grip – Foreperson in charge of grips during principal photography.

Line producer – On-set administrator who oversees principal photography, during which he or she manages the logistics of the shoot and the budget of the production.

Magazine – Lightproof attachment to a movie camera that holds the film negative. The film is threaded out from the magazine so that it feeds into the camera and returns back into the magazine after exposure in the camera.

Matte – A partial covering in front of the lens that blocks light from reaching the corresponding area of the image. This blocked area of the frame can be replaced with a painting (known as a "matte painting") or other prepared visual to create a composite image.

Model – A miniature, or scale model, of an object to appear life-size or to fit into a normal scale production through the use of perspective or visual effects.

Net – A mesh surface used to partially diminish light from a lamp source.

Optical effects – Effects achieved through the printing stages of film processing, such as fades or dissolves.

Producer – Administrator of all budgetary and supervisory aspects of production from development to distribution.

Production designer – Department head responsible for the creation and decoration of the physical appearance and design of interiors and exteriors in a production.

Production value – Term used to describe the overall quality of a motion picture production as it is seen on the screen, including sets, design excellence, costumes, vehicles, and historical, fantastical, or futuristic details.

Rear projection – Optical effect in which the actors are filmed in front of a screen onto which a film is projected from the other side of the screen, most commonly used in scenes with actors in a moving car. This "process shot," whose use began in the 1930s, had distinct flaws because of the unavoidable lower light level of the background image. Rear projection was improved by front projection, in which the image is projected from the front, as used in films such as *2001: A Space Odyssey*.

Reflector – Surface used to reflect light toward subjects in a scene, such as a bounce board used to brighten a certain part of the scene or a character. Reflectors can be positioned to bounce light back from illumination units that face away from the scene.

Schüfftan process – Optical technique that allows the combination of live action with miniature sets and paintings through the use of a mirror placed at a 45-degree angle in front of the camera with part of its surface scratched away to leave transparent glass. The mirrored section of the surface shows whatever image is bounced off at the 45-degree angle, such as a miniature or a scene with actors, while the transparent glass portion reveals what is behind the glass.

Scrim – Circular screen that slides into place in front of a light to lower its intensity.

Second assistant camera – The second AC, also known as clapper/loader, assists the first AC by setting up the camera, loading and removing film from magazines, and preparing and clapping the slate, although there may be a separate film loader.

Second assistant director – The second AD assists the first AD on the set and creates call sheets daily to inform the crew and actors about the locations and schedule.

Set designer – Member of the art department in charge of drafting blueprints and plans from the directions of the production designer. Set designers create drawings and scale models for the construction of sets and props.

Sound stage – Acoustically designed soundproof studio engineered for ease of motion picture production and construction of sets.

Special effects – Until the advent of digital effects, special effects were understood to be any illusionist technique in a motion picture achieved by optical or mechanical means. Since the turn of the twenty-first century, special effects are understood as any optical effects performed directly with the camera and physical effects created during production by mechanical, pyrotechnic or artificial means.

Special effects coordinator – Supervises the creation of fire, snow, explosions, and all other effects necessary during production.

Stunt coordinator – In charge of safely preparing and executing any stunts in coordination with the camera crew, special effects team, and other departments.

Unit production manager – Supervisor of personnel and physical aspects of principal photography, including adherence to schedule and budget.

Visual effects – Since the integration of digital manipulation of motion pictures and the advent of computer-generated images, all effects that are created for implementation during post-production, such as digital compositing and CGI, are known as visual effects.

Visual effects supervisor – Department head in charge of all visual effects work, planning all work with the director, cinematographer, and other necessary personnel, and overseeing budgeting and execution of these procedures for the project.

Wardrobe supervisor – Individual in charge of inventory and maintenance of wardrobe and timely and accurate costuming of actors during principal photography.

Wild wall – A movable wall constructed for a film set.

Just another day on the set for director Nash Edgerton. He has served as actor, stunt performer, editor, writer, director, and other roles on a long list of movies including music videos for Bob Dylan, Ben Lee, and other artists, the shorts Spider *and* Fuel, *and his feature* The Square. *(Courtesy of Nash Edgerton and Blue-Tongue Films)*

Close-Up
Behind the Scenes with Film Director
Nash Edgerton

Q How did you start getting into stunt performing and filmmaking?

A I kind of got into stunts in an old-fashioned approach, learning from people that had done it before. I would get the concept by helping out, and then get training by working with different people. I think one of the most important aspects of it is being adaptable because there are things that are always changing and things don't always go to plan or you're working against time or weather or various other things. As you work, you can get better at finding solutions. Having learned to be adaptable, as director you can get better ideas on that day when you're in actual situations.

Q What lessons did you learn as you moved into directing?

A It's quite daunting running the show, so the fact that I was already comfortable being around a crew really helped. I think it's always kind of scary trying to get your head around how to tell the story. You have to make sure to do as much homework as possible so you can approach the day of filming with fresh ideas.

The best thing I learned is to be open to accidents, to things going wrong or not your way. Instead of resisting it, maybe it's meant to be that way. If you're open to things that change or don't go your way, maybe you'll find a better idea. Rather than just being disappointed because it's raining or you can't have this tool or something is broken, there is always a solution. It's good to have a plan, but ideas are always evolving and part of it is always out of your control.

Filmmaking is such a collaborative process. You try to hire the right people to be around you because they're going to bring something to it and help you get the best of your day. What I like about filmmaking in general is that it does take more than just one person to do it. It's working as a team made of different people who all have different skills. It's a combination of these contributions that creates what it becomes.

There's a bunch of guys that I work with, and we all work on each other's films in different aspects. What's great is you learn from each other, and we have a good shorthand with each other that makes it easier. They have a good way of challenging you and asking why you want to do something a certain way. It helps you to be the best that you can be and next time you want to do something even better than that.

For films I have made with my brother what will usually happen when I read the script during the different drafts is that I will be thinking about it as a director. If I can see it when I'm reading it, then I know how to make it. If I can't see it, for a particular scene, then I fear there's something that's not working for me in it so that's how I talk about it with the writers. I know it's not right because I can't visualize it. If I can't see it, there must be another way of doing it or it doesn't need to be there. I'd rather say it at that point than try to shoot it without any idea on how to.

Q   What have been some of the greatest challenges you have faced?

A   Usually on any kind of shoot day you get challenges, where you're trying to get everything you need to shoot in that one day. The challenge all the time is if you have a plan like "the way I want to cover this scene is in five shots," you have to be ready for complications. There was a day we were shooting *The Square* in a small apartment, and we had gotten really far behind. My plan was to get five or six shots, and with the amount of time I had left, I was forced to try and cover the scene in one shot. I think sometimes the pressure can help, and because I was forced to do it in a shorter space of time, I got something better than anything I had come up with before.

Filmmaking is always ups and downs, but I find that there's always at least one good thing that happens in a day, and it's enough to keep you going. Something good happened or something worked out how you planned it. You try to savor that when other things don't work out.

Visit the textbook website to read the entire interview with Nash Edgerton.

Bibliography

Ahmad, Yasmin. "Mee Sup and Mise-en-Scène." *Yasmin the Storyteller.* Blogspot, 12 Oct 2006. Web. 10 Aug 2009.

Alekan, Henri. *Des Lumières et des Ombres.* Paris: Librairie du Collectionneur, 1991.

Alton, John. *Painting with Light.* Berkeley, CA: University of California Press, 1995.

Amidi, Amid. *Cartoon Modern: Style and Design in Fifties Animation.* San Francisco: Chronicle Books, 2006.

Anderson, Joseph and Barbara Anderson. "The Myth of Persistence of Vision Revisited." *Journal of Film and Video* Spring 1993: 3–12.

Arnold, Brian and Brendan Eddy. *Exploring Visual Storytelling.* Clifton Park, NY: Delmar Cengage Learning, 2007.

Aronson, Linda. *Screenwriting Updated: New (and Conventional) Ways of Writing for the Screen.* Los Angeles: Silman-James Press, 2001.

Ascher, Steven and Edward Pincus. *The Filmmaker's Handbook: A Comprehensive Guide for the Digital Age.* New York: Plume, 2007.

Atchity, Kenneth and Chi-Ling Wond. *Writing Treatments that Sell.* 2nd Ed. New York: Henry Holt, 2003.

Axelrod, Mark. *Character and Conflict: The Cornerstones of Screenwriting.* Portsmouth, NH: Heinemann, 2004.

Bacher, Lutz. *Max Ophuls in the Hollywood Studios.* New Brunswick, NJ: Rutgers University Press, 1996.

Barnouw, Erik. *Documentary: A History of the Non-Fiction Film.* 2nd Ed. New York: Oxford University Press, 1993.

Barron, Craig and Mark Cotta Vaz. *The Invisible Art: The Legends of Movie Matte Painting.* San Francisco: Chronicle, 2002.

Barsacq, Leon. *Caligari's Cabinet and other Grand Illusions: A History of Film Design.* Boston: Little, Brown and Company, 1978.

Baxter, Peter. *Just Watch! Sternberg, Paramount, and America.* London: British Film Institute, 1993.

Béchade, Chantal de. "Alexandre Trauner." *La Revue du Cinéma* Dec 1984.

Bogdanovich, Peter. *Who the Devil Made It: Conversations with Legendary Film Directors.* New York: Alfred A. Knopf, 1997.

Bobker, Lee R. *Making Movies: From Script to Screen.* New York: Harcourt Brace Jovanovich, 1973.

Boorman, John and Walter Donohue, eds. *Projections 1.* London: Faber and Faber, 1992.

——. *Projections 2.* London: Faber and Faber, 1993.

——. *Projections 3.* London: Faber and Faber, 1994.

——. *Projections 4 ½.* London: Faber and Faber, 1995.

——. *Projections 5.* London: Faber and Faber, 1996.

——. *Projections 6.* London: Faber and Faber, 1996.

———. *Projections 7.* London: Faber and Faber, 1997.

———. *Projections 8.* London: Faber and Faber, 1998.

Boorman, John, Fraser MacDonald, and Walter Dohohue, eds. *Projections 12.* London: Faber and Faber, 1999.

Boorman, John, Tom Luddy, David Thomson, and Walter Dohohue, eds. *Projections 4.* London: Faber and Faber, 1995.

Bordwell, David. *On the History of Film Style.* Cambridge: Harvard University Press, 1997.

———. *The Way Hollywood Tells It.* Berkeley: University of California Press, 2006.

Bordwell, David and Kristin Thompson. *Film Art: An Introduction.* 8th Ed. New York: McGraw-Hill, 2008.

———. *Film History: An Introduction.* 3rd Ed. New York: Mc-Graw-Hill, 2009.

Brady, Ben and Lance Lee. *The Understructure of Writing for Film and Television.* Austin: U of Texas, 1988.

Brady, John. *The Craft of the Screenwriter.* New York: Simon and Schuster, 1981.

Brion, Patrick, Dominique Rabourdin, and Thierry de Navacelle. *Vincente Minnelli.* Paris: Hatier, 1985.

Brody, Richard. *Everything Is Cinema: The Working Life of Jean-Luc Godard.* New York: Metropolitan, 2008.

Burton, Tim. Mark Salisbury, ed. *Burton on Burton.* Boston: Faber & Faber, 1995.

Cantine, John, Susan Howard, and Brady Lewis. *Shot by Shot: A Practical Guide to Filmmaking.* 2nd Ed. Pittsburgh: Pittsburgh Filmmakers, 1995.

Card, James. *Seductive Cinema: The Art of the Silent Film.* New York: Alfred A. Knopf, 1994.

Ceram, C.W. *Archaeology of the Cinema.* New York: Harcourt, Brace & World, 1965.

Ciment, Michel and Noël Herpe. *Projections 9: French Film-makers on Film-making.* London: Faber and Faber, 1999.

Cook, David A. *A History of Narrative Film.* 4th Ed. New York: W.W. Norton, 2004.

Coursodon, Jean-Pierre and Bertrand Tavernier. *50 ans de Cinéma Américain.* Paris: Nathan, 1995.

Dancyger, Ken, and Jeff Rush. *Alternative Scriptwriting.* 4th Ed. Burlington, MA: Focal, 2007.

Dick, Eddie, Andrew Noble, and Duncan Petrie. *Bill Douglas: A Lanternist's Account.* London: British Film Institute, 1993.

Dickinson, Thorold. *A Discovery of Cinema.* London: Oxford, 1971.

Donati, Jason. *Exploring Digital Cinematography.* Clifton Park, NY: Delmar Cengage Learning, 2007.

Dreyer, Carl Th. *Réflexions Sur Mon Métier.* Paris: Cahiers du Cinéma, 1983.

Dumont, Hervé. *Frank Borzage: Sarastro à Hollywood.* Milan: Mazzotta, 1993.

Field, Syd. *Screenplay: The Foundations of Screenwriting.* New York: Delacorte, 1982.

——. *The Screenwriter's Problem Solver.* New York: Dell, 1998.

Fujiwara, Chris. *Jacques Tourneur: The Cinema of Nightfall.* Baltimore: Johns Hopkins University Press, 2000.

Geffner, David. "Shooting Stars, Part II (The Women)." *MovieMaker* Jun 30, 1999.

Gondry, Michel. *You Like This Film Because You're In It: The Be Kind Rewind Protocol.* New York: PictureBox, 2008.

Goodell, Gregory. *Independent Feature Film Production.* New York: St. Martin's Griffin, 1998.

Gurskis, Dan. *The Short Screenplay.* Mason, OH: Cengage Learning, 2007.

Harrod, Horatia. "Ken Adam: The Man Who Drew the Cold War." *Telegraph.co.uk* 28 Sep 2008. Web. 15 jun 2009.

Hauge, Michael. *Writing Screenplays that Sell.* New York: HarperPerennial, 1991.

Hausman, Carl and Philip J. Palombo. *Modern Video Production: Tools, Techniques, Applications.* New York: HarperCollins, 1993.

Hay, Stephen. *Bertrand Tavernier: The Film-Maker of Lyon.* New York: I. B. Tauris, 2000.

Horowitz, Josh. *The Mind of the Modern Moviemaker: 20 Conversations with the New Generation of Filmmakers.* New York: Plume, 2006.

Horton, Andrew. *Writing the Character-Centered Screenplay.* Berkeley: University of California Press, 1994.

——. "The 'How to Write the Best Ever Screenplay' Book Biz." *Cineaste* Nov 1992: 12–14.

Houston, Penelope. *Keepers of the Frame: The Film Archives.* London: British Film Institute, 1994.

Howard, David and Edward Mabley. *The Tools of Screenwriting.* New York: St. Martin's, 1993.

Hunter, Lew. *Screenwriting 434.* New York: Perigree, 1993.

Huver, Scott. "Interview with 'Batman Begins' Batmobile Designer Nathan Crowley." *Hollywood.com* 17 jun 2005. Web. 15 jun 2009.

James, Christopher. *The Book of Alternative Photographic Processes.* 2nd Ed. Clifton Park, NY: Delmar Cengage Learning, 2009.

Jarecki, Nicholas. *Breaking In: How 20 Film Directors Got Their Start.* New York: Broadway Books, 2001.

Jarman, Derek. *War Requiem: The Film.* London: Faber and Faber, 1990.

Kay, Karyn and Gerald Peary. *Women and the Cinema: A Critical Anthology.* New York: Dutton, 1977.

Kleinhans, Chuck. "Barbara Kopple Interview Making *Harlan County, USA.*" *Jump Cut* 14 (1977): 4–6.

Kobel, Peter and the Library of Congress. *Silent Movies: The Birth of Film and the Triumph of Movie Culture.* New York: Little, Brown and Company, 2007.

Konigsberg, Ira. *The Complete Film Dictionary.* 2nd Ed. New York: Penguin, 1997.

Levy, Frederick. *Hollywood 101: The Film Industry.* Los Angeles: Renaissance Books, 2000.

Lippy, Todd, ed. *Projections: 11.* London: Faber and Faber, 2000.

Loos, Anita and John Emerson. *How to Write Photoplays.* New York: James A. McCann Company, 1920.

Lowenstein, Stephen. *My First Movie: 20 Celebrated Directors Talk about Their First Film.* New York: Penguin Books, 2000.

———. *My First Movie: Take Two.* New York: Pantheon, 2008.

Lumet, Sidney. *Making Movies.* New York: Alfred A. Knopf, 1995.

Macdonald, Kevin. *Emeric Pressburger: The Life and Death of a Screenwriter.* London: Faber and Faber, 1996.

Mackendrick, Alexander. *On Film-Making.* London: Faber and Faber, 2004.

Malkiewicz, Kris. *Film Lighting.* New York: Fireside, 1986.

Malkiewicz, Kris and M. David Mullen. *Cinematography: Third Edition.* New York: Fireside, 2005.

Mamet, David. *Bambi vs. Godzilla: On the Nature, Purpose, and Practice of the Movie Business.* New York: Pantheon, 2007.

Mayne, Judith. *Directed by Dorothy Arzner.* Bloomington, IN: Indiana University Press, 1994.

McChesney, Robert. *Rich Media, Poor Democracy: Communications Politics in Dubious Times.* Urbana: University of Illinois Press, 1999.

McGilligan, Patrick, ed. *Backstory 1: Interviews with Screenwriters of Hollywood's Golden Age.* Berkeley, CA: University of California Press, 1986.

———. *Backstory 2: Interviews with Screenwriters of the 1940s and 1950s.* Berkeley, CA: University of California Press, 1991.

———. *Backstory 3: Interviews with Screenwriters of the 60s.* Berkeley, CA: University of California Press, 1997.

———. *Backstory 4: Interviews with Screenwriters of the 1970s and 1980s.* Berkeley, CA: University of California Press, 2006.

McMahan, Alison. *Alice Guy Blaché: Lost Visionary of the Cinema.* New York: Continuum, 2002.

McKee, Robert. *Story: Substance, Structure, Style, and the Principles of Screenwriting.* New York: Regan, 1997.

Miller, Katie. *Photography for the 21st Century.* Clifton Park, NY: Delmar Cengage Learning, 2007.

Modine, Matthew. *Full Metal Jacket Diary.* New York: Rugged Land, 2005.

Murch, Walter. *In the Blink of an Eye: A Perspective on Film Editing.* 2nd Ed. Los Angeles: Silman-James Press. 2001.

Norman, Marc. *What Happens Next: A History of American Screenwriting.* New York: Harmony Books, 2007.

Nowell-Smith, Geoffrey, ed. *The Oxford History of World Cinema.* Oxford: Oxford University Press, 1999.

Oldham, Gabriella. *First Cut: Conversations with Film Editors.* Berkeley, CA: University of California Press, 1992.

Oumano, Ellen. *Film Forum: Thirty-Five Top Filmmakers Discuss Their Craft.* New York: St. Martin's Press, 1985.

——. *Movies for a Desert Isle.* New York: St. Martin's Press, 1987.

Packard, William. *The Art of Screenwriting.* New York: Thunder's Mouth, 1997.

Peet, Bill. *Bill Peet: An Autobiography.* Boston: Houghton Mifflin, 1989.

Phillips, William. *Writing Short Scripts.* 2nd ed. Syracuse: Syracuse UP, 1999.

Pierson, Michelle. *Special Effects: Still in Search of Wonder.* New York: Columbia University Press, 2002.

Powell, Michael. *A Life in Movies: An Autobiography.* London: Faber and Faber, 2001.

——. *Million Dollar Movie.* New York: Random House, 1995.

Rabiger, Michael. *Directing: Film Techniques and Aesthetics.* 4th Ed. Burlington, MA: Focal Press, 2007.

Restuccio, Daniel. "A Chat with Editor Thelma Schoonmaker: Edit This!" *Post Magazine* Apr 2003: 45–49.

Robinson, David. *From Peep Show to Palace: The Birth of American Film.* New York: Columbia University Press, 1996.

Rose, Jay. *Producing Great Sound for Film and Video.* 3rd Ed. Burlington, MA: Focal Press, 2008.

Sayles, John. *Thinking in Pictures.* Boston: Houghton Mifflin, 1989.

Schaefer, Dennis and Larry Salvato. *Masters of Light.* Berkeley, CA: University of California Press, 1984.

Scorcese, Martin and Michael Henry Wilson. *A Personal Journey with Martin Scorcese through American Movies.* New York: Hyperion, 1997.

Seger, Linda. *Creating Unforgettable Characters.* New York: Henry Holt, 1990.

Seger, Linda and Edward Jay Whetmore. *From Script to Screen: The Collaborative Art of Filmmaking.* New York: Henry Holt, 1994.

Shamas, Laura. *Playwriting for Theater, Film, and Television.* Crozer, VA: Betterway, 1991.

Shyles, Leonard. *Video Production Handbook.* Boston: Houghton Mifflin, 1998.

Sitney, P. Adams. *Visionary Film: The American Avant-Garde, 1943–2000.* New York: Oxford University Press, 2002.

Soderbergh, Steven. "Academy Award Acceptance Speech for Best Director." *73rd Academy Awards Ceremony.* ABC, 25 Mar 2001. Television.

Soderbergh, Steven and Richard Lester. *Getting Away With It.* London: Faber and Faber, 1999.

Spoto, Donald. *The Art of Alfred Hitchcock: Fifty Years of His Motion Pictures.* New York: Anchor Books, 1992.

Sternberg, Josef von. *Fun in a Chinese Laundry.* San Francisco: Mercury House, 1965.

Sweeney, Kevin W. *Buster Keaton: Interviews.* Jackson, MI: University Press of Mississippi, 2007.

Tavernier, Bertrand. *Amis Américains: Entretiens avec les grands Auteurs d'Hollywood.* Paris: Actes Sud, 2008.

Teasley, Alan and Ann Wilder. *Reel Conversations: Reading Films with Young Adults.* Portsmouth, NH: Heinemann, 1997.

Thompson, Kristin. *Storytelling in the New Hollywood.* Cambridge: Harvard University Press, 1999.

———. *The Frodo Franchise.* Los Angeles: University of California Press, 2008.

Tirard, Laurent. *Moviemakers' Master Class.* New York: Faber and Faber, 2002.

Tummunello, Wendy. *Exploring Storyboarding.* Clifton Park, NY: Delmar Cengage Learning, 2008.

Vick, Tom. *Asian Cinema: A Field Guide.* New York: Harper, 2008.

Warren, Bruce. *Photography.* 2nd Ed. Clifton Park, NY: Delmar Thomson Learning, 2002.

Weinraub, Bertrand. "At the Movies." *The New York Times* Jan 30, 1998.

Wheeler, Paul. *High Definition Cinematography.* 3rd Ed. Burlington, MA: Focal Press, 2009.

Wilder, Billy and I.A.L. Diamond. "Dialogue on Film." *American Film* Jul–Aug 1976: 33–48.

Wise, Robert. "An American Film Institute Seminar with Robert Wise and Milton Krasner." *American Cinematographer* Mar 1980: 248–249, 269–274, 291–295.

Index

Information presented in figures is indicated by *f*.